MANIFESTATIONS OF HISTORY

Manifestations of History

Time, Space, and Community in the Andaman Islands

edited by

FRANK HEIDEMANN

PHILIPP ZEHMISCH

PRIMUS BOOKS

PRIMUS BOOKS

An imprint of Ratna Sagar P. Ltd.
Virat Bhavan
Mukherjee Nagar Commercial Complex
Delhi 110 009

Offices at
CHENNAI LUCKNOW
AGRA AHMEDABAD BENGALURU COIMBATORE DEHRADUN
GUWAHATI HYDERABAD JAIPUR JALANDHAR KANPUR KOCHI
KOLKATA MADURAI MUMBAI PATNA RANCHI VARANASI

First published 2016

ISBN: 978-93-84092-04-7 (hardback)
ISBN: 978-93-84092-41-2 (POD)
ISBN: 978-93-84092-44-3 (e-book)

Published by Primus Books

Lasertypeset by Shine Graphics
Amar Colony, East Gokalpur, Delhi 110 094

Printed and bound by Sanat Printers, Kundli, Haryana

Contents

Plates, Figures and Maps

PLATES

FIGURES

MAPS

Acknowledgements

From 21 to 24 June 2013, twenty-five scholars met in Munich to discuss the significant, yet underestimated, place of the Andaman Islands within the historiography of the British Empire, the Indian nation state, and the Indian Ocean. This conference—the first of its kind outside of South Asia—brought together scholars from anthropology, history, sociology, human ecology, literature, political science, and geography. The always lively, and at times controversial, discussions centred on the appropriation, negotiation and representation of the past in the present. It became clear that history, as a process in the making and as a contested field of interpretation, is inscribed and manifested in the public and the private spheres, as well as in the ongoing research in various disciplines. We realized that according to the specific maritime environment and geographical location of the Andamans, history works both temporally and spatially. More importantly, the implicit assumption of the pre-eminence of time over space needs to be questioned. The dominant quality seems to appear according to the context. This volume, *Manifestations of History: Time, Space, and Community in the Andaman Islands*, is the outcome of the said conference.

First, we would like to thank all those interlocutors, colleagues and government servants on the Andamans who have generously supported social and cultural research in the last decades. Without them, the work presented in this volume would not have seen the light of the day. We are grateful to all participants of the conference for their engaged contributions, for sharing their insights and for all their critical comments. Beyond the contributors to this volume, the following scholars acted as chairs, discussants and speakers: Swapan Kumar Biswas, Palash Chandra Coomar, Samit Ghosal, Jens-Uwe Hartmann, Lydia Icke-Schwalbe, Richard Janney, Carola Krebs, Manju Ludwig, Madhumita Mazumdar, Johannes Moser, Madhusree Mukerjee, Katja Müller, Vishvajit Pandya, Roderich Ptak, Pankaj Sekhsaria, and Uditi Sen.

Generous financial support was granted by the German Research Foundation (Deutsche Forschungsgemeinschaft), the University of Munich (Ludwig-Maximilians-Universität München), and the Department of Social and Cultural Anthropology, Munich. The Internationales

Begegnungszentrum der Wissenschaft München (IBZ) provided the venue for the conference. Saskia Brill, Smitha Muttanoly, and Christine Omeltschenko were part of the organizing team. Michaela Appel, Curator in the Munich State Museum of Ethnology, now the Five Continents Museum, created a special exhibition of objects from the Andamans for the participants of the conference and guided us through the Oceania Section of the Museum. Emma Batell Lowman revised all texts in this volume and was much more than a copyeditor.

Munich

FRANK HEIDEMANN
PHILIPP ZEHMISCH

1

Introduction
Manifestations of History

PHILIPP ZEHMISCH and FRANK HEIDEMANN

NARRATIVES AND THE PAST

History is writ large in the remote archipelago of the Andaman Islands. It is inscribed in the architecture and the layout of the town of Port Blair, in documents and monuments, and even in classifications of the population. For example, the term 'Pre-42' refers to families settled before the Japanese occupation of the islands in 1942. It indicates, on the one hand, a specific social status as a 'local' person, who belongs to the Andamans and nowhere else. On the other hand, the Pre-42 administrative category grants privileged access to the local quota system in the fields of higher education and employment at public institutions.[1] Further, the legacy of the British penal colony appears in almost all narratives and in complex processes of identification. No doubt, one precondition for our ethnographic fieldwork was knowledge of the socio-political terrain involved in recollections of the past in the Andamans, and a willingness to engage with and discuss these themes.

When talking about the past to our contemporaries in the Andamans, we experienced rather strange or even paradoxical situations. Our interlocutors, informants and friends, as well as officials, businessmen and politicians, had a rich reservoir of references to the past, which caught our interest. However, our questions and their answers did not always correspond. We enjoyed friendly relationships and agreed on most things we talked about, but with regard to history, our expectations and their views did not always meet. A strange undercurrent crosscut our shared interest. Without identifying the foundation of this paradox, we continued our work, each of us among a particular community. Only later, when we analysed our data from

* Appearing in reverse order, both authors have equally contributed to this Introduction.

the field, did we realize that we had not had a communication problem with our interlocutors. But, we had, without thinking, applied different concepts of history.

Our attempt to address this disjuncture involves reflecting on the epistemic legacy of conceptualizations of the past. We shared a basic understanding of history with our friends and informants in the Andamans: a model or narrative of the past used to understand the present by looking back in time. However, the main difference between our interlocutors and us was that we applied different strategies to reduce the complexity of historical narratives. Our, i.e. the fieldworkers', understanding of history was dominated by timelines. Our questions presupposed a linear succession of events and periods ordered by time. This is due to our educational upbringing within hegemonic Western frameworks, which were dominated by science, post-Enlightenment rationalism and reason. At school, we learned history by year dates, genealogies or rulers; diagrams in mathematics and physics usually included a horizontal axis of time. To us, time was the prime means of bringing order to complexity.

In contrast, our contemporaries in the Andamans laid more emphasis on places, locations, regions, territories, and other spatial dimensions. What mattered was their ancestors' region of origin and residence, which served to identify both individuals and groups. By and large, their perceptions of the past were built on localized memory. Sites and regions mattered more than time. In sum, markers with a clear reference to space (such as language) were highly important means of identification. In spite of the omnipresent dichotomy between the colonial and the post-colonial period, we argue that, in contemporary Andaman society, spatial aspects overshadow temporal aspects. References to spatiality can be found in everyday life, in administrative and policy matters, and in popular conceptualizations of history. Taking these empirical findings seriously and reflecting on them compelled us to question and reconsider the validity of Eurocentric perceptions of history, in which time is regarded as the structured and structuring element that serves to explain the present.

As a consequence of these insights, we propose an analytical alternative: as memories of the past are to a certain extent spatially oriented, there is, consequently, a need to recognize that history is space-bound, too. By doing so, we do not intend to ignore the temporal aspects of history. We are aware that temporal and spatial dimensions are irreversibly interconnected, both in philosophical debates and in daily experience, and we will not comment on the long-standing academic debates in this field. Instead, we would like to discuss the possibility of a space-bound history: an approach to the past which the contributors of this volume encountered in the Andamans in many different forms. Local people, both subaltern and elite, tend to experience history less as a temporal progression of events and more as a structured and structuring *space*. Their perceptions of the past are based on localized memories in which sites and regions matter more than time. Migrants' places of origin on the Indian subcontinent appear to be more important for locals than the time of their arrival on the islands. Settlement structures and residential patterns suggest the emergence of a characteristically Andaman social order in which groups' spatial locations in the islands and the islands' geographical location within the boundaries of the Indian Union count more than the time span of colonial rule. Seeking approximations to this emic view, we found observable manifestations of history: man-made settlement structures, state monuments, meaningful local artefacts, situated social performative acts, and so forth.

Proposing that there is another form of historical consciousness in far off islands does not imply another East-West dichotomy. The opposite is the case. Our fieldwork was based on a common ground of communication with our interlocutors, and we hope to extend this shared experience by discussing different efficacious ways of understanding history, time, and space. This volume seeks to achieve a better understanding of 'our' own ideas by discussing 'their' concepts, based on emic experiences. The different emphasis on space and time in history is less a question of 'them and us' and more about the relational position of the speakers. We assume (1) that telling one's own history might give greater weight to space, while time seems to be helpful, as a more neutral dimension, when constructing someone else's history. In addition, (2) we see parallels to other places that have experienced large-scale migration. Societies with a heterogeneous migrant population, such as Israel, Singapore and California, display origin and movement in space as more important than timelines. Last but not least, (3) we argue that certain interests influence the emphasis on time or space, in politics and in academia.

HISTORIOGRAPHY FROM AN INTERDISCIPLINARY PERSPECTIVE

This book explores alternative analytical avenues opened by a space-bound concept of history. We argue against a monopolist, Euro-American, time-centred history and suggest that there are other ways of explaining the present based on the past. The goal is to offer a view of the Andamans' contemporary historical legacy informed by empirical work. *Manifestations of History* fills two gaps in the hitherto under-represented scholarship on the contemporary legacy of history in South Asia: first, the gap between research rooted in historical theory and research stemming from ethnographic observation; second, the gap between macro-level studies of South Asian nation states and micro-level studies of local communities. The question at issue throughout is the analytical usefulness of Eurocentric perceptions of time-structured historical models as the only valid means of explaining the present.

Until now, scholars studying the contemporary historical legacy of South Asia have tended to concentrate mainly on trying to understand either its historical past or its ethnographic present.[2] In 1980, Bernard Cohn reflected on the relationship of history and anthropology. He argued that the academic traditions, methodological training, and particular cultures, within the different faculties, have produced different approaches. In his words: 'anthropologists work in space and historians work through time in their respective construction of accounts of "otherness".'[3] From a contemporary perspective, we would like to 'bury' this opposition in the past. We seek to establish various interfaces between the two perspectives, combining insights from cultural historians and ethnographers in order to discover common ground and reassess how ideas and categories *about* the past, and objects *from* the past, gain powers of definition in the here and now.

Almost all fields of ongoing research on the Andamans deal with historical questions in one way or another. Beyond the academic discipline of historical science, most researchers in the social sciences and humanities regard historical events and legacies of the past as useful for their work about the present. Initially, traces and legacies of the past produce plural versions of historical events that researchers consider as implicit or even explicit forms of historiography. A broadened, interdisciplinary approach that enquires into historical manifestations, therefore, needs to consider the overlap of several conflicting conceptualizations of understanding and writing history. Investigating the rich, and under-researched historicity of the Andaman and Nicobar Islands, all contributors had to deal with demotic and dominant discourses about the past. On the one hand, everyone is confronted with a legacy of popular, hegemonic versions of 'history', often connected to nation building, which are based on a periodization of time structured by periods of rule. In these dominating forms of narrating the past, important personalities are presented as the main actors of historical events, while the participation of the vast majority of the population is undermined and silenced. On the other hand, there are approaches such as social history and Subaltern Studies that aim to counter such imbalances in dominant representations.[4] In order to decolonize the hegemonic episteme of elite history, they highlight the agency of lower classes and subaltern groups in the past whose own voices were not recorded in the archives. Apart from archival work, these approaches also turn to oral histories and life histories.

The authors of this volume propose that there are further levels of analysis to which we need to pay attention. History has to be regarded as a process in the making, and a field of contested interpretations. The production of oral, written or symbolic reminders of the past in the present can have cultural, social, economic or political motivations. These ways of constructing history can be regarded as giving meaning to the present by referring to the past. Words and objects are used to manifest claims and to reinterpret rituals and bodily practices. They can manifest in written documents or oral narrations, both of 'big' events in History and 'smaller' experiences in life history. Further, history can become manifest in popular memory through physical markers such as monuments, shrines, and artefacts, while on a more abstract level, the integration of a historical consciousness into people's everyday life can also be detected in legends, myths, rituals, songs, and kinship structures. Here, a consideration of the diverging perceptions, narrations, and practices of memorization among the elite, middle, and lower classes has crucially affected our academic practices of writing and representing history.

DIMENSIONS OF ANDAMAN HISTORY: TIME, SPACE, AND COMMUNITY

This volume focuses on the nexus between empirically observable and socially efficacious phenomena relating to the islands' historicity. The contributions in this book are an attempt to represent some of the diverse overlapping conceptualizations and various entanglements of past and present, both among the Andaman people and their historiographers. It needs to be emphasized that all contributions highlight several of the manifold, entangled discourses and coexisting perceptions of the past. Three dimensions or structuring patterns of history can be identified. They relate to time, space, and community. The first two dimensions are primarily structuring elements while the third can be regarded as a focus or a frame of history. The order in which we introduce these dimensions does not reflect their importance or ontological status.

The first of the three dimensions structuring history is time. Historiographers and the Andaman people themselves feel constrained in following a linear, Eurocentric conceptualization of history as the advance of time and a temporal succession of events. As a broad generalization, Andaman history can be compartmentalized into five periods: pre-colonial, colonial, under Japanese occupation, post-colonial, and post-tsunami. Historiographers wrote about the Andaman and Nicobar Islands long before the advent of colonialism. However, early seafarers, explorers, and geographers created an enduring image of the islands that has leaked into the colonial and post-colonial imagination, too. Accounts produced by the Cholas (in the tenth century), Arab, Chinese, and Greek writers as well as medieval explorers, such as Marco Polo and Niccolò dei Conti,[5] fixed the representation of the Andamans and Nicobars as a wild, untamed Oriental space, inhabited by savage cannibals.[6] This perception of the indigenous people as 'savages' and the islands as a wild place has influenced their popular perception in colonial and post-colonial times, for example through collections and displays of 'primitive' objects. In Chapter 4, Claire Wintle explores how representations of material culture in colonial collections and museums have persistently shaped the contemporary imagination of the indigenous islanders as exotic, evolutionarily backward, and static. As a concomitant to this process of representing 'nature' as opposed to 'culture', the geographical space of the Andamans and Nicobars itself has been branded as peripheral, marginal, and in-between world regions.

In colonial times, the British erected two penal settlements in the islands, one from 1789–96, which was abandoned,[7] and a second permanent and enduring one in 1858. The transportation of convicts from many castes, regions, religions, and linguistic groups from the Indian subcontinent and Burma contributed to the formation of a settler colony with distinct socio-cultural features. While prominent scholars of Andaman history have so far largely concentrated on the history of colonized populations,[8] Clare Anderson's contribution (Chapter 3) discusses texts, objects, images, and material traces of a British family that was part of the colony's administrative establishment. Her chapter points to the imperial connectedness of the Andamans with larger parts of the British Empire through affective relationships, as well as through travel and mobility. She investigates how the discovery of the family's initials carved in a rock caused a lively discussion among local intellectuals about the lifeworlds of British families in colonial Andamans.

The Japanese occupation of the islands between 1942 and 1945 is another topic of local debate because of the atrocities committed in the context of World War II.[9] The older generation of islanders has kept alive the memory of the Japanese occupation, especially that of violence against the local population. The fact that they remained in the islands and endured Japanese rule was, according to some old inhabitants, proof of their patriotism. They claim that without their sacrifices (some even called it 'martyrdom'), the Andamans would have never become part of the Indian nation state after Independence. More than a decade ago, several hundred local citizens collected money for a still pending court case against the Government of India with the aim of finding out where the compensation payment for Japanese atrocities against the Andaman population had gone. According to the initiators of the case, the compensation never reached the 'martyrs'' families.

After the Japanese capitulation in 1945, the Andaman and Nicobar Islands were reoccupied by the British. Following an intermediate period in which their future status was uncertain, they were finally handed over to the Indian nation state. In this period, Britain, Burma, Pakistan, and India negotiated their rival claims to the islands. According to Uditi Sen, the most important element in these negotiations was the characterization of the Andamans as an 'empty space', or *terra nullius*.[10] It was conceptualized as devoid of any history prior to the arrival of external colonizing forces. The representation of the indigenous population as 'people without history'[11] and the silencing of their voices have had a considerable impact on post-colonial settlement processes. Rival groups of settlers constructed competitive narratives demonstrating their contribution to the islands' spatial development and colonization in order to claim recognition and resources from the state.

Satadru Sen's contribution to this volume (Chapter 5) directly joins the argument about the Andamans being rendered a space 'emptied' of indigenes. Investigating the meaning and place of 'aboriginality' within the ideology and practice of nationhood in post-colonial India, Sen locates the indigenous Andaman islanders within global debates about governance and citizenship. He criticizes that policies aiming to protect and isolate the Andamanese hunters and gathers from the local migrant and settler society have actually worked to keep them in a 'cage' of 'primitivism' satisfying the (post-)colonial desires of tourists, bureaucrats and others to see 'exotic' ethnographic objects 'alive'. Sen argues that the Andamanese should instead be educated to become aware of their rights as citizens of India and to articulate a political voice like other Adivasi groups on the Indian mainland.

Concerning the concept of time, we discovered that the islanders themselves have introduced an additional periodization of their history. The 2004 tsunami needs to be considered as a watershed in the islands' history: when narrating the past, islanders resort to a periodization of time that divides into before and after the tsunami. Following the destructive waves, a 'tsunami of aid'[12] not only provided considerable funds for accelerated economic development, but also brought massive social and cultural transformations, which islanders broadly refer to as 'modernization'. Further, the post-tsunami period can be regarded as the islands' virtual entrance into the global public sphere. It went along with increasing transnational attention via the mass media, especially through the World Wide Web, the advent of private airlines allowing mass tourism, and steadily rising numbers of metropolitan tourists.

The second of the three dimensions structuring history is space and spatial relationships, an omnipresent and graphically structuring pattern. A spatial history takes topography as a point of departure and subordinates time. On the islands, land is a scarce and crucial resource. Administrative power is expressed in the control of territories, access to hinterlands, movements along the contested Andaman Trunk Road (ATR) leading through the reserve of the indigenous Jarawas (see Map 3), permits to visit the Nicobar Islands and of course—as in all Indian states—the granting of land rights. Structural power leads to systems of land classification, creating revenue land, reserved forest, protected forest, tribal areas, buffer zone, biosphere reserves and UNESCO World Heritage sites. Opposition and resistance are expressed in the form of encroachments and the trespassing of laws restricting access and resource utilization of government owned land. Memories of the past are dominated by power struggles over land. Settlements, creeks, coastlines, slopes and islands are habitats, agricultural fields, hunting grounds or ritual spots. Remembering such localities turns these grounded objects into named entities. At the same time, they become static, eternal and above history. People and groups pass through such spatial units like empires pass through centuries.

Compared to the Indian mainland, the physical environment of the archipelago is more strongly pre-structured. Islands and coastlines cannot be pushed like the boundaries of kingdoms or administrative units. Compared to time, space seems to be more 'real'. A piece of land can be identified, occupied, modified and even be sold. Its physical features are discernible to the senses. Soil, for example, has agency, as it can grow trees and fruits. Based on such experiences, the dominance of spatial dimensions in explaining the past comes as no surprise. Space matters, time passes.

Manish Chandi (Chapter 9) provides us with such a conceptualization of space-bound history. Based on extensive fieldwork in the Nicobars, Chandi analyses how legends about 'uninhabited' islands serve to imbibe a sense of conserving these places among those who use them as a resource base. In these legends, an ancestral past is resurrected to establish the control of resources in the present, interweaving behavioural norms, taboos, and means of ensuring compliance with customary laws. Their function is to create a situation of 'epiphenomenal' conservation.

An orientation towards space also holds true for Sri Lankan repatriates, as described by Frank Heidemann in Chapter 6. The history of Sri Lankan repatriates has become manifest in their name, settlement pattern, and social strategies to claim rights from the state. After their so-called 'repatriation' to south India, from which their Tamil-speaking ancestors once migrated to Sri Lanka to work on coffee and tea plantations, the administration rehabilitated repatriate families in Katchal Island (Nancowry group of the Nicobars) and Little Andaman. Being settled on the islands, Sri Lankan repatriates have no grand narrative about the past, no cultural or political hero, no statue and no ritual uniting them in public spaces. Instead, narratives about places of origin and places of residence dominate. Comparisons of past

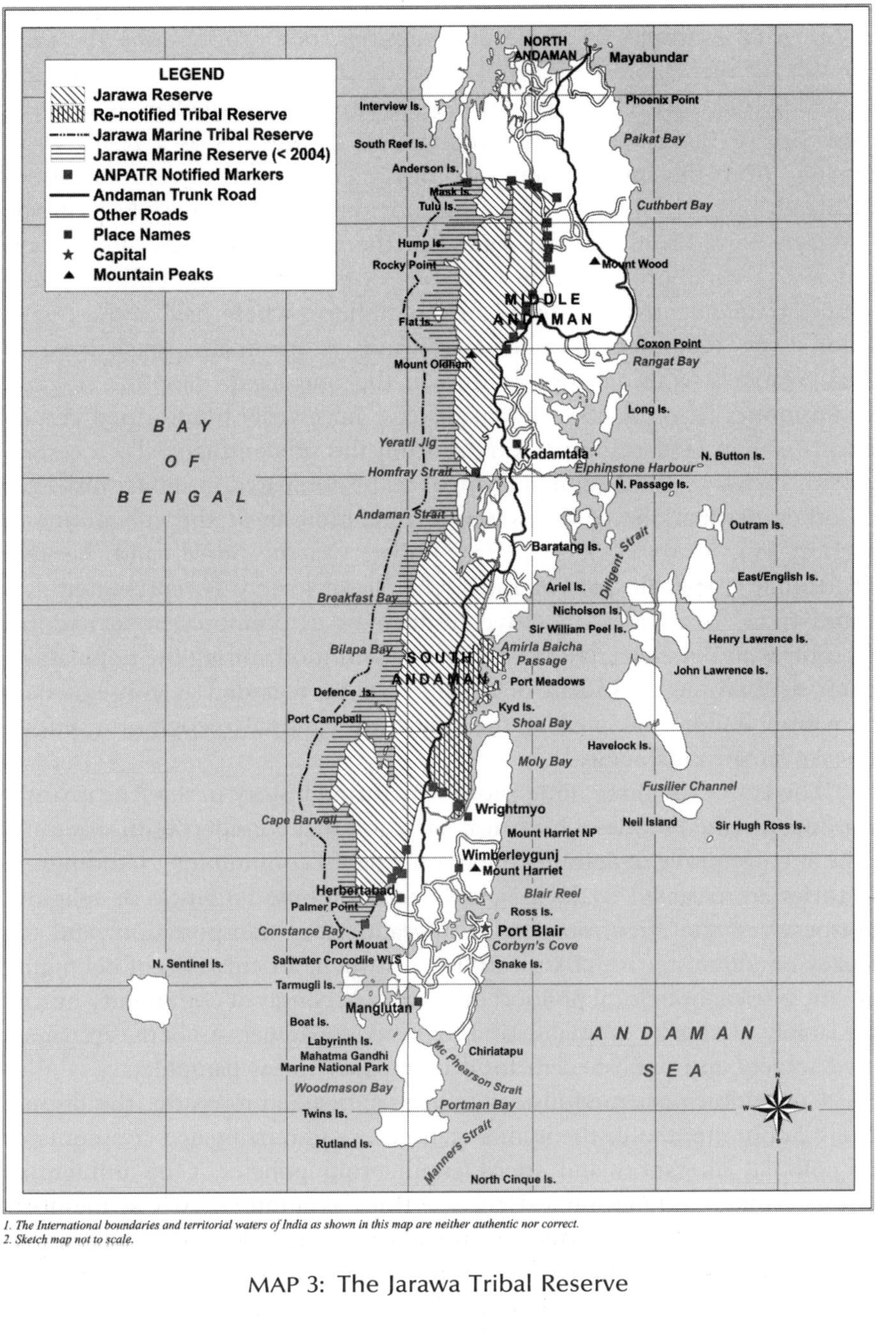

1. The International boundaries and territorial waters of India as shown in this map are neither authentic nor correct.
2. Sketch map not to scale.

MAP 3: The Jarawa Tribal Reserve

events do not follow strict timelines but juxtapose events in a geographical arena. As Heidemann argues, their conceptualization of history is oriented towards space and their movement as migrants.

Beyond examples of single communities, one can describe the relationship of the whole island society to the Indian nation state as clearly shaped by spatiality. Discourses on the Andamans and Nicobars as a Union Territory of India, located in geographical marginality as a result of its distance from the subcontinent, are firmly entrenched in representations of island history. There is, of course, not only a centre–periphery divide between New Delhi and the capital of the Union Territory, Port Blair, but also a rural–urban divide between Port Blair as the only city and administrative centre and the islands' periphery, where half of the population lives. Representations of the islands as nationalist space have to deal creatively with a conundrum. On the one hand, diasporic migrant communities living in the Andamans have necessarily transformed certain norms, values, and practices coming from the subcontinent. To a certain extent, such social and cultural change can be compared to similar processes in other destinations of transoceanic migration from the subcontinent, such as Fiji, Malaysia or the West Indies. On the other hand, because of forming a specific part of India, the island society is represented as a 'Mini-India' overseas. A decisive 'Indianness' is omnipresent in national discourses and in collective modes of self-definition among the population. Such declarations of Indian belonging can be regarded as consequences of nation building as well as the desire for cultural recognition among the Andaman inhabitants.[13]

The last of the three dimensions structuring history in the Andamans is a group-oriented mode of historical narration that considers both space and time as constitutive of defining the boundaries of communities. Community histories are narrated by local actors who combine linguistic or religious perspectives, the circumstances of migration and transportation, and the legacy of administrative classifications.[14] As such, articulations of belonging are most relevant in local political discourse. Accounts of community history are largely written by journalists and respected spokespersons of the Andaman civil society and published in local newspapers or as pamphlets.

Community-oriented history concerns, first and foremost, the distinct Pre-42 communities of the islands, who came into being as a consequence of colonial migration and social engineering policies. One influential, characteristic Pre-42 group is the 'Local Born' community, whose members largely descend from unions solemnized between convicts.[15] Congruent to the larger trend in India around the writing of popular social history,[16] intellectual spokespersons of the Local Born community have started to re-inscribe the history of their subaltern ancestors into the national history of the anti-colonial struggle, so as to gain recognition and to counter negative perceptions of Local Borns as descendants of criminals.[17] There were also attempts to write the history of two other convict communities transported by the British, the Bhantu, a 'criminal tribe' from north India,[18] and the Moplah, Muslim rebels from the Malabar Coast.[19] Among the free communities coming to the islands under the British were the Karen, a 'hill tribe' from Burma, who started settling in Middle Andaman from 1925 onward,[20] and the so-called 'Ranchis' or 'Ranchiwallahs', aboriginal contract labourers from the Chotanagpur Plateau in middle India, who were recruited as coolies in the town of Ranchi (see Chapter 7 in this volume).[21]

Kanchan Mukhopadhyay (Chapter 8) investigates the effect of the colonial social engineering policies on contemporary perceptions of identity among the Pre-42 communities. He explores how conceptualizations of space and time have affected the cultural genesis of different Pre-42 communities in specific ecological and social niches. Mukhopadhyay devotes special attention to a demotic discourse classifying the Pre-42 populace not only according to 'ethnic' criteria but also by the spaces people inhabit. Specifically, this refers to the divide between town dwellers (*bajarwalas*), the village population (*bastiwalas*), and forest dwellers (*jangalwalas*) who live at the fringes of settled zones.

The larger argument about space as major component of empirically-oriented historiography also applies to the communities settled in the Andamans as a result of mass migrations from different parts of South Asia after independence. The post-colonial policy of 'social uplifting' and territorial expansion, named rehabilitation and colonization schemes, led to the 'emplacement' of altogether 4,531 impoverished families on cleared plots of forests.[22] More than 86 per cent of these families were Bengali refugees.[23] Moreover, landless Malayalis and Ranchis, Tamil Sri Lankan repatriates (see Chapter 6), as well as Telugu and Tamil repatriates from Burma, were rehabilitated as settlers. The main reason for the massive demographic increase from 30,971 in 1951 to an official count of 3,79,944 in 2011 was, however, the result of self-motivated, independent migrations from all over South Asia.[24]

Ranchi labour forces played a crucial role in this process of territorial colonization. These contract workers cleared the Andaman forests to create spaces for settlements, roads, and agricultural zones as well as to generate revenue for the timber industry. Philipp Zehmisch (Chapter 7) elaborates on the epistemic and material legacy of the exploitative history of coolie transportation from Chotanagpur to the Andamans. He argues that the current socio-economic and political marginalization of the Ranchi community, as well as their discrimination as 'primitive tribals', can be traced back to the racial stereotype of aboriginality, which had accompanied coolie transportations across the British Empire. Further, he highlights the way Ranchi politics of recognition are influenced by attempts to evoke a popular memory acknowledging the role of subaltern Ranchi labourers in the history of island colonization. Similar to self-definitions of Bengali settlers as agricultural pioneers,[25] Ranchis regard themselves as builders of the islands' infrastructure and desire to be recognized accordingly.

In contemporary Andamans, a diverse social, cultural, and political landscape has emerged. Numerous diasporic communities from across South Asia are represented through associations and political parties, temples, churches, gurudwaras, and mosques.[26] An outstanding example of religious identification is the cultural memory of Islam. In Chapter 2, Jamal Malik elaborates on the historical legacy of the famous Muslim scholar Fadl-e Haqq Khairabadi, who was transported as a political offender to the Andaman penal colony after the 'mutiny/rebellion' of 1857. Malik's contribution demonstrates how transnational, national and local perceptions entangle when it comes to the declaration of the Andamans as a place of Muslim cultural memory with specific forms of religious and cultural pluralism.

MANIFESTATIONS OF HISTORY

Localities remain, even if their meanings change. The Cellular Jail, built in Port Blair as a penitentiary to house criminals and political prisoners, was turned into a national monument to commemorate 'freedom fighters'. Today, the building hosts a museum and a library. Every night, a sound-and-light show takes place in the courtyard of the former jail. Special effects lead visitors into the past of the place. This 'true-to-life' setting serves to inform the visitor about Andaman history and to create an affective connection with the revolutionaries' struggles against the colonial state and the jail authorities. Further, localities such as the remains of colonial buildings on Ross Island, housing the administrative headquarters and a small settlement with European facilities, are experiencing a similar semantic transformation. As a result, the currently uninhabited island has been turned into a tourist destination and functions as a large outdoor museum.

One material legacy of Japanese rule is the bunkers that are spread out all over the islands. For locals, the solidly constructed bunkers not only visibly embody the bygone strength and endurance of the Japanese, they have also turned into objects of local myths that are spun around mysterious hoards of gold supposedly buried underneath them. Moreover, military objects such as tanks and torpedoes, 'testimonies' of World War II, are exhibited in the Marina Beach Park. In physical proximity to statues of Indian leaders, these objects are placed on pedestals with a metal table indicating technical details. They face the ocean and in a metaphysical sense they protect Port Blair. On a slope planted with grass next to Marina Beach Park, a giant map of India using colourful flowers and a slightly over-dimensioned representation of the Andaman and Nicobar Islands indicates the unity of the mainland and the islands. Museums, monuments and flowerbeds are objects of the present. Institutions care for them. They share the attribute of marking places and the past.

These forms of historicization can be considered 'manifestations' of the past. This term is useful to elaborate different semantic contexts. First, it explains the phenomenon whereby imagined dimensions such as ideas, visions or ghosts appear (by an invisible hand) in a perceivable form. Second, it describes how ideas can be consciously expressed in action, in terms or in a text, for example, at a rally or in a political manifesto. Third, and less frequently, the term is used to mean a mechanical or chemical trace in the physical environment or in biological bodies, as a kind of proof of a past process. In most cases, visible bodies are transformed by a particular human, numinous, or 'natural' force. An impact of the past is present, and the present form relates to the past.

Quite often, the term 'manifestation' is used in religious contexts, when a numinous being appears in a material form. We do not want to suggest that the origin of history lies in belief systems. The very process of manifestation indicates a transition from mind to matter, and—what seems even more important—from matter to mind. Museums, monuments, and flowerbeds are creations of the present and refer to the past. Contrary to religious contexts, where the major trajectory is directed towards the material form (God appears in material form), the dominant indicator of the manifestation we talk about is directed towards the imagined. The same applies to timelines. Unlike geological layers or tree rings—physical forms produced over time—the manifestations of history are created in the present and tell us about a present state of mind. The material might be old (bunkers and tanks), but the process of selection and presentation happens now.

Most of the manifestations we discuss have a physical form. They exist in places or spatial patterns. In the non-indigenous world of the Andamans, settlements are comparatively young. The growth of settlements is often the major indicator for local history. The naming or renaming of places or locations must be seen as a struggle to control history. On Little Andaman, Burmese and Sri Lankan repatriates have debated toponyms and the resettled Ranchi village of Birsanagar has been named after the Adivasi freedom fighter Birsa Munda. The naming of settlements refers to the space between material and immaterial aspects of manifestation. The physical village is locally understood as a reference to the past, but the act of naming evades a clear reference to the material world. Therefore, we explicitly include immaterial forms of manifestation in our discussion. The term 'Pre-42' is a powerful marker of history, created after Independence, and refers to a distinct contemporary person with a local family history on the islands before 1942. Terms, classifications, categories, toponyms, and settlement names need to be included in any comprehensive discussion of manifestations of history.

As Sita Venkateswar states in her Afterword to this volume, the authors of this book offer more than one approach to history. They refer to various forms of historical manifestation and describe the complex entanglement of social groups, time, and space. Venkateswar expands to consider similar processes in other places, but her own ethnographic work is focused on the Andamans. She reminds us of our common task to reflect on the various shades and modes of history in academic and demotic contexts. The Andamans offer a large variety of materials on manifestations relating to the past. In everyday life and on special occasions, ideas of history fuse with its material signs and new forms emerge. *Manifestations of History* takes up these processes and brings together the empirical research, analysis, and reflections of a multidisciplinary group of scholars whose work on the Andamans will manifest further in future perceptions of history.

NOTES

1. The islanders are classified by the administration by settlement categories such as 'Pre-42', 'Settler', '10 Years of Continuous Education', and 'Migrant'. Beyond that, larger categories of quota reservation, 'Scheduled Tribes' (ST) for the indigenous population and 'Other Backward Classes' (OBC), were introduced by the central government. Both the local administration's and the central government's categorization matter crucially for people's access to seats in higher education and government postings. Therefore, in the political field, people base their self-identification on these pre-fabricated bureaucratic categories of belonging. See Philipp Zehmisch, 'A Xerox of India: Policies and Politics of Migration in the Andaman Islands', *Working Papers in Social and Cultural Anthropology*, vol. 2, Ludwig-Maximitious-Universität München (hereafter, LMU Munich), 2012 [http://www.ethnologie.uni-muenchen.de/forschung/publikationen/studien/bd2_zehmisch_andamanen.pdf], accessed 8 May 2015.
2. Nicholas Dirks accused Louis Dumont of neglecting historical dimensions when describing caste as a pan-Indian institution (Louis Dumont, *Homo Hierarchicus: The Caste System and its Implications*, Chicago and London: University of Chicago Press, 1980). In Dumont's view, power struggles occur within a relatively stable world of values and ideas, while Dirks claimed that power struggles generate change and therefore new systems of thought (Nicholas B. Dirks, *Castes of Mind: Colonialism and the Making of Modern India*, Princeton, NJ and Oxford: Princeton University Press, 2001).
3. Bernard S. Cohn, *An Anthropologist Among the Historians and Other Essays*, Delhi: Delhi University Press, 1980, p. 42. Like his student Dirks, Cohn took history seriously. Both had a long-lasting influence on anthropology. However, their views remained within a chronological framework of history.

In continuation of their approaches, we consider history as dynamic and driven by a power struggle for resources and dominance.

4. For a comprehensive discussion of the Subaltern Studies Project, see David Ludden, *Reading Subaltern Studies: Critical History, Contested Meaning and the Globalization of South Asia*, London: Anthem Press, 2002.
5. F.A.M. Dass, *The Andaman Islands*, 1937; 2nd repr., New Delhi: Asian Educational Services, 2001, p. 9.
6. Aparna Vaidik, *Imperial Andamans: Colonial Encounter and Island History*, Hampshire and New York: Palgrave Macmillan, 2010, p. 17.
7. Satadru Sen, 'On the Beach in the Andaman Islands: Post-mortem of a Failed Colony', *Economic and Political Weekly*, vol. XLVI, nos. 26–27, 25 June 2011, pp. 177–86, see especially p. 177.
8. Clare Anderson, *Legible Bodies: Race, Criminality and Colonialism in South Asia*, Oxford and New York: Berg, 2004; Satadru Sen, *Disciplining Punishment: Colonialism and Convict Society in the Andaman Islands*, New Delhi: Oxford University Press, 2000; Vaidik, *Imperial Andamans*.
9. Sugata Bose, *A Hundred Horizons: The Indian Ocean in the Age of Global Empire*, Cambridge, MA and London: Harvard University Press, 2006; Laxman P. Mathur, *Kala Pani: History of the Andaman and Nicobar Islands with a Study of India's Freedom Struggle*, New Delhi: Eastern Book Corporation, 1984; B.R. Tamta, *Andaman and Nicobar Islands*, Delhi: National Book Trust, 1991.
10. Uditi Sen, 'Developing *Terra Nullius*: Partition, Independence and the Andaman Islands', presentation delivered at the conference 'Manifestations of History in the Andaman Islands', LMU Munich, 22 June 2013.
11. Eric Wolf, *Die Völker ohne Geschichte. Europa und die andere Welt seit 1400*, Frankfurt and New York: Campus, 1986.
12. Venkat Ramanujam, 'Gifts without Dignity? Gift-giving, Reciprocity and the Tsunami Response in the Andaman and Nicobar Islands, India', M.Phil. thesis, University of Cambridge, 2010, p. 10.
13. Zehmisch, 'A Xerox of India'.
14. The Andaman and Nicobar issue of K.S. Singh's famous 'People of India' project can be regarded as an administrative attempt to document the history of the majority of island communities (Kumar Suresh Singh, ed., *People of India: Andaman and Nicobar Islands*, vol. XII, New Delhi: Anthropological Survey of India, 1994). The ethnographic project had the intention of covering all 4,365 communities of India in 43 volumes (Partha Chatterjee, *The Politics of the Governed: Reflections on Popular Politics in Most of the World*, Delhi: Permanent Black, 2004, p. 37). The 'Andaman and Nicobar Islands' volume covers ethnographic descriptions of 19 communities, including the indigenous groups, by putting otherwise more diverse identifications into ethnic 'containers'. There have been complaints that some communities, such as the Nepalis, were not considered.
15. Because these unions regularly crossed ethnic, religious, linguistic, and caste boundaries, the Local Borns appropriated various cultural elements and developed a cosmopolitan creole culture (Samit Ghosal, 'An Event of Cultural Creolisation in Port Blair, Andaman and Nicobar Islands', *Man in India*,

vol. 81, nos. 1–2, 2001, pp. 203–8, see especially p. 206). The *lingua franca* of the Andamans, Andaman Hindustani, became the Local Borns' mother tongue.

16. Partha Chatterjee, 'Introduction: History and the Present', in *History and the Present*, ed. Partha Chatterjee and Anjan Ghosh, London and Des Plaines: Anthem Press, 2006, pp. 1–18, see especially p. 13.
17. Philipp Zehmisch, 'Freedom Fighters or Criminals? Postcolonial Subjectivities in the Andaman Islands, South-East India', *Kontur, Nr. 22: Colonial and Post-Colonial Subjectivities*, 2011, pp. 4–16 [http://kontur.au.dk/fileadmin/www.kontur.au.dk/Kontur_22/ZEHMISCH_MOD1.pdf], accessed 8 May 2015.
18. The nomadic Bhantu community was transported from north India in order to be reformed with the help of the Salvation Army. Despite mingling increasingly with the island population, they have maintained a separate group identification. This is the subject of a monograph by Coomar (Palash Chandra Coomar, *Migration and Social Change: A Study of the Bhantu of Andaman Islands*, Calcutta: Anthropological Survey of India, 1997).
19. The Moplah were brought to the Andamans for rehabilitation between 1921 and 1926 and settled on agricultural land (Chhanda Mukhopadhyay, 'Economic Profile of Port Blair Town', *The Journal of the Anthropological Survey of India*, vol. 51, no. 4, December 2002, pp. 27–46, see especially p. 29). They speak a dialect of Malayalam, which, according to some interlocutors, is clearly reminiscent of their region in the 1920s. The Moplah are today the biggest Muslim community in the islands. So far, there is no monograph on the Moplah. The journalist, Ahmed Zubair, has published two articles about his community (Ahmed Zubair, 'Moplahs in 1922', 25 March 2011 [http://vehicleferry.blogspot.com/2011/03/moplahs-in-1922.html], accessed 8 May 2015; idem, 'The Moplah Rebellion and Andamans: Moplah Colonisation Scheme 1921–30', 2 September 2012 [http://vehicleferry.blogspot.de/2012/09/the-moplah-rebellion-and-andamans_2.html], accessed 8 May 2015. In 2013, Smitha Muttanoly, an undergraduate student in the Department of Social and Cultural Anthropology at Munich, conducted fieldwork among the Malayali-speaking migrants in the Andamans. Her thesis about transformations of Moplah identity was submitted in 2015.
20. Coomar published a monograph on the Andaman Karen (Palash Chandra Coomar, Manis Kumar Raha, and Sudip Bhui, *Tradition and Transformation in an Immigrant Island Society: The Karen of Andaman Islands*, Delhi: Abhijeet Publications, 2009). Also, see Mary Pee, 'The Karen Tribe Of The Andaman Islands: Lest We Forget!', *Andaman Chronicle*, 4 October 2012 [http://www.andamanchronicle.net/index.php?option=com_content&view=article&id=71:community-newspaper-hamara-nicobar-second-edition66&catid=19&Itemid=147], accessed 8 May 2015.
21. There were attempts to write the Ranchis' history by Agapit Kujur and Benjamin Barla, both respected community elders from the Andamans. Their accounts, however, were never published. Only a few copies of a pamphlet, authored by Barla, were distributed to distinguished members of the Ranchi Association and the Catholic Church in Port Blair. Philipp Zehmisch's yet

unpublished Ph.D. dissertation (Philipp Zehmisch, 'Mini-India: The Politics of Migration and Subalternity in the Andaman Islands', Department of Social and Cultural Anthropology, Ludwig-Maximilians-University, Munich, 2015) provides the first detailed ethnographic account of the Andaman Ranchis.

22. Kiran Dhingra, *The Andaman and Nicobar Islands in the Twentieth Century: A Gazetteer*, New Delhi: Oxford University Press, 2005, p. 167.
23. Swapan K. Biswas, *Colonization and Rehabilitations in Andaman and Nicobar Islands*, Delhi: Abhijeet Publications, 2009, p. 90.
24. Zehmisch, 'A Xerox of India'.
25. Uditi Sen, 'Dissident Memories: Exploring Bengali Refugee Narratives in the Andaman Islands', in *Refugees and the End of Empire: Imperial Collapse and Forced Migration in the Twentieth Century*, ed. Panikos Panayi and Pippa Virdee, Basingstoke: Palgrave Macmillan, 2011, pp. 219–44, see especially p. 222.
26. In the 1991 Census, the main spoken languages enumerated were Bengali (64,706), Tamil (53,356), Hindi/Hindustani/Urdu (50,961), Telugu (32,979), Nicobari (26,142), Malayalam (26,075), and Kurukh/Oraon (9,253) (Directorate of Statistics, Port Blair, cited in Dhingra, *The Andaman and Nicobar Islands in the Twentieth Century*, p. 168). The 2001 Census counted 69.20 per cent Hindus, 8.20 per cent Muslims, and 21.70 per cent Christians (Census of India 2001, cited in R.V.R. Murthy, *Andaman and Nicobar Islands: A Geo-political and Strategic Perspective*, New Delhi: Northern Book Centre, 2007, p. 95). While identifications with most forms of community and linguistic and religious groups can be observed in public life, most of their histories are still to be written.

2

The Andaman Islands in Muslim Cultural Memory and Fadl-e Haqq Khairabadi

JAMAL MALIK

In January 1858, the British arrested the scholar Fadl-e Haqq (1797–1861) in his home *qasbah* Khairabad,[1] Uttar Pradesh, because of a legal opinion (*fatwa*) that he is said to have decreed against them in Delhi in 1857. This was seen as an alleged incitement of treason against colonial power. Within the same time frame, a colonial settlement began in November 1857 at Port Blair, using inmates' labour. By March 1858, the islands were thoroughly colonized followed by deforestation and settlement projects. Already by the end of the eighteenth century—or by 1789, to be more precise—the East India Company had toyed with the idea of sending convicts to the islands, but due to the unfavourable climate and local diseases, they were soon forced to leave. Against the background of rising turmoil and the events of 1857, their intention started materializing. Initially some 200 Indians were transported to the islands. More prisoners arrived from India and Burma as the settlement grew. Local people were compensated through donations and pacified by offers to send their children to Christian schools. Christian catechism in local languages was soon made available. Spreading across varied ethnic and social groups and nationalities, the *lingua franca* was Hindustani.[2] Later, as the independence movement picked up momentum, the number of prisoners rose, requiring an accessible high-security prison of sorts on the Andaman Islands.

THE ANDAMAN ISLANDS AND THE NEHRUVIAN PROJECT

Kept under detention and tossed into different Indian prisons for quite some time, Fadl-e Haqq Khairabadi arrived at Port Blair on board the steamer 'Fire Queen', after five days of an arduous journey. On reaching the South

Andaman Islands' fateful soil in October 1858, he had no idea that his grave would eventually become an important site for peaceful encounters between Hindus and Muslims—just in line with the secularism that Nehru had proposed as a guiding principle of the Indian nation state.

Over the years, a number of players have admittedly tried to appropriate and reinterpret the records of the profound scholar Fadl-e Haqq Khairabadi. Muslim narratives as well as state institutions, such as Ministry of Minority Affairs, Departments of Religious Affairs or State Waqf Boards, endowed him and his material remnants with a major historical dimension in public debates. These reinterpretations of popular discourses have produced notions of history that have also served different Muslim historical consciences for various reasons, and continue to do so. Khairabadi's alleged involvements in the 1857 Uprising and his detention on the islands have become major fields of contested interpretation from within Muslim communities, and have provided multiple meanings in the construction of an array of histories.

Colonized as a penal settlement following the events of 1857, the Andaman Islands, meanwhile, have evolved into a main locus for the historicization of diverse movements, non-governmental as well as governmental. Part of the post-colonial nation building process, the islands have been integrated into India's arsenal of symbolic sites reflecting the experience of colonial wrath and disgrace, and subsequently of anti-colonial struggle. The dreaded Cellular Jail, built between 1896 and 1906, has been culturally reconfigured as the 'Indian Bastille' in the fight against colonial oppression. Subsequently, much has been invested in sanctifying the islands with memories of 'the dust of Martyrs' feet and their sweat and blood'.[3]

KALA PANI AND DETENTION

The reshaping of the Andaman Islands is compounded by the perception that crossing *kala pani*—black waters—results in the loss of one's varna status, in pollution and impurity. The transportation of convicts can be considered as punishment and dislocation by removing people from society, isolating them from their families, as prescribed in brahmanic texts, and placing them in distant settlements so as to put them to work. Ritual purification from this inflicted pollution is absolutely essential before the travellers can be accepted back into their home communities.[4] Fears of deviation from customs, especially those concerning food and purity, aroused severely frightening effects, so that *kala pani* or sea voyage came to represent the taboo of the sea in Indian culture. It was subsequently discussed as a controversial issue in Indian media by the end of the nineteenth century.[5] The colonial power resorted their project to this lingering ban, unscrupulously making use of prisoners in chain gangs to construct buildings, harbour facilities, and prisons. Convicts, accordingly, worked to colonize the islands for the British, bearing in mind the misery of the stigmatizing taboo that made transportation to the Andaman Islands the epitome of *kala pani*.

Presented as a harmonious model of 'unity in diversity' for all India, and a key site of the struggle and resistance against the British Empire, the Andaman Islands today offer compensation for the taboo. It appears that the official version of Andaman history has been successful in doing so by constructing a continuous historical narrative from the quarry of shared tradition. Yet, in spite of having acquired a generic meaning in Indian cultural memory, *kala pani*, i.e. the Andaman Islands, has hardly been represented in school textbooks, which have otherwise elaborated quite a bit on the events surrounding 1857.[6] Further—and even more disturbingly—little is known about the lives of the convicts and their experiences of confinement in the early years, immediately following the events of 1857.

THE ROLE OF WRITTEN TESTIMONIES

A productive source for the reconstructing of the life in early colonial Andaman and the convicts' experiences is prison literature.[7] In this genre, generally, the penitentiary is conceived as a liminal site, neither here nor there, with its own laws pertaining to time and space. This heterotopos or 'space of otherness', containing deviant people outside the norm, can become an important source for making a real utopian realm possible.[8] Together with the mythical origins and whereabouts of prison literature and the contingent process of its ingenious reconstitution, it takes on a central meaning in the collective memory, bestowing identity and inspiring solidarity—not only for the author, but also for the readers.

However, such literature remains utterly internalized and deeply silent until it is 'heard' from its concealment. Only when made audible and publicly accessible to an imagined, implied or even idealized audience, can the text become virulently active and alive to exhibit its versatile meaning. Its liberation from the constraints of a unique and dramatically constructed spatio-temporal setting is essential to create a link with the outside world. The subversive circumstance of its smuggling from the place of the 'other' is for that reason the *leitmotiv* of prison literature. Its encoding and decoding, as well as the enigma attached to its reconstruction and non-publication, help the text all the more in stimulating curiosity and demanding significance, offering a specific—albeit biased and highly personalized—version of history. Such subjective authorship and wording must obstruct the view of other historical realities, but at the same time it nonetheless creates room for new insights.

Moreover, the reference to an—often imaginary—sacred centre such as Jerusalem, Mecca, or Varanasi can animate towards uniting and mobilizing the addressees. Finally, the use of a liturgical language, such as Latin, Arabic or Sanskrit, proves its worth all the more. The prison literature in hand, Fadl-e Haqq Khairabadi's untitled Arabic poems about the Andaman penal colony, confirms such attributes in the process of reconstruction of history and reinvention of tradition; the cultural and linguistic anachronisms, emphasized, silenced, and distorted in the process of becoming and their subsequent promotion, make the corpus prone to being used by the range of actors involved in the contested field of historiography, competing for the power of agency, truth, and funds.

As a matter of fact, the specific text in question exhibits an interesting trajectory. It is said to have been penned by a member of the Muslim service elite, a reputed scholar and son of arguably the first grand-mufti of the East India Company in Delhi, Fadl-e Imam Khairabadi (d.1828),[9] a man who adhered to the traditional interpretation of Islam. Fadl-e Haqq Khairabadi's Arabic poems or *qasidas* (a classical form of Perso-Arabic lyric poetry often used as a petition to a patron) draw a remarkably dramatic picture of the earliest colonial settlement on Andaman Islands, bemoaning the situation of confinement. It stands, therefore, in contrast to a much later convict autobiography written by the 'Wahhabi'[10] Muhammad Ja'far Thanesari (1838–1905),[11] who was arrested in 1863 for conspiring to smuggle funds to anti-British *mujahidin* in Afghanistan.[12] Detained on Andaman Islands from 1866 to 1883, Thanesari's portrayal of the islands attests to a lively scholarly infrastructure, in a surrounding that virtually resembles paradise, with tall trees ostensibly 'conversing with the heavens', in a wonderful climate, that would be the envy of Kashmir, somehow divinely administrated.[13] The ethnographic account anticipates his ability to overcome the latent and open antagonisms between Muslims and Hindus against the background of a waxing cultural and religious racism under colonial administration. Eventually, Thanesari's intellectual and linguistic faculties offered him unprecedented social mobility to readjust his identity as a member of the convict elite,[14] almost resembling traumatic bonding.

In contrast, Fadl-e Haqq's account is as depressing as prison literature can be. A revenant of Greek *hypomnemata*, that is, a record and means of preserving information and memory for later generations, and an important relay in the subjectivation of discourse, it expresses a heightening interiority to form 'a raw material for the drafting of more systematic treatises, in which one presented arguments and means for ... overcoming some difficult circumstance (a grief, an exile, ruin, disgrace) ... deeply lodged in the soul ... [and which] detaches the soul from concern for the future and redirects it toward contemplation of the past'.[15] The contemplation of the past or imaginative anamnesis, thus, plays an important role in the retention of one's memory.

Yet, neither was Khairabadi able to resort to the 'web of lateral goodwill and kindness between the prisoners and their native jailors',[16] like the inmate, Mufti 'Inayat Ullah Kakorwi (d.1863),[17] who, upon his early release is said to have been instrumental in smuggling the untitled poems, secretively written with pencil and charcoal on shreds of cloth and paper, to the Indian mainland. It is said that the poems were handed over to Fadl-e Haqq's son, 'Abd al-Haqq Khairabadi (d.1899), a teacher at the Delhi College, who allegedly pieced the scattered text together and decoded most of it.[18] For this process of additional revision and edition, he must have used the notes as mnemonic aids for which he probably had a key of some description. The additions and amendments transmitted thus make it difficult to establish the original 'authorship'.

Nor was Fadl-e Haqq able to re-socialize in the wake of the disciplinary power of prison authorities. As a matter of fact, his recounting of the fatal climate, the poisonous diseases and hostile wardens in the 'barren' islands, where the only intellectual source was that of memory, echoes the notorious Indian Muslim discourses of self-victimization. Yet, the mysterious description ascribed to him assumed momentum and eventually became a prominent point of reference in Indian Muslim historiographies,[19] pervading the Islamicate[20] island's—nay South Asia's—sacred geography.

The process of printing and publishing the Arabic poems has a long and intricate genealogy; the procedure of collating, editing, translating, and publishing then has provided a scope for semantic shifts and displacements reflecting contemporary concerns that have been politically deployed. Depending on different points of view, the text was received as a 'mutiny', or named a 'freedom struggle', thereby turning local activists into agitators with quasi proto-nationalist agendas. Thus, the poems' titles oscillated between an apparent colonial perspective, such as *Risala ghadariyya* ('Mutinous Epistle'), *al-Fitna al-hindiyya* ('The Indian Sedition'), or *Baghi Hindustan* ('Rebellious India') on the one hand, and distinct nationalist comprehensions like *al-Thaurat al-hindiyya* ('The Indian Revolution') and 'War of Independence' on the other.

But why would Muslims consider the struggle of 1857 a despicable crime against authority, epitomized in the metaphor of 'mutiny' and 'sedition' (*ghadr*, *fitna*) in the first place, and rename this precious piece of prison literature 'Indian Revolution' (*thaura*) and 'War of Independence' only later? After all, the author, Fadl-e Haqq, is said to have depicted in quite some detail his appalling experiences during 1857, his subsequent detention in a number of prisons before embarking for the Andaman Islands and his misery in detainment there.

PROPHET MUHAMMAD ON THE ANDAMAN ISLANDS

The reconstruction of these trajectories can properly be understood only if semanticized in the context of intra-Muslim debates—to which the site of the Andaman Islands was to become witness, albeit indirectly but not unintentionally. The bone of contention in the *qasidas* is a reference to a debate on the nature of Prophet Muhammad that has kept alive memories of emigration (*hijrat*), persecution, and discrimination until quite recently, connecting the local debates on freedom fighters with global Islamic discourse on prophethood. It is argued that the primary titles bore specific witness to secession or *fitna* and *ghadr* caused by the so-called Wahhabis, held responsible for the colonial onslaught in 1857. As a matter of fact, the text and more particularly its commentaries, were written much later by the author's sympathizers, and his detention is thought to have been part of a malicious intrigue initiated by contentious 'Wahhabi apostates'. These 'apostates' are said to have once disputed with Fadl-e Haqq regarding a verse of the Koran (5:51) on the difficulty of accepting Jews and Christians as friends.[21] It is also asserted that these 'unbelievers' had betrayed Fadl-e Haqq to the British authorities.[22] Hence, the concepts of mutiny and *fitna* were applied to Khairabadi's 'Wahhabi' enemies only.

This drastic accusation (of apostasy and unbelief) goes back to the disputes between two contesting parties: on the one hand, those who do not acknowledge the authority of the four Sunni Muslim legal schools and consider Sufism and folk religious practices heretical innovation (*bida*'), and on the other, those who tend towards popular Indian interpretations of Hanafi Islam and attach great importance to the omnipresence of Prophet Muhammad invested with God's pre-eminent light. While the first category belongs to the puritan branch of the Naqshbandi Sufi order and its contemporary local and global network known as Tariqah-ye Muhammadiyya, the latter subscribes to the Qadiri Sufi order, which tried to reconcile traditionalist legalism with ecstatic mystic individualism. The first (Naqshbandis) were followers of the unity of witness, a metaphysical doctrine of phenomenological monism called Wahdat al-Shuhud; the latter (Qadiris) submitted to the unity of being, a metaphysical doctrine of ontological monism known as Wahdat al-Wujud.[23] Around the 1870s, those following Wahdat al-Wujud came to be solidified under the popular name of Barelwis, a toponym derived from Bareilly in Uttar Pradesh, the birthplace of their central figure Ahmad Rida Khan (1855–1922).[24]

The vivid debate between these two groups—that is, between representatives of the service elite and those of socio-religious revival—reached its peak in Mughal India; the 1820s and 1830s culminating in public *munaziras* (disputes) in Delhi. The issue pertained to the long-established position of Prophet Muhammad in Islamic cosmology,[25] which was questioned by a preacher from Rae Bareli near Lucknow, Shah Ismail (d.1831), actually a companion of Thanesari, in his polemic called *Taqwiyat al-Iman* ('The Strengthening of Faith').[26] In this book—which is basically an Urdu edition of the *Kitab al-Tawhid* written in Arabic by the eighteenth-century Arab puritan reformer, Muhammad b. 'Abd al-Wahhab (1703–92)[27]—the iconoclast Shah Ismail condemned the belief in the intercessory power (*tawassul*) of holy men, images, places or objects. He also argued that God was capable of creating another Muhammad—the Seal of the prophets (*khatam al-anbiya*)—but would not make him appear on earth. This sort of puritanism challenged the well-known prophetology, which had evolved from the mystical idea of the pre-existent Muhammadan light, as represented in a rich and eminent literary tradition, such as in *shama'il* and *fada'il* literature.[28] Fadl-e Haqq, by contrast, maintained that it was impossible that the Prophet should have a match; the creation of a peer of the Seal of the prophets was beyond even God's power[29] and also contrary to Koranic injunctions. In fact, his argument added to the filial attachment to the Prophet, and was part of a larger complex of mimetic engagement emulating the embodied virtues set by the Prophet for Muslims.[30]

In this avowedly vehement and incidentally violent dispute, a number of scholars and literary personalities got involved as well, such as the mufti of Delhi, Sadr al-Din Azurdah (d.1868)[31] and the famous Urdu poet Mirza Ghalib (d.1869), for whose aliment Khairabadi arranged princely funds. Arguably, Ghalib had no religious predilection whatsoever, but was nevertheless pushed by Khairabadi to write an anti-Wahhabi poem along such lines. Revising his *Mathnawi-ye shasham* for reasons of friendship, the poet closed the composition with the assertion that even if there were hundreds of worlds, Muhammad was singular and unique.[32]

As the debate flared, Fadl-e Haqq wrote a detailed Persian treatise in 1824/5 disqualifying the reformer as an unbeliever.[33] Theologically bested, the 'Wahhabi' sympathizers subsequently tried to deny Khairabadi's erudition, disavowed his political activities, and made him responsible for the death of hundreds of Muslims on account of the events around the Hanuman Temple in 1855 in Faizabad, Uttar Pradesh.[34] They even spread the idea that Khairabadi in hindsight had regretted his argument against Shah Ismail during his time in detention at the Andaman Islands.[35]

In fact, the debate around these two opposing positions is still very lively in South Asia and beyond, with recurrent reference to *kala pani*.[36]

Some of Fadl-e Haqq's followers have rallied behind the Barelwi movement and recently have tried styling the scholar from Khairabad as a solidarity-creating figurehead by, for example, expensively republishing all of his works, thereby historicizing popular discourses.[37] In this way, they invent a genealogy for themselves, one that harks all the way back to the first half of the nineteenth century, in an attempt to monopolize the heritage of Fadl-e Haqq and his family.

THE MAKING OF MAZAR-BABA

Notwithstanding this acrimonious debate amongst Sunni Muslims, the Waqf Board administrating the religious endowments at the Andaman and Nicobar Islands characterizes Khairabadi as a 'great Sufi saint of that time', who 'had issued "Fatwa-E Jehad" (a religious sanction) for initiating war of independence to liberate India from British yoke' and who 'confessed his guilt without fear or fret'. However, he was not a great Sufi, and his issuing of the *fatwa-ye jihad* cannot be attested to with surety. In fact, he was instead known for his rather worldly scholarship and his *bon vivant* ways.[38] There is also high probability of a judicial error on the part of the colonial administration. This is more likely than the alternatives mentioned above, since there had been a namesake from Shahjahanpur active in 1857, also alluded to in the *qasida*s. Consequently, Khairabadi never confessed his guilt but was busy writing petitions to prove his innocence until his death.

Regardless of these lasting disputes, Khairabadi's grave has become an essential element in the state clientelistic networks like many other sacred spaces that occupy public meaningfulness.[39] Under the management of the local Waqf Board,[40] it has advanced into a realm of and for peaceful encounter between Hindus and Muslims, serving the idea of a composite nationalism of sorts. A fairly large board at the burial ground praises the site as one:

> visited by hundreds of persons regardless of caste, creed or religion every day. It is also very dear to non-Muslim brothers who visit the Dargah in large numbers. The people of the Andamans have the belief that on visit to Dargah of Mazar-Baba, their miseries are taken care of. On fulfillment of their desires, they happily arrange a feast at Dargah and invite friends and poors to enjoy the feast. Fact remains that the Mazar of Allama Fazal-Haq-Khairabadi exists as a true symbol of Hindu-Muslim unity in these islands.[41]

The allegedly shared tradition perforating cultural boundaries, however, has frequently been questioned in the story ascribed to Fadl-e Haqq.

Assiduously ignoring Khairabadi's denunciation of 'Wahhabi' and also Hindu traitors during 1857, the official narrative has actually bestowed a generic term upon the shrine: Dargah of Mazar-Baba. In a de-historicized turn, this personification and generification of Khairabadi into the shrine's (*mazar*) old venerable man (*baba*) suggests that his is the place of pilgrimage to be visited by Hindus and Muslims at all costs, if only for reasons of purification and redemption.

This politics of piety is enmeshed in post-colonial governance. It constitutes an attempt to mobilize popular and renowned citizens—such as Khairabadi's famous great-great grandson, the Indian lyricist and scriptwriter Javed Akhtar—to commemorate the death anniversary of Mazar-Baba on 12 February, as the rituals perfectly provide for the (re)production of a common cultural identity and secure coherence in time and space. As a matter of fact, myths and legends constitute fundamental figures of memory. As Jan Assmann puts it, their 'constant repetition and actualization is one of the ways in which a society or culture affirms its identity'.[42] Arguably, the ritualized and collective visits to the holy place can help transcend individual limitations and social/ethnic/caste barriers—at least for a limited time. Egalitarian identity is facilitated by the common kitchen (*langar*) where community food is served to all the visitors for free, imbued with purity and spiritual power (*baraka*), to acquire dharma. Buying one's way out of the looming excommunication by alimenting *langar* helps conciliate even orthodox sections. The Sufi song (*qawwali*) performed there proclaims an ethics of brotherliness.[43] The religious poetry in praise of the Prophet (*na't*), for which the founder of the Barelwi movement was an acclaimed master, helps render the Prophet an *avatar* welding together a variety of local religious identities, such as Sunni, Shia and Hindus.[44] What is even more important is that the shrine—as the survivors' endowments of meaningfulness as it were—can operate as a centre for the consolidation and expansion of religious social capital and networks of loyalty, support and trust that involves an array of social groups including religious, social and political elites. Such a process of framing and shared understanding regarding intention and content can insinuate a common validity, attaching meaning and order to the particular social practice and symbolic communication for the visitors performing *ziyarat*, the pilgrimage or pious visitation. Given the fact that the normal means of disposal of the dead in the Indian context is cremation, the existence of tombs and their reverence might lead to raised eyebrows. Yet, as a tomb has structural similarity in Indian architecture with palaces, temples and hero-stones, 'it is natural to find the popular imagination attributing both royal heroism and saintliness to the tomb-dweller, regardless of who it may have been'.[45] Richard Eaton concisely analyses this phenomenon: 'For it was through its rituals that a shrine made Islam accessible to nonlettered masses, providing them with vivid and concrete manifestations of the divine order, and integrating them into its ritualized drama both as participants and as sponsors.'[46]

Historiographical endeavours at both the official and unofficial level suggest that the Andamans have been pregnant with iconic representations, viable enough to reiterate constructions of the past so as to capture a prominent role in cultural memories.[47] It is functionally endowed with normative properties attached to contemporary societal discourses, and it covenants a collective moral order projected onto a teleologically perceived communion. In the Muslim perspective, this validity is compounded by normative historical thinking. It is characterized by a history of salvation, epitomized in postulating the finality of Muhammad's prophethood and celebrated in the *na't*. In the nationalist Indian view, this is embedded in a similarly normative historical thinking, one of composite nationalism. In both consciousnesses, this is monumentalized in the sacralized terrain of this place of pilgrimage, connecting the local with the global and linking the religious practice in the new homelands to ancestral traditions in the old ones.[48]

Consequently, history, as it is constructed in historiographical writings within a spatio-temporal setting, never merely represents facts of the past, but is always also a reflection of the context of its creation. The trajectory of the titles of the Arabic poems show these contesting negotiations of collective memories and ways of dealing with the past. It is based on sedimentary religious vocabulary and symbolism around the Prophet, and is superimposed by the events of 1857 and their tragic figure, Fadl-e Haqq Khairabadi. These phenomena of change might well be banal, but the colonial and post-colonial period of South Asian history and its historiography illustrate the cognizant and strategic entanglement of these sorts of negotiations in current discourses of power; and one must add, increasingly of sectarian violence—as can be traced in nationalist historiography, and as has been elaborated in post-colonial discourses.

Such narratives inevitably become rhetorical, since the complex processes of self-canonization are informed by self-referential normative functions in people's collective memory, and can be traced in semantic displacements of the sort encountered in this discussion between competing and disputing groups in a contested field; the intra-Muslim debate, as well as the Waqf Board's policy of fraternization are each cases in point. The latter is supported by the larger process of conventionalizing the cultural geography of Andaman into the 'Indian Bastille', the former by the broader dispute on the nature of the Prophet and on freedom fighters.[49] As such, Sufism is considered a proven device to this end, whereas the conflict between Sufis and Wahhabis is perceived as emblematic of a larger struggle between fundamentalism and syncretism.[50]

At any rate, the diverse historiographical narrations are refreshed in situations of increasing depravity, unassertiveness, harassment, and renewal—such as the events surrounding 1857, Partition or the nation building process. Given the contingency and complexity of Indian historiography with reference to the Andaman Islands, one can say in fairness that tradition serves as a 'quarry' for the construction not only of hermetically sealed differences and boundaries, but also of shared tradition and creative mutuality. In consequence, for the making of the future, the designing of the past is as ideologically relevant as the political convenience of its imagination. The past ought to be plausible and operational, informed by Nehruvian dictates that can facilitate expansive and sweeping claims to interpretation. As a result, a hermeneutics of suspicion is well placed.

CONCLUSION

To conclude, transposing appropriated events into a modus of the past does produce meaning and relevance. Proven devices to that extent include: strategic mimesis, such as meticulously following the example of the Prophet, respectively *avatar*; structural amnesia, such as silencing deviant accounts, e.g. Fadl-e Haqq's plea for innocence; and imaginative anamnesis, or rather, the remembrance and visualization of the events of 1857 during the collective rituals at the death anniversary (*'urs*) of Mazar-Baba. Thus, the social performance[51] and the supportive mnemonic systems at the shrine can effectively translate the missions of different players into practice, thereby generating lingering imageries, narratives and identities that include both the past and the present, just as shrines in other Muslim areas.[52] Viewed in this light, the sanctuary has come to play a role in both collective memory and collective amnesia, remaining the focal point for devotion and communication. As such, it is an important integrating space in the face of the highly stratified immigrant society in Andaman.

Historiography meets the function of building identity and generating solidarity, and it is often focused on a place beyond or outside history, such as Andaman, the 'space of otherness'. Further, it is always informed by the past, and enmeshed in questions and interests that are of and in the present, in order to serve future goals. To quote Jörn Rüsen: 'By remembering, interpreting and representing the past peoples understand their present-day life and develop a future perspective on themselves and their world. "*History*" in this fundamental and anthropologically universal sense is a culture's interpretive recollection of the past serving as a means to orient the group in the present.'[53]

So, it is not a historical record of things that happened that is of the highest significance, rather it is the construction of the past and the potential meanings with which this construction can be invested. Writing the history of the Andaman Islands is, therefore, far from an unpretentious and unemotional fact-finding mission. On the contrary, it is carefully conceptualized, reconstructed and re-narrated, referring to specific notions of a past that hark back—in this case—not only to inclusivist traditions of Sufism and its critics' exclusivism, but also to the Hindu tradition of the sea-taboo as represented in the conception of *kala pani*. Undergoing expiatory ceremonies is facilitated by certain rituals and impositions, including financing the common kitchen. The modulation of such sacralized space of the *dargah*, its beckoning catharsis and embracing liminality, one must hasten to say, would not have been possible in case of a 'Wahhabi' site.[54]

It is, therefore, the social location of historical narratives and procedures of remembrance of the groups involved in the process of composing the history of Andaman—for example, ascertainable in historical sources of Wahhabis, Barelwis, and the state—that must all be investigated. This is especially the case as the actors have been prone to constructing Andaman's past with contesting references, thus arguing for a plethora of normative historiographies and various concepts of agency and authenticity. It is only a matter of time before the graveyard is converted into a prestigious mausoleum, serving as, repository of sacred charisma 'beyond Turk and Hindu'.[55] All of this is a far cry from the situation in the time of Khairabadi, who is now remembered more than he ever was in his own lifetime.[56]

NOTES

1. Khairabad was a famous *qasbah* (garrison town) in Awadh, about 80 km. north-west from Lucknow where in the nineteenth century many public officers of the British service used to live. It was attractive for investment due to its many Hindu temples, mosques, shrines, markets and manufacturers, but after crushing the revolt of 1857, it became the target of British writ. See Iqbal Husain, 'A Calendar of Khairabad Documents: Sixteenth-Nineteenth Century', *Islamic Culture*, vol. 53, 1979; Muhammad Siddîq Khairâbâdî, *Dâr al-Khair Khairâbâd*, Karâchî: Sûfî 'Abd al-Rashîd, 1976; Abū l-Fadl 'Allāmī, *The Ā'īn-i Akbarī*, 3 vols., tr. Heinrich Blochmann and Henry S. Jarrett, Calcutta: Asiatic Society of Bengal, 1877, vol. 2, pp. 93, 176, 278; 'Abd al-Qādir Ibn-i-Mulūk Shāh Badā'ūnī, *Muntakhab-ut-Tawarikh*, tr. vol. 1 George S.A. Ranking, tr. vol. 2 W.H. Lowe, tr. vol. 3 T. Wolseley Haig, Calcutta: Asiatic Society of Bengal, 1898–1925; repr., Delhi: Atlantic, 1990, vol. 2, p. 51f. H.R. Nevill, *Sitapur, a Gazetteer*, vol. XL of the District Gazetteers of the United Provinces of Agra and Oudh, Allahabad: Government Press, 1905, p. 135f. S.W.H. Sleeman, *The Kingdom of Oude*, vols. I–II; repr., Lucknow: Helicon, 1989, vol. 1, p. 135f.

2. In 1881, the Andaman population consisted of some 7,440 convicts (one-third Muslims, two-third Hindus), yet only 1,300 local peasants; 9 Muslim and 3 Hindu moneylenders; nearly 400 Muslim and approximately 600 Hindu employees; and three times more Hindu than Muslim artisans. For the Andaman Islands, see Government of India, *Selections from the Records of the Government of India*, Home Department, no. XXV: *The Andaman Islands with Notes on Barren Islands*, Calcutta: Lewis, 1859. According to reports of the Census of 1881, there was a little autonomous world on the islands which was particularly designed for the detainees: see Census of India 1881, *Statistics of the Population Enumerated in the Andamans, 1881*, Calcutta: Superintendent Government Printing, 1883; Khushî Râm Shâhjahânpûrî, *Târîkh-e Jazîrah-ye Andamân*, s.l., s.d., 1861; Muhammad Ja'far Thânesarî, *Kâlâ pânî ma'ruf beh tawârîkh 'ajîba*, Delhi, 1879; repr., Lahore: Iqbal Academy, 1993; Muhammad Ayyûb Qâdirî, *Jang-e Azâdî*, Karachi: Pâk Akademî, 1976, pp. 429–37.
3. Thus, the author of the celebrated 'The Heroes of Cellular Jail', S.N. Aggarwal, considering the islands, as cited by Clare Anderson, 'The Politics of Convict Space: Indian Penal Settlements and the Andaman Islands', in *Isolation: Places and Practices of Exclusion*, ed. Alison Bashford and Carolyn Strange, London, New York: Routledge, 2003, p. 45.
4. See Anderson, 'The Politics of Convict Space', p. 37f. This taboo might have had historical roots and resulted among others in the reluctance to engage in maritime trade.
5. See Susmita Arp, *Kâlâpânî: Zum Streit über die Zulässigkeit von Seereisen im kolonialzeitlichen Indien*, Stuttgart: Franz Steiner Verlag, 2000. I am thankful to Heinz Werner Wessler for having drawn my attention to this publication.
6. See, for example, *Themes in Indian History Part III: Textbook in History for Class XII*, New Delhi: National Council of Educational Research and Training, 2007, see esp. pp. 288–315.
7. There is a long tradition of prison poetry, *habsiyyat*. See J.T.P. de Bruijn, 'Habsiyya', in *The Encyclopaedia of Islam*, new edn., vol. XII, Supplement, Leiden: Brill, 2004, p. 333f. For contemporary Islamist prison literature, see Miriam Cooke, 'Ayyam min hayati: The Prison Memoirs of a Muslim Sister', *Journal of Arabic Literature*, vol. 26, Leiden: Brill, 1995.
8. For the concept of heterotopia, see Michel Foucault, *Surveiller et punir. Naissance de la prison*, Paris: Gallimard, 1975, German translation *Überwachen und Strafen: Die Geburt des Gefängnisses*, Frankfurt: Suhrkamp, 1976, pp. 305, 342.
9. He was praised by S. Ahmad Khan (d.1898) and Mirza Ghalib (d.1869) and later scholars called him the apex of the rational sciences. After his studies, Fadl-e Imam came to Delhi, where (after 1807) he became *sadr al-sudur* (literally, 'eminent of the eminents', a title of Mughal origin referring to the person recommending appointments of *qadi*s (judges) and *mufti*s (interpreters of law and customs), though he had himself no judicial functions) of the East India Company in Delhi, though the report on Hindu-Muslim agitation in Delhi in 1807 does not mention his name (see India Office Library and Records: Board's Collection 1796–1810: F/4/217 4758: 'Outbreak of a riot at Delhi on 1 May 1807 caused by Muslim antagonism towards Hindu religious practices').

He was dismissed from this job around 1825 due to allegations of corruption. After short stays in Patiala and Calcutta, he returned to Khairabad, where he died in 1829. Fadl-e Imam was an ardent follower of the metaphysical doctrine of ontological monism (Wahdat al-Wujud, 'unity of being'). In 1808, he challenged the followers of the 'unity of witness', Wahdat al-Shuhud—a metaphysical doctrine of phenomenological monism—surrounding Shah 'Abd al-'Aziz (1746–1824), arguably the most important Sunni Muslim scholar living in early nineteenth-century Delhi and son of Shah Wali Allah. Fadl-e Imam was eventually countered by the puritan preacher Shah Ismail's (1779–1831) first polemic pamphlet *Izhar al-Haqq*. Fadl-e Imam's son Fadl-e Haqq pursued this debate (see section on 'Prophet Muhammad on the Andaman Islands'). For Fadl-e Imam Khairabadi, see Rahmân 'Alî, *Tadhkirah-ye 'Ulamâ-ye Hind*, Urdu by Muhammad Ayyûb Qâdirî, Karachi: Pakistan Historical Society, 1964, pp. 376–8; Sayyid 'Abd al-Hayy, *Nuzhat al-khawātir wa-bahjat al-masāmi' wa al-nawāzir*, 8 vols., Dâ'ira al-Shaikh 'Alam Ullâh: Maktabah Dâr 'Arafât, 1962–92, vol. 7, p. 412; Fadl-e Imâm Khairâbâdî, *Tarâjim al-Fudalâ*, partly edited by Mufti Intizamullah Shihabi with an English translation and additional notes by A.S. Bazeem Ansari, Karachi: Pakistan Historical Society, 1956. For *Wahdat al-Wujud* and *Wahdat al-Shuhud*, see W.C. Chittick, 'Wahdat al-Shuhûd', in *The Encyclopaedia of Islam*, new edn., vol. XI, Leiden: Brill, 2002, pp. 37–9.

10. The influential book by W.W. Hunter (*The Indian Musalmans*, London: Trübner and Co., 1876) had quite some impact in introducing the term 'Wahhabi' to Indian soil with a rather derogatory meaning. For the genealogy of the term 'Wahhabi' in the Indian context, see Marcia Hermansen, 'Fakirs, Wahhabis and Others: Reciprocal Classifications and the Transformation of Intellectual Categories', and Marc Gaborieau, 'Muslim Saints, Faquirs, and Pilgrims in 1831 According to Garcin de Tassy', in *Perspectives of Mutual Encounters in South Asian History 1760–1860*, ed. Jamal Malik, Leiden: Brill, 2000, pp. 23–48 and 128–56 respectively.
11. He had been Chief Accountant of the municipal administration (*nambardar*) of Thanesar, was incarcerated on Andaman but returned from there with significant funds and a new wife.
12. Muhammad Ja'far Thânesarî, *Kâlâ pânî ma'ruf beh tawârîkh 'ajîba*; Muhammad Jafar Thanesari, 'Kala Pani: Tavarikh-e Ajib', *The Annual of Urdu Studies* 26, tr. S. Kamal Abdali, Madison, WI, 2011, pp. 167–216.
13. One can add that while a Hindu might well hate the island for religious reasons, a Muslim might in contrast love it for his own religious reasons. In Muslim philosophy, there is the concept of an island paradise, where one can come to enlightenment through philosophical and solitary contemplation of God. See, for example, Joshua Parens and Joseph C. Macfarland, 'Ibn Tufayl, Hayy the Son of Yaqzan', in *Medieval Political Philosophy: A Sourcebook*, ed. Joshua Parens and Joseph C. Macfarland, Ithaca, NY: Cornell University Press, 2011. I am thankful to David Doss for drawing attention to this issue.

14. See Satadru Sen, 'Contexts, Representation and the Colonized Convict: Maulana Thanesari in the Andaman Islands', *Crime, History & Societies*, vol. 8, no. 2, 2004, pp. 117–39 [http://chs.revues.org/index467.html], accessed 12 June 2013.
15. See Michel Foucault, 'Self Writing', *Dits et écrits*, vol. IV, Paris: Gallimard, 1983, pp. 415–30 [http://www.foucault.info/documents/foucault.hypo Mnemata.en.html], accessed 27 June 2013.
16. Masood A. Raja, *Texts of a Nation: The Literary, Political, and Religious Imaginary of Pakistan*, Ph.D. diss., Florida State University, 2006, p. 61.
17. Kakorwi was interned because he had issued a *fatwa* in favour of Nawwab Khan Bahadur Khan Ruhella (hanged 1860). Kakorwi wrote a number of books in the Andamans and was finally released because he translated Abu al-Fida Imad al-Din al-Aiyubi's (d.1331) *Taqwim al-buldan*, a standard book on geography, from Arabic into English. See *Freedom Struggle in Uttar Pradesh; Source Material*, ed. S.A.A. Rizvi and M.L. Bhargava, Lucknow: Publications Bureau, 1957, pp. 170–5.
18. For 'Abd al-Haqq Khairabadi, who in 1887 was honoured with the title of *Shams al-'Ulama* by Viceroy Dufferin (d.1902) and who was returned parts of the confiscated land of his father, see Muhammad 'Abd al-Shâhid Khân Sherwânî, tr. and ed., *Al-Thaurat al-Hindiyya; bâghî Hindûstân*, Mubarikpur: Al-Majma'al-Islami, 1985 (4th edn.), pp. 232, 328f. Rahmân 'Alî, *Tadhkirah-ye 'Ulamâ-ye Hind*, p. 279f.
19. For an analysis of the text, see Jamal Malik, 'Letters, Prison Sketches and Autobiographical Literature: The Case of Fadl-e-Haqq Khairabadi in the Andaman Penal Colony', *Indian Economic and Social History Review*, vol. 43, no. 1, 2006, pp. 77–100.
20. For the term 'Islamicate', see Marshall Hodgson, *Venture of Islam: Conscience and History in a World Civilization*, vols. 1–3, Chicago: University of Chicago Press, 1975, vol. 1, p. 59.
21. The dispute was about verse 5:51: 'Oh you who believe! Take not the Jews and Christians for friends. They are friends one to another. He among you who takes them for friends is (one) of them. Allah guides not wrongdoing folk.' This verse is made into an issue by Ghulâm Mihr 'Alî (*Al-thaurat al-hindiyya, ya'nî al-risâla al-ghadariyya, ma' sharhiha yawaqiyat al-mihriyya*, Chishtiyân sharîf: al-maktabat al-mihriyya, *c.*1964), a follower of Khairabadi, who maintained that the debate displayed the struggle between Wahhabis led by Shah Ismail and Shah Ahmad Shahid (e.g. 'wrongdoing folk'—both men being leading figures of the *mujahidin* movement in 1820s) on the one hand, and the Khairabadis (subsequently Barelwis—e.g. the 'righteously guided') on the other.
22. This has been championed by Ghulâm Mihr 'Alî, *Al-thaurat al-hindiyya.*
23. For these important concepts, see W.C. Chittick, 'Wahdat al-Shuhûd', in *The Encyclopaedia of Islam*, new edn., vol. XI, Leiden: Brill, 2002, pp. 37–9.
24. The Barelwi movement has been portrayed by Usha Sanyal, *Devotional Islam and Politics in British India: Ahmad Reza Khan Barelwi and his Movement 1870–1920*, Delhi: Oxford University Press, 1996; also see Jamal Malik,

'The Luminous Nurani; Charisma and Political Mobilisation among the Barelwis in Pakistan', in *Person, Myth and Society in South Asian Islam*, ed. Pnina Werbner, Adelaide: University of Adelaide, 1990, pp. 38–50.

25. For the importance attached to the Prophet, see Annemarie Schimmel, *And Muhammad is His Messenger*, Chapel Hill: University of North Carolina Press, 1985.
26. First published in 1824; see Shah Muhammad Ismail, *Support of Faith*, tr. Mir Shahamat Ali, Lahore: Muh. Ashraf, 1969.
27. For the Wahhabiyya, see Esther Peskes, *Muhammad B. 'Abdalwahhab (1703–92) im Widerstreit*, Wiesbaden: Frant Steiner Verlag, 1993.
28. For these important genres, see, for example, Schimmel, *And Muhammad is His Messenger.*
29. Also, see S.A.A. Rizvi, *Shah 'Abd al 'Aziz: Puritanism, Sectarian Polemics, and Jihad*, Canberra, ACT.: Ma'rifat Publishing House, 1982, pp. 518–22.
30. This has been discussed for reading and media practices along religious lines in the context of *The Satanic Verses* (Salman Rushdie, 1988) as well as the cartoons of the Prophet Muhammad published by the Danish newspaper *Jyllands-Posten* in 2005; see Pnina Werbner, 'Allegories of Sacred Imperfection: Magic, Hermeneutics, and Passion in *The Satanic Verses*', *Current Anthropology*, vol. 37, Supplement, February 1996, pp. 55–86; Saba Mahmood, 'Religious Reason and Secular Affect: An Incommensurable Divide?', in *Is Critique Secular? Blasphemy, Injury, and Free Speech*, ed. Talal Asad, Wendy Brown, Judith Butler, and Saba Mahmood, Berkeley: University of California Press, 2009, pp. 64–100.
31. Also, see Rizvi, *Shah 'Abd al-'Aziz*, pp. 517f. Afdal Haqq Qarshî, ''Allâmah Fadl-e Haqq Khairâbâdî; Jihâd-e Azâdî awr Shâh Ismâ'îl Shahîd', in *'Allâmah Fadl-e Haqq Khairâbâdî awr Jihâd-e Azâdî*, ed. Muhammad Sa'îd al-Rahmân 'Alawî, Lahore: Sunni Publications, 1987, pp. 11–70, see especially pp. 39–51.
32. See *Ghalib; 1797–1869*, tr. and ed. Ralph Russell and Khurshid Islam, London: Allen & Unwin, 1969, vol. I, pp. 32–4; Altaf Hussain Hali, *Yadgar-e Ghalib*, tr. K.H. Qadiri, Delhi: Idarah-i Adabiyat-i Delli, 1990, p. 95f. Sakhawat Mirza, 'Ghâlib awr Iqbâl men mas'alah-e imkân-e nazîr o imtina'-e nazîr kâ 'ilmî pas-e manzir' (The Problem of the Possibility or Impossibility of the Creation of a Peer [*nazir*] according to Ghalib and Iqbal), *Iqbal Review*, Karachi, July–October 1971, pp. 1–34.
33. Fadl-e Haqq Khairâbâdî, *Tahqîq al-Fatwâ fî Ibtâl al-Taghwâ*, 3rd edn., Lahore: Maktabah Qadiriyyah, 2000.
34. For the incident, see J.R. Cole, *Roots of North Indian Shi'ism in Iran and Iraq: Religion and State in Awadh, 1722–1859*, Berkeley, Los Angeles: University of California Press, 1988, pp. 244–50; Michael H. Fisher, *A Clash of Cultures: Awadh, the British, and the Mughals*, New Delhi: Manohar, 1987, pp. 227–36; Najm al-Ghanî, *Tarîkh-e Awadh*, Lucknow: Nawal Kishore, n.d., vol. V, p. 183f. also Qâdirî, *Jang-e Azâdî*, pp. 92–116; *'Allâmah Fadl-e Haqq Khairâbâdî awr Jihâd-e Azâdî*, pp. 306–28.

35. Amîr Shâh Khân, *Amîr al-Riwâyât fî Habîb al-Hikâyât*, Delhi n.d., p. 161.
36. The nexus of *kala pani* and the 'Wahhabiyya' has been reinforced by Thanesari himself when publishing books entitled *Kâlâ Pânî ma'rûf beh Tawârîkh 'ajîba* (see note 2) and *Tawārīkh-e 'Ajība, Mausūm beh Sawāniḥ Aḥmadī*, Delhi: Matba' Fārūqī, 1891, thereby deliberately juxtaposing the Andaman Islands and Shah Ismail's companion, Sayyid Ahmad, though the latter text actually is a biography of Sayyid Ahmad rather than an account of the Andamans.
37. See, for example, *'Allâmah Fadl-e Haqq Khairâbâdî, awr Jihâd-e Azâdî*; Qamar al-Nisâ, *Al-'Allâma Fadl Haqq al-Khairâbâdî: hayâtuhu wa ma'athiruhu ma'tahqîq kitâbihi al-thaurat al-hindiyya*, Lahore: al-Maktabah al-Qâdiriyya, 1399/1989; Mahmûd Ahmad Barakâtî, *Fadl-e Haqq Khairâbâdî awr sann satâwan*, Karachi: Barakât Akademî, 1975; Râjâ Ghulâm Muhammad, *Imtiyâz-e Haqq*, Lahore: Maktabah Qâdiriyya, 1979; *Maulana Fadl-e Haqq Khairâbâdî: aik tahqîqî jâ'izah*, ed. Afdal Haqq Qarshî, Lahore: Zâhid Press, 1992; Mushtâq Ahmad Nizâmî, *Sîrat 'Allâmah Fadl-e Haqq Khairâbâdî*, Karachi: Jam'iyyat Isha'at Ahl-e Sunnat, 1997 [http://de.slideshare.net/themrtariq/seerat-allama-fazl-e-haq-khairabadi], accessed 2 June 2013.
38. Even enjoying chess and dance party: *'Yal'abu bi al-shatranj . . . wa al-hudûr fi majâlis al-raqs'*. See 'Abd al-Hayy, *Nuzhat al-khawātir*, vol. 7, p. 413. Also, Rahmân 'Alî, *Tadhkirah-ye 'Ulamâ-ye Hind*, p. 383.
39. There is a vast literature on shrines. See *Muslim Shrines in India*, ed. Christian W. Troll, New Delhi: Oxford University Press, 1989; *Manifestations of Sainthood in Islam*, ed. C.W. Ernst and G.M. Smith, Istanbul: The Isis Press, 1993; P.M. Curie, *The Shrine and Cult of Mu'în al-Dîn Chishtî of Ajmer*, New Delhi: Oxford University Press, 1989; *Ritual and Religion Among Muslims of the Subcontinent*, ed. Imtiaz Ahmad, Lahore: Vanguard, 1985; also, see Helene Basu, *Habshi Sklaven, Sidi-Fakire: Muslimische Heiligenverehrung im westlichen Indien*, Berlin: Das Arabische Buch, 1994; Dale F. Eickelman and James Piscatori, eds., *Muslim Travellers: Pilgrimage, Migration, and the Religious Imagination*, London: Routledge, 1990.
40. On the notorious policy of Waqf boards or Auqaf departments, see Jamal Malik, *Islam in South Asia: A Short History*, Leiden: Brill, 2008, p. 234f.
41. While the nameplate at the shrine entrance introduces 'Hazrat Allama Fazal Haq Khairabadi' in Hindi, English, Bengali and two other regional languages, it ignores the name in the Persian script, though the Bay of Bengal was part of the Persephone world for many centuries.
42. Jan Assmann, *The Mind of Egypt: History and Meaning in the Time of the Pharaohs*, Cambridge: Harvard University Press, 2003, p. 10.
43. See Pnina Werbner, 'Langar: Pilgrimage, Sacred Exchange and Perpetual Sacrifice in a Sufi Saint's Lodge', in *Embodying Charisma: Modernity, Locality and the Performance of Emotion in Sufi Cults*, ed. Pnina Werbner and Helene Basu, London: Routledge, 1998, pp. 95–116; R. Burckhardt Qureshi, *Sufi Music of India and Pakistan: Sound, Context and Meaning in Quawwali*, Cambridge: Cambridge University Press, 1986; Adam Nayyar, *Qawwali*, Islamabad: Lok Virsa Research Centre, 1988.

44. This policy of semiotics is not new. Even Mahmud al-Ghazni, the archetypical Islamic warrior of Zia al-Din al-Barani (1285–1357) and others, issued a Sanskrit version of the Islamic profession of faith, a bilingual Indian coin with a Sanskrit legend describing the Prophet as the *avatar* of God. Cf. Hirananda Shastri, 'Devanagari and the Muhammadan Rulers of India', *Journal of the Bihar and Orissa Research Society*, vol. 23, 1937, pp. 492–7, see especially p. 495; Carl W. Ernst, *Eternal Garden: Mysticism, History and Politics at a South Asian Sufi Centre*, Albany: State University of New York, 1992, p. 52f.
45. Ernst, *Eternal Garden*, p. 104.
46. Richard M. Eaton, 'The Political and Religious Authority of the Shrine of Baba Farid', in *Moral Conduct and Authority: The Place of ADAB in South Asian Islam*, ed. B.D. Metcalf, Berkeley: University of California Press, 1984, pp. 333–56, see especially p. 334.
47. The historical memory creates the sources it needs for its own reproduction and is equipped with normative properties.
48. Nile Green, 'Geography, Empire and Sainthood in the Eighteenth-Century Muslim Deccan', *Bulletin of the School of Oriental and African Studies*, vol. 67, no. 2, 2004, pp. 207–25 [http://journals.cambridge.org/action/display Journal?jid=BSO], accessed 12 January 2016.
49. An interesting study on the political negotiations of locality is Philipp Zehmisch, 'Freedom Fighters or Criminals? Postcolonial Subjectivities in the Andaman Islands, South-East India', in *Kontur* 22, ed. P. Pannu, 2011, pp. 4–16 [http://kontur.au.dk/fileadmin/www.kontur.au.dk/Kontur_22/ZEHMISCH_MOD1.pdf], accessed 4 January 2016.
50. See Saba Mahmood, 'Secularism, Hermeneutics, and Empire: The Politics of Islamic Reformation', *Public Culture*, vol. 18, no. 2, 2006. The conference 'Understanding Sufism and its Potential Role in US Policy', held in Washington in October 2003, is very specific about this dichotomy. See [http://www.worde.org/publications/commentary/empowering_asj__sufi_muslim_networks/understanding-sufism-and-its-potential-role-in-u-s-policy/], accessed 8 May 2015.
51. For the process of effective translation of an institution's mission into practice in line with accepted social values, that is, social performance, see, for example, Jeffrey C. Alexander, 'Cultural Pragmatics: Social Performance Between Ritual and Strategy', *Sociological Theory*, vol. 22, 2004, pp. 527–73.
52. See, for example, the role of shrines in post-Yugoslav Bosnia-Herzegovina: Catharina Raudvere, 'Claiming Heritage, Renewing Authority: Sufi-oriented Activities in Post-Yugoslav Bosnia-Herzegovina. Collective Memory and Collective Amnesia', *European Journal of Turkish Studies*, December 2012, p. 5 [http://ejts.revues.org/index4602.html], accessed 12 June 2013.
53. Jörn Rüsen, 'Some Theoretical Approaches to Intercultural Comparative Historiography', *History and Theory*, vol. 35, no. 4, 1996, pp. 5–22, see especially p. 8. Also, see Jörg Rüpke, 'History', in *The Routledge Handbook of Research Methods in the Study of Religion*, ed. Michael Tausberg and Steven Engler, London: Routledge, 2011, pp. 285–309.

54. It might well be that the official narrative deliberately links the *dargah* to a Hindu tradition that tried to prove that sea voyages were in perfect accordance with tradition, such as *The Hindu Sea-Voyage Movement in Bengal* in 1894; for the discussion on the movement and its critic, see Arp, *Kâlâpânî*, Chapters VII-VIII.
55. This notion of shared history refers to David Gilmartin and Bruce B. Lawrence, eds., *Beyond Turk and Hindu: Rethinking Religious Identities in Islamicate South Asia*, New Delhi: Research Press, 2002. Gilmartin and Lawrence take seriously the term 'Islamicate culture' as suggested in Hodgson's *Venture of Islam*. For similar perspectives, also, see Richard M. Eaton, ed., *India's Islamic Traditions, 711–1750*, New Delhi: Oxford University Press, 2003.
56. Also, see 'Allama Fazl-e-Haq Khairabadi Convention at Delhi' on the occasion of his 150th death anniversary [http://sunnimuslimsnews.blogspot.de/2011/09/allama-Fazl-e-haq-khairabadi-convention.html; http://www.youtube.com/watch?v=3jf7F_srZsg], accessed 11 June 2013.

3

In Search of Black Rock

History in and of the Andaman Islands

CLARE ANDERSON

The India Office Records of the British Library in London hold a set of brown boxes catalogued as 'MSS Eur F388'. They are part of the unusually rich and wide textual, visual and material archive of one colonial family, the Warnefords-cum-Nightingales. The boxes contain hundreds of items of correspondence between the Revd Thomas L.J. Warneford and his daughter Alice Maude, written during the period 1875–82.[1] In 1866, Warneford had been appointed Chaplain to the troops in the Indian Presidency of Bengal, and from there he had been posted to the Andaman Islands. He lived in Port Blair for almost a decade with his wife Charlotte and their two children, Reginald (Reggie) and Alice (known as Maude or Maud). Following the death of their mother in 1874, Warneford sent Reggie and Maude to the English county of Berkshire to live with a Revd Buckley. He stayed in the Andamans until the end of 1878, served in the Second Afghan War (1878–80), and then in Calcutta. Reggie and Maude returned to India in 1880 and 1884 respectively, whilst Warneford went back to England. He became Vicar of St. Cuthbert's, in the town of Satley, County Durham, in 1889. By this time, he had clocked up over twenty years of Indian service.[2]

* This research forms part of a larger project, 'Integrated Histories of the Andaman Islands', supported by the Economic and Social Research Council (ESRC) (award no. RES-000-22-3484). I thank the ESRC and the project co-investigators, Madhumita Mazumdar and Vishvajit Pandya. I am deeply grateful also for the assistance of archivists and counter staff at the British Library's Asia Pacific and Africa Collections, which include the India Office Records, and at The National Archives, London. Finally, I thank Zubair Ahmed, Frank Heidemann, Emma Battell Lowman, Margaret Makepeace, Francis Neelam, and Philipp Zehmisch.

The family archive spreads beyond the British Library, and is also located in the British National Archives, London's Imperial War Museum, and the India Museum in Calcutta. It comprises more letters as well as Maude's memoir, photographs and photograph albums, and small objects including dried flowers and ferns, feathers, collections of seashells and even military paraphernalia—a machete, a Russian sword, a Turkish bayonet and knife, and a Burmese sword. And, at picturesque Mount Harriet in the Andamans, there remain today family inscriptions carved into a rock at a local beauty spot. Together, these texts, objects, images, and material traces illuminate a great deal about the everyday life of one colonial household in the peculiar situation of the penal colony. Used for the first time in this chapter, these unusually rich, diverse, expansive, and non-officially generated archives open up a means of exploring manifestations of history in and of the Andaman Islands in interesting and new ways.

This chapter centres on some of the key themes of this volume: space, time, materiality, and commemoration. It examines the familial and other affective relationships that connected the islands to Asia and the British metropole during the 1870s and 1880s.[3] It considers how the exchange of letters, objects and photographs were used as a means to collapse both distance and the passing of childhood and adolescence, for one separated family. Further, it asks questions about historicity in the Andamans, discussing the meaning of the Warneford archive in all its materiality for the making of histories in and of the present. The local discussion that emerged from my search for the family inscriptions in the islands in 2012, following my chance finding of reference to them in the India Office's collection of Warneford letters, facilitates discussion of how the British Raj is simultaneously remembered and forgotten in the islands today.

LETTERS, OBJECTS, PHOTOGRAPHS

The 1857 Revolt that catalysed the British decision to colonize the Andamans in part had been a violent reaction to colonial interventions into social and caste strictures. These included the East India Company's introduction of common messing in jails, through which prisoners from all communities were forced to share cooking fires, pots, bowls, and utensils.[4] In the aftermath of the revolt, as India was transferred from East India Company to British Crown control, the colonial administration became nervous about accusations of interference in matters of Indian religion. Thus, Revd Warneford was forbidden to proselytize amongst the Indian convicts who had been transported to the penal colony, including the many hundreds of rebels and mutineers who were still in the islands when he arrived in

1866. His role was to minister to the islands' British residents, including elites like the chief commissioner and senior medical officer; Anglo-Indians, who were present in the islands as convicts and guards; and ordinary sailors and soldiers. Warneford also chaired the local education board, which uniquely in the Indian Empire provided free education for the freeborn children of convicts, who were gradually increasing in number even in the 1870s.

In a later memoir, J.H. Titcomb, first Bishop of Rangoon, wrote of a visit to the Andamans in 1878–9. He described Warneford as 'rooted to [the islands] with all the affection of one who could make it his home for life'. He described the 'lovely situation' of the parsonage, perched high on a cliff, with blue sea in front and rich tropical vegetation at the back. He detailed how the two men had rowed across the bay, enjoying the rainbow colours of the coral reef. Visitors were often surprised at the freedom of movement enjoyed by convicts in the penal colony, and Titcomb was no exception. He expressed his astonishment that Warneford's convict boatmen were murderers, and described the Reverend's laughter when he asked if he was apprehensive of danger.[5]

Warneford's letters to his daughter, written at this time and when she was living in England, give further details of the family's life in the islands. He sent Maude news of the household pets she had left behind in Port Blair—dogs, rabbits, cats, goats, parrots, pigeons, tortoises—and wrote in detail of the plants in the garden that they had created together. He described the scriptural readings, music and hymns sung in Christ Church. He frequently implored her to remember her experiences—the way she had decorated the church altar for services, the *chapatis* (flat breads) that she had eaten each morning for breakfast, the friends that she had made. He passed on Maude's greetings to his convict boatmen, and to her former nursemaid (*ayah*), and servants; and he reminded her that she used to teach them their 'English letters'. He told her that his recently released convict servant, a man called James, wanted to go back to England, 'to see Miss Maud or Missie Baba as he calls you.... He often talks of you'. He usually signed his letters with rows of kisses, with sighs about how much he missed his daughter, and longed to see her again. He thanked her for her many letters and complained that Maude's older brother, Reginald (Reggie), also then in England, did not write to him as often as he would have liked.

Warneford wrote little about his work in the Andamans, though he described visits to the jungles, if he met indigenous islanders known to Maude. He was not allowed to set up a mission for convicts, but he was permitted to minister to one 'friendly' tribe, the Great Andamanese. Warneford baptized at least one girl ('Martha'), the daughter of the Chief of Rutland Island, Maia Biala. She had previously lived in an institution of forced indigenous confinement called the Andaman Orphanage (or 'Home') on Ross Island, the headquarters of the penal colony. As part of the colonial desire to 'civilize' indigenous islanders, like many others from the 1860s on, there she learnt to sew, to recite the Lord's Prayer, to say Grace, and to repeat the first lesson of the Bible.[6] It seems that her conversion was short-lived, though. 'I am so sorry to say Martha has given up wearing clothes again,' Warneford wrote to his daughter in January 1875.[7] The Bishop of Rangoon also noted his surprise at meeting 'Martha' in native dress, a few years after her marriage to Bfa Boi, Chief of Kyd Island:[8] 'I shall never forget what a shock it gave me as she approached, presenting exactly the same appearance as her sisters by her side. It was indeed sad to see this poor sheep wandering forlorn and uncared for in the wilderness.'[9]

Warneford mentioned only briefly what we might call other 'public' matters. He noted the shifting of Andamanese children between Ross and Viper Island, which was a site of chain gang labour for Indian convicts who had committed further offences. He also wrote of the freeing of over three hundred convicts in January 1875—likely because Maude knew two of them: the family's *mali* (gardener) and a servant called Sobram.[10] A devastating night-time fire in 1879 that engulfed half of Aberdeen Bazaar in Port Blair, where many ex-convicts and their families lived, was also described. 'It was', wrote father to daughter, 'a magnificent sight but very hot work.'[11] Otherwise, his main topic was the comings and goings of other colonial officers and their families, especially Maude's childhood friends. He wrote of the clock gifted by Deputy Commissioner E.H. Man for the church.[12] He described croquet and badminton with 'the general' (Chief Commissioner Donald Stewart)[13]—and how much he missed him and his family when they left Port Blair for England.

The Reverend mentioned the children of British officers, indigenous Andamanese and transportation convicts: Chendi, Maggie, Ma, Zoe, Robert, Ti, Nicholas, Sobram, Lucy, Tumbee, Martha, Minnie, Nora, Rajah, and The Old Boy Tom.[14] Moreover, from the letters we know that these men, women and children watched for the arrival of the monthly steamship in the harbour; awaited eagerly the unloading and delivery of letters; listened attentively as the Reverend read Maude's letters out loud; heard Maude's messages to them; and spoke of their own good wishes. The Reverend wrote their words down and sent them back to his daughter. The letters, thus, facilitated the continuation of various kinds of friendships and relationships in the face of Maude's absence.[15] Letter writing and reading collapsed the distance between these most unlikely of companions: indigenous peoples, transported convicts, boys and girls, a man of the church, Maude and her wayward brother. They enabled the crossing of space, spanning and networking jungles and settlements, islands and oceans, colony and metropole.[16] If within the discipline of history such letters are most usually seen as a source for writing about culture and society in particular locales during particular historical time frames, here they might also be conceptualized as attempts to collapse the geographical distance and long periods of time implied by the extended separation of family and kin.

In a recent theoretical intervention into the anthropology of photographs, it has been suggested that we should see images as *sensible objects*, for their circulation, mobility and ordered display in albums lend them meanings that go beyond visual representation.[17] And, as argued recently for nineteenth-century India, letters must be interpreted in the same frame of analysis as objects, for they frequently accompanied money and gifts.[18] Such methodological integration in the use of texts, images, and goods here enables a consideration of the spatial dynamics that connected the Andamans to the Indian Empire (which included at this time Burma), India to metropolitan Britain, and the colonies and spheres of influence of the empire to each other.

Warneford's letters to Maude frequently listed the contents of parcels that he had posted to England, and detailed how she should distribute them. A 'list of things sent March 1875' is quite typical:

One dark embroidered shawl for Mrs Berkeley
One blue *do do* for Miss Maudie with her papa's best love
Two silk Neckties for Mrs Berkley and Maud
One pair slippers for Reggie
One Japanese spray for Maud
One megapod[e]'s egg for me
Some photographs and 'odds and ends' to be kept by Maudie for me
Photograph of your mamma's grave for you

The global character of these and other objects sent from Port Blair to England is striking, with the Andamans clearly networked into the Asian trade in luxury goods. Gifts sent included a nine-yard length of Burmese *putso* silk, with 'a very curious pattern', apparently given to a soldier by the King of Mandalay;[19] Japanese boxes and trays; Chinese spoons; Chinese pictures; a polished mussel shell; a scarf;[20] a Burmese doll; Chinese paint-brushes; a silver Burmese ring; and a monkey skin pouch. And, from the Andamans: tortoiseshell combs; Andamanese bird skins (shaped to be worn on hats); coins; crocodile, kingfisher and megapode eggs; and an edible birds' eggs nest, with the egg still in.[21] Charlotte's personal effects were also gradually sent: a hymnbook and *Guide to Knowledge*;[22] a fan ('take care of it'); a pocket handkerchief embroidered with the letters 'C.W.'; a ribbon ('you keep it and wear it for her sake');[23] and a shawl—'worn by your mamma the last time she went out in Calcutta. You will value it therefore for her sake.'[24] Just one parcel was posted in the other direction, with Warneford noting the arrival of 'valuables in the way of gifts from little Maudie' and knives sent by Reggie. Reggie had directed his father to give the latter to his Great Andamanese friends.[25]

Father and daughter also folded small items into their letters. These included many photographs. 'I think very often of you, and look at your photograph nearly every day. I wish I could see you again, and I hope I shall some day next year,' Warneford wrote in mid-1875.[26] He sent a picture of Maude sitting beside her *ayah* and dog;[27] and another of her mother—'it will remind you of her'.[28] Though both father and daughter expressed pleasure at being able to 'see' each other in the pictures, they also mused on the disappointments of photographs, which despite their promise of visual proximity could not prevent the passing of time, or bridge the months and then years of separation. 'So you did not like my photograph . . . ?', Warneford wrote after receiving letter. 'Very well, I will try and get a better one taken another day and send to your ladyship, and then see what you say.'[29] And, a week or so after noting how grown-up Maude looked in one picture, he wrote, 'The more I look at your photograph the less I like it, because the photographer has touched up your eyes and eyebrows and so has taken away your natural expression. He has made you stand stiff.'[30] Subsequently, on the promise of new pictures from Maude she tells her, 'Mind you look very nice and don't go screwing up your little nose, like you used to out here, when you were going to be taken.'[31]

Pressed snowdrops, dried leaves, moss and ferns also travelled between the Andamans and England, picked from the garden that Maude and her father had planted together. Enveloped in one small piece of paper, folded into three, remains still a dried flower: 'The first violet ever grown in the Andaman Islands, 18 July 1877. For dear little Maudie. TW.' Even peacock feathers—which Warneford wrote had fallen into the garden as the birds flew overhead—were collected, snipped down to size, and posted in a letter.[32] The letters, gifts, photographs, feathers, flora, and fauna connected Maude to her father, colonial household and childhood friends. With their textual, photographic and other references to the past—everyday life, Charlotte, Maude's growing up, and their shared garden—they described it textually and visually, and marked it materially. This represented an effort to shrink the geographical distance between the Andamans and England, and simultaneously to both note and arrest the passing of time. The sending of letters, photographs and objects had the intention of bringing the islands closer to Maude, and of bringing Maude closer to the islands, across both space and time.

NETWORKED ISLANDS

In 1878, as Warneford's service in the islands was coming to an end, his old friend General Donald Stewart, who had been Chief Commissioner of the Andamans during 1872–5, wrote to him from Kandahar, where he was commanding the Southern Field Force in the Second Anglo-Afghan War. Stewart asked Warneford to consider joining him as chaplain to the troops. He readily agreed.[33] From his new posting, the Reverend continued to receive and to send on news of the Andamans, including in 1880 a letter from 'the Old Boy, Tom Rungiah', a convict servant.[34] Maude's letters also circulated around the region. Warneford wrote in 1879 that, from Calcutta, '[Mrs Man] sent one of your letters out to her son at Port Blair, who sent it on to me here—fancy that! You never thought your letter to Mrs Man would ever reach me in Afghanistan.'[35]

Warneford's former convict servant James accompanied him to the war, following his release in April 1878 at Warneford's behest. 'I am so glad the poor boy has got his freedom', he wrote at the time, 'for he has behaved very well.'[36] At the start of 1879, the Reverend stated that James enjoyed camp life. However, by the end of the year he reported that James did not like Afghanistan at all, and called it 'a very bad country'.[37] He continued, 'I don't think James likes this soldiering and fighting much but would far rather be back quietly in some civilized land.' Warneford told his daughter, 'he remembers you very well, and always asks after Mees Maud.'[38] For his part, Warneford longed for 'home' (England), writing that he could hardly wait to see his Andaman shell collection again.[39] He planned to take James back with him.[40]

At the end of 1880, the two men returned to Calcutta to meet Warneford's son Reggie, who had finished school and returned to India. Warneford found him work on the East Indian Railway. He took lodgings, and James (whom he had known as a child in Port Blair) went to work for him.[41] James held out hopes of visiting Maude in England, but by the end of 1880, Warneford had decided that he would 'not be able' to take him, though he did not specify why.[42] The Reverend travelled to England and spent the summer of 1881 with Maude, but went back to India without her.[43] Warneford quickly resumed his letter writing, first on the return voyage, writing from Aden that he felt very 'down'.[44] And, later, 'You don't know how I felt that parting from you in London. It seemed as if my days of happiness were all over.'[45] 'I never can get out of my mind your face as I left you in 1874. I somehow always see you in my dreams as I saw you then . . . I like to think of you as you were . . . because you were something like the Maud of my former remembrances.'[46] For her part, Maude wanted to join her father and brother in India, though Reggie warned her that she would soon tire of Calcutta.[47]

News to and from the Andamans continued to flow, with letters from brother to sister as well as from father to daughter: General Stewart's daughter Minnie got married in Calcutta, and went to the Andamans on her honeymoon. She returned to the mainland with an Andamanese servant, a man that both the children had known, 'Jerry'.[48] Warneford hosted visits from serving Andaman officials, including E.H. Man and senior medical officer Dr Reid.[49] By this time (1882), James had married a woman called 'Fanny', and Warneford thought that she would make a good *ayah* for Maude when he would be able to bring her to Bengal.[50]

Maude sent news to James through her father, but she also wrote to him directly, and the ex-convict was apparently very proud of her letters.[51] James seems to have regarded Maude with great affection, once sending her a nautilus shell that he had picked up in Aberdeen,[52] and writing her at least one letter, from Afghanistan. It is difficult to overstate how remarkable this short text is, for it is the only personal correspondence addressed by an ordinary Andamans convict that I have ever located. It offers glimpses of his unhappiness in Afghanistan, as well as details of his ongoing communication with indigenous Andamanese working as servants in the islands, or in Burma:

26th May 1880, Logar Valley near Cabul.

My Dear Miss Maud

I just going to write you a few lines in hoping to find you and Master R[eggie]. H.W[arneford]. quiet [quite] well through the Blessing of almighty God.

I have received your message from Papa this morning, and I was so glad of that you are still remembers me.

This is miserable country sandstorms day and night alike we see nothing but that Rocky Hills standing from 100 feet to 8000 in height without a bit green of any sort we live in a small tent 6 feet in length and 4 feet in breadth papa lives inside with 2 Boxes (small) 1 camp cot and I live side off it outside. I am glad to say Papa T is quiet well He is getting rather grey not much I dont mind that if we only get out this country soon.

I cant write and tell you the state I am undergoing but I will be able to explain it to you when we meet to gether and now I will leave that matter alone I heard from Lucy last week she is quiet well Tiye [her daughter] is married poor Thumbee [her son] is died last year I suppose papa has told you that I been to Rangoon before I left Port Blair I had 18 days leave than I saw Lucy and Tye, I hear from

Port Blair twice a month Timothy writes very often he is the old boy Tom's son used to be inn Mrs Stewarts service.

My Dear Miss

It cools my heart to think the fine days we all spent in Port Blair, but to think the present days which I am undergoing it is awful the weather is getting very hot now.

Paper [papa] told me that you have to a higher school lately, what master Reggie going to be his he going to a engineer or what papa tells me he doing nothing at present what his Idea I cant mak[e] out please give my kind respects to him tell him that I am very glad to hear from him at any time too glad to get a letter from you all and now I got nothing more to say at present.

Your[s] truly

James

Please except this poor letter of mine which his full of error James

Now I say good bye James[53]

The Reverend wrote of James as a faithful man, 'who looks after things capitally', even remembering to serve him his favourite dinner of duck and green peas every year on his birthday.[54] As noted in his letter, James had travelled to Rangoon, and he also went back to Port Blair on at least one occasion.[55] A second ex-convict servant, Tom, arrived on Warneford's doorstep one day in 1883, asking for work, but the Reverend did not think he could get along with James and so he turned him away.[56]

In 1884, finally, Warneford sailed to England to collect his daughter. She delighted in the journey to India, and in a later memoir wrote of her enjoyment of the 'kaleidoscopes of colour' and 'spicy scents' that she encountered. She soon became part of the Calcutta scene. She was presented at court in 1884, chaperoned by Mrs Stewart—ex-Andamans Chief Commissioner General Stewart's wife—who had been a friend of her mother's in Port Blair. It was not long before she became engaged, and in 1887, she married a man called Walter Nightingale. They left Calcutta, initially for Bhagulpur and later on Darjeeling and Assam. 'My Hindustani came back to me as if by magic,' she wrote of this period. The couple had two children, both born in Calcutta: Margaret (Meta) Warneford Nightingale (1888) and Guy Warneford Nightingale (1890).[57]

MATERIALITY AND COMMEMORATION

I had been working with the letters of Eur MSS F388 for several weeks, when on a cold day in London, in December 2010, I read the following lines:

4 May 1876: Went to the 'rock' at Mount Harriet and cut out your name MAUD about 4 inches long. Near Miss Stewart's, Reggie's is also there and the mark of the bullet he fired from my rifle into the tree at the sides of the rock.[58]

It was as though in the context of their then two-year separation that the father had inscribed his daughter's presence on a spot that he knew she loved; and that he had *remembered* her there. I resolved to try and find the inscriptions on my next visit to the Andamans, two months later.

Mount Harriet is a well-known scenic spot in the Andamans. The tallest peak on South Andaman, it was in the nineteenth century—and remains today—a popular picnic place. Officials and their families enjoyed—and now locals and tourists enjoy equally—the brisk climb up, the opportunities for birdwatching, the cool breezes, and the stunning views. At the end of the nineteenth century, a house there was used to confine the royal princes of Manipur, exiled from Assam to the Andamans for supposed treason. And, most famously of all, Mount Harriet is the last place that the Viceroy of India, the Earl of Mayo, visited before convict 'fanatic' Shere Ali killed him in 1872. The viceroy had surveyed the peak as a potential site for a European sanatorium. He enjoyed a beautiful sunset, and after descending to Hope Town where his launch was waiting, he was taken by surprise and stabbed in the back.[59]

Less well known, perhaps, even amongst locals, and though it is sign-posted, is a trail at the top of the mountain that leads to *kala pathar*—black rock (Plate 3.1). Indeed, when I first read Warneford's description of 'the rock' I did not know of it either. But during my next trip to Port Blair, I invited two friends, educationist, civil servant and historian Francis Xavier Neelam and journalist Zubair Ahmed, to come with me to Mount Harriet, to see if we could find the inscriptions. Francis and Zubair were sceptical about whether the carvings existed and, even if they did, they were doubtful that we would be able to find them. Francis later wrote an account of our trek for Zubair's newspaper, *Light of Andamans*:

I was not interested. How could some graffiti, written more than a hundred years ago, be still there on a rock! But that would be a nice trek, and an opportunity to watch some rare birds.... I started doubting the wisdom of trekking all the way to a black rock and look for some graffiti mentioned in the letter of [a] pastor to his daughter that Professor Clare had dug out in the British Library. It was clear that many British families stayed in the bungalows on the top of Mt. Harriet during the hot season. They would explore the forest and shoot pigeons. But a visit to the 'Rock' to cut one's name has not been mentioned anywhere in the records or the books *I* have read.[60]

I was more optimistic, remembering the soldiers' names that as a Ph.D. student in 1995 I had seen cut into fortifications at Île de la Passe,

Mauritius. They had dated from the period of the Napoleonic Wars (1810–15). I also knew that Australian archaeologists had been logging historic inscriptions from North Head Quarantine Station in New South Wales, and interpreting them as 'commemorative gestures, or mementoes of passage'.[61] So, for me, it was not such a stretch of historical imagination to fancy that we might find the names of Maude, Nora and Reggie on the mountain.

I take up the story, once again in Francis's words:

> Professor Clare increased her pace as she sensed we were approaching the rock. A sudden shout announced that she had found what she was looking for. 'I found it!—the graffiti!—it's there!', an excited Clare said. When I reached the rock a little later I couldn't believe my eyes. In front of us, was a huge black rock, worn smooth by the weather, but with not just WARNEFORD 1876 but many more names cut into its surface.

We were all delighted with the find. We were able to match some of the other initials to those of European officials, though we could not find the names (or initials) of Maude, Reggie or Nora. We assumed that

PLATE 3.1: *Kala pathar* (black rock), Mount Harriet, South Andaman, January 2011.

Source: Courtesy of the author.

they had been cut into a part of the rock that had broken off and fallen into the valley below—perhaps during the great earthquake of 1945—for it was clear from the lines of fracture on the surface that part of the rock had formerly split.[62]

The inscriptions on the rock aroused much local interest. Francis and Zubair posted descriptions and photographs onto the social networking site Facebook, and they were soon read, 'liked' and commented on by their 'friends'.[63] Some were astonished at the pictures of the names and letters; others lamented that they had missed the hike. As I elaborated on the contents of the boxed-up Warneford collections in the far-distant British Library in my discussions with them, and with others including the Curator of the Cellular Jail National Memorial, Dr Rashida Iqbal, it became clear that what was interesting locally was the discovery of material traces of Empire that have not been engineered by the Indian state. In this respect, their manifestation of the history of the penal colony revealed some of the tensions of post-colonial practices of commemoration.

The Andamans have played a central role in the making of a shared history for the new Indian nation, since Independence in 1947. The islands have become famous as the site of the notorious Cellular Jail (established in 1906), where some of the mainland's most famous freedom fighters against British rule were incarcerated. From the very first Independence Day celebrations in 1947, continuing into the 1950s and up to the present day, a series of plaques, memorials, and statues have been commissioned, constructed and positioned across the landscape of Port Blair. These memorialize the islands as a place of Britain's repression of anti-colonialism. Thus, the islands have acquired enormous symbolic importance on the mainland to larger post-colonial histories of nationalist struggle. However, locals, including the descendants of convicts ('Local Borns') and other colonial-era settlers, have not always supported this mainland-generated commemorative agenda. Some align themselves to it by claiming that ordinary criminal convicts were freedom fighters too, while others draw attention to their sacrifices during the Japanese occupation of the islands in the Second World War (1942–5). These tensions have set the stage for the production of several, locally constructed commemorative sites that have different kinds of meaning to different island residents.[64]

The inscriptions at black rock are entirely separate from this commemorative agenda. They are quite simply material traces of the British colonial elite that once administered the islands, of moments in time when the Warneford family and their acquaintances marked their presence at a popular leisure spot. Warneford at least returned to the place, to re-read the inscriptions and to remember and to recall family events from the past. About a year after our hike to black rock, as I was drafting this chapter, Francis and Zubair wrote to me details of a second trip to Mount

Harriet. They had found more letters: on a second smooth rock close to *kala pathar*: 'T.L.J.W.' (Thomas L.J. Warneford). There was something peculiarly apt about their communication of their visit and find, which so mirrored that of Revd Warneford to his daughter. As they remembered our collective presence at the same place twelve months earlier, history, I felt, really had come full circle.

This chapter has, thus, explored Revd Warneford's correspondence with his daughter Maude, and the carved inscriptions of their presence in the Andamans, as a means of unpacking some of the ways in which space, time, materiality and commemoration have been manifested in the islands. I have argued for an expansive definition of the archive, to incorporate textual records, images, objects and graffiti, and explored themes of separation and connection; the passing of time; and Empire and its aftermath.

The enduring material presence of the Warneford family in and beyond the Bay of Bengal reach much further than the small objects enclosed in the letters exchanged between father and daughter, in the presents sent from India to England, and the photographs that were exchanged and treasured by the Reverend and his children. And yet, the survival of these objects, and the lists of gifts and images in the archives is entirely incidental to their intended purpose: as conductors of affect and the cementing of personal relationships across a long period of time and distance. The inscriptions at Mount Harriet are quite different, for they were carved as intentional, lasting trace of physical presence, to be seen by others, and upon Warneford's subsequent views, to prompt memories of times past. Of course, Revd Warneford and his children could not have known that I would happen upon a few lines describing them, buried among hundreds of pages of personal letters thousands of miles from the 'black rock'. Nor could I have anticipated that I would decide to look for them almost 150 years later. But in writing of the context in which his letters came to pass, and of embedding them within a much larger story of family, Empire, and the separation and reunification of kin, not only do we see that textual archives are intertwined with objects and pictures, but that they can acquire a material presence and reality in a post-colonial Andamans that their authors and senders could never have imagined.

NOTES

1. T.L.J. Warneford is listed in *Burke's Peerage* [http://thepeerage.com/p39678.htm#i396778], accessed 16 May 2012. The archive does not include letters written from Alice Maude to her father.
2. *The Indian Army and Civil Service List, July 1869*, London: W.H. Allen, 1869, p. 21; 'India Deaths and Burials, 1719–1948' [https://familysearch.

org/search/records/index#count=20&query=%2Bgivenname%3Acharlott e%20%2Bsurname%3Awarneford%20%2Bdeath_place%3Aindia], accessed 9 February 2012; Certificate of service and residence of Revd T.L.J. Warneford, a Chaplain of the Bengal Establishment, and of the annuity for which he is eligible (£365), L/PJ/6/269 file 105, India Office Records, British Library, London (hereafter, IOR, BL).

3. For a recent historiographical intervention on family and Empire, see Esme Cleall, Laura Ishiguro and Emily J. Manktelow, eds., 'Imperial Relations: Histories of Family in the British Empire', *Journal of Colonialism and Colonial History*, vol. 14, no. 1, 2013.
4. Clare Anderson, *The Indian Uprising of 1857–8: Prisons, Prisoners and Rebellion*, London: Anthem, 2007, Chapter 2.
5. The Right Revd J.H. Titcomb, *Personal Recollections of British Burma and Its Church Mission Work in 1878–79*, London: Society for the Propagation of the Gospel in Foreign Parts, 1880 [http://anglicanhistory.org/asia/burma/titcomb1880/05.html], accessed 3 February 2012.
6. For a more expansive discussion of the forced confinement of Indigenous Andamanese, see Clare Anderson, 'Colonization, Kidnap And Confinement In The Andamans Penal Colony, 1771–1864', *Journal of Historical Geography*, vol. 37, no. 1, 2011, pp. 68–81.
7. MSS Eur F388/1, Letters of the Revd Warneford, 1874–7 [to Maude], 12 January 1875, IOR, BL.
8. M.V. Portman, *A History of Our Relations with the Andamanese, Vol. II*, Calcutta: Superintendent of Government Printing, 1899, p. 353.
9. *The Gospel in All Lands: Methodist Episcopal Church Missionary Society*, A.D.F. Randolph, 1883, p. 167. The bishop's visit was noted by Warneford in a letter to Maude, MSS Eur F388/1, 7 May 1878, IOR, BL.
10. MSS Eur F388/1, 12 January 1875, IOR, BL.
11. MSS Eur F388/1, [date illeg.] 1879, IOR, BL.
12. MSS Eur F388/1, 9 February 1875, IOR, BL.
13. For example MSS Eur F388/1, 26 August 1875, IOR, BL.
14. Maggie, Minnie, and Nora were children of British officers; Martha, Nicholas, Zoe, Robert, Ti, Tumbee, Lucy were Andamanese; Chendi, Sobram, Rajah, and The Old Boy Tom were convict servants.
15. Warneford wrote in 1879: 'They remember you very well.' MSS Eur F388/1, 31 May 1879, IOR, BL.
16. For a wonderful cultural analysis of a set of letters written by an unhappily married British woman in mid-nineteenth-century Bombay, see Erika Rappaport, '"The Bombay Debt": Letter Writing, Domestic Economies and Family Conflict in Colonial India', *Gender and History*, vol. 16, no. 2, 2004, pp. 233–60.
17. Elizabeth Edwards, Chris Gosden and Ruth B. Philipps, eds., *Sensible Objects: Colonialism, Museums and Material Culture*, Oxford: Berg, 2006. Note the significance also of Arjun Appadurai, ed., *The Social Life of Things: Commodities in Cultural Perspective*, Cambridge: Cambridge University Press, 1986.
18. Rappaport, '"The Bombay Debt"', p. 234.

19. MSS Eur F388/1, 11 May 1876, IOR, BL. I thank Sandra Dudley for detailed information on the likely provenance of this cloth. She tells me that if woven near Mandalay, it was likely an 'acheik' weave—well known as the classic pattern produced for male and female skirt-cloth silks of high quality, even today.
20. MSS Eur F388/1, 25 January 1877, IOR, BL.
21. MSS Eur F388/11, Letters to Reggie from his father, n.d., 29 June [1877?], IOR, BL. The British had granted Chinese collectors gathering rights for the valuable cooking ingredient, edible birds' nests, in the Nicobar Islands.
22. MSS Eur F388/1, 25 January 1877, IOR, BL.
23. MSS Eur F388/1, 7 March 1875, IOR, BL.
24. MSS Eur F388/1, 12 June 1876, IOR, BL.
25. MSS Eur F388/1, 5 September 1878, IOR, BL.
26. MSS Eur F388/1, 29 June 1875, IOR, BL.
27. This is the only photograph included in the collection.
28. MSS Eur F388/1, 12 June 1876, IOR, BL.
29. MSS Eur F388/1, 19 November 1875, IOR, BL.
30. MSS Eur F388/1, 13 January 1876; 21 January 1875, IOR, BL.
31. MSS Eur F388/1, 13 December 1875, IOR, BL.
32. MSS Eur F388/1, 26 July 1876, IOR, BL.
33. MSS Eur F388/2: Letters to Maude, 17 January 1879, IOR, BL.
34. IOR MSS Eur F388/2, 31 March 1879, IOR, BL; MSS Eur F388/3, Letters for Maude from Calcutta, and from North Afghan Field Force, 1880, 22 July 1880, IOR, BL.
35. MSS Eur F388/2, 31 March 1879, IOR, BL. Mrs [Emma] Man's husband Henry formally annexed the Andamans for the British Crown in 1858. Their son E.H. Man later worked in the islands as assistant and then deputy superintendent.
36. MSS Eur F388/1, 5 April 1878, IOR, BL. 'James' cannot be found in transportation or release records, probably because in Warneford's service, he converted to Christianity and changed his name.
37. MSS Eur F388/2, 2 February 1879, IOR, BL; 31 March 1879; 21 September 1879, IOR, BL.
38. MSS Eur F388/2, 24 May 1880, IOR, BL.
39. Ultimately, Warneford donated his collection to the India Museum, Calcutta, and to what is now the Natural History Museum, London. See, *Hand List of Mollusca in the Indian Museum, Calcutta*, Calcutta: Superintendent of Government Printing, 1884. E.H. Man noted that Warneford had assisted him with identifying shells. See *The Aboriginal Inhabitants of the Andaman Islands*, London: Trübner, 1883, p. 214.
40. MSS Eur F388/3, 6 January 1880, 1 December 1880, 8 December 1880, IOR, BL.
41. MSS Eur F388/3, 12 November 1880, 1 December 1880, 8 December 1880, IOR, BL.
42. MSS Eur F388/3, 15 December 1880, IOR, BL.
43. MSS Eur F388/4, Letters to Maude from Calcutta, and en route to England 1881, 3 February 1881, 26 February 1881, 24 November 1881, IOR, BL.

44. MSS Eur F388/4, 11 January 1881, 24 November 1881, IOR, BL.
45. MSS Eur F388/5, 16 May 1882, IOR, BL.
46. MSS Eur F388/4, 6 December 1881, IOR, BL.
47. MSS Eur F388/5, Letters to Maude from Fort William, Calcutta, 1882, Letter from Reggie to Maude, 6 February 1882.
48. MSS Eur F388/5, Letter from Reggie to Maude, 6 February 1882 IOR, BL.
49. MSS Eur F388/5, 26 September 1882, 18 December 1882, IOR, BL.
50. MSS Eur F388/5, 16 May 1882, 21 June 1882, 18 December 1882, IOR, BL. On Andamanese journeys overseas and employment as servants in South and South-East Asia, see Clare Anderson, 'Colonization, Kidnap and Confinement in the Andamans Penal Colony, 1771–1864'; idem, 'Writing Indigenous Women's Lives in the Bay of Bengal: Cultures of Empire in the Andaman Islands, 1789–1906', *Journal of Social History*, vol. 45, no. 2, 2011, pp. 480–96.
51. MSS Eur F388/5, 22 July 1882, IOR, BL.
52. MSS Eur F388/1, 31 January 1879, IOR, BL.
53. MSS Eur F388/17, Letter to Maude from James, an old servant, 26 May 1880, IOR, BL.
54. MSS Eur F388/5, 4 April 1882, IOR, BL; MSS Eur F388/6, 14 July 1883, IOR, BL.
55. MSS Eur F388/6, 9 January 1883, IOR, BL.
56. MSS Eur F388/6, 3 June 1883, IOR, BL.
57. PRO30/71/6, 'Mrs Nightingale's essay, My childhood and upbringing at Kingsclere-Woodlands Vicarage, Hants. Beginning 1874 and ending 1884 by Alice Maude Nightingale née Warneford', The National Archives, London; [http://archiver.rootsweb.ancestry.com/th/read/NIGHTINGALE/2009–05/1241253414], accessed 2 February 2012; 'India Marriages, 1792–1948, Alice Maude Warneford [https://familysearch.org/pal:/MM9.1.1/FGJP-RN1], accessed 11 July 2012. Joanna Bourke discusses Guy's later military career in *An Intimate History of Killing: Face-to-face Killing in Twentieth-century Warfare*, London: Granta, 2000, p. 216. Maude's brother Reggie married one Alexandra Campbell, the daughter of a captain in the Royal Indian Marine. They had five children, four girls and a boy [http://thepeerage.com/p39678.htm], accessed 2 February 2012. Reggie's son, Rex Warneford, is well known as a recipient of the Victoria Cross for bringing down a Zeppelin over enemy lines during the First World War. He died a few days later in a tragic air crash.
58. MSS Eur F388/1, 4 May 1876, IOR, BL.
59. Clare Anderson, *Subaltern Lives: Biographies of Colonialism in the Indian Ocean World, 1790–1920*, Cambridge: Cambridge University Press, 2012, pp. 130–2.
60. Francis Xavier Neelam, 'The Quest for Kala Pathar', *Light of Andamans*, 27 January 2012; emphasis added.
61. Anne Clarke, Ursula Frederick and Anna Williams, 'Wish You Were Here: Historic Inscriptions from the North Head Quarantine Station, Manly,

NSW', *Australasian Historical Archaelogy*, vol. 28, 2010, pp. 77–84, see especially p. 77.

62. Also, see the piece written by Francis Neelam and me for the British Library's *Untold Lives* blog [http://britishlibrary.typepad.co.uk/untoldlives/2012/02/index.html], accessed 10 July 2012.
63. Facebook post, 17 February 2011 [https://www.facebook.com/francis.neelam], accessed 15 August 2014.
64. These themes are elaborated in Clare Anderson, Madhumita Mazumdar and Vishvajit Pandya, *Integrated Histories of the Andaman Islands: Landscapes in the Bay of Bengal, 1780–2012*, Cambridge: Cambridge University Press, 2016, Chapters 1, 3, 4 and 5. Also, see Philipp Zehmisch, 'Freedom Fighters or Criminals? Postcolonial Subjectivities in the Andaman Islands, South-East India', in *Kontur* 22, ed. Paula Pannu, 2011, pp. 4–16 [http://kontur.au.dk/fileadmin/www.kontur.au.dk/Kontur_22/ZEHMISCH_MOD1.pdf], accessed 4 January 2016.

4

Material Histories

Objects and Imaginings of the Andaman and Nicobar Islands

CLAIRE WINTLE

> 'Is that an English thorn?' [Sherlock Holmes] . . . asked.
> 'No, it certainly is not.'
>
> —ARTHUR CONAN DOYLE, *The Sign of Four.*

The Andaman Islands were perhaps most famously projected onto the popular European imagination in Arthur Conan Doyle's 1890 Sherlock Holmes novella, *The Sign of Four.*[1] In this account of a wronged woman, a glorious, twice-stolen treasure, and the deadly revenge of four conspirators, the Andaman Islands and Tonga, the Andaman islander, loom large as central components of the story's narrative. Despite the text-based form of *The Sign of Four*, material culture plays a crucial role in the construction and climax of the drama: it is Tonga's personal possessions that first provide Holmes with the required insight into the 'ungovernable' character of the mysterious assassin; it is an arrow and blowpipe which allow the detective to make his final conclusion about the origin and ethnicity of the objects' owner. As Holmes concludes, the dart is not English; it is from the Andamans. Once this is established, the motivation for murder quickly emerges and the case is solved.

Arthur Conan Doyle and his characters are quite typical in their use of material culture to establish identity and place. It is perhaps the visible and enduring character of the material world that encourages the universal

*I would like to thank the colleagues who offered their time to be interviewed, especially Brian Durrans, who also read the manuscript and offered his valuable critique. Thanks also to Jim Hamill for assisting with image sourcing. Some of this research was funded by the Arts and Humanities Research Council, UK.

tendency to make assumptions about the character and status of others according to the objects they own and make. Indeed, to take another example from the Andaman Islands' 'British period', colonial officials often used material culture to facilitate their initial understandings of remote Andamanese communities. Given the impracticality of directly observing newly 'discovered' but still hostile groups, stray objects were often employed as factual data in the identification and classification of disparate communities that used such items.[2] Conversely, it is also common to use the things we produce and the things we possess in order to perform facets of our own gender, class, and values: objects are constantly used to assert individuality and to affirm or reject social connections to others.[3] Vishvajit Pandya's Onge informants, for example, have explained that after the British visited Little Andaman Island with their Great Andamanese 'assistants' in the late nineteenth century, the Onge no longer produced ornaments made with human skulls. This was specifically in order to assert their distinctiveness from the Great Andamanese who were seen as co-opted by British colonial administrators.[4]

Objects, thus, have a special quality in communicating the character of their makers and users, although they are not always 'honest'. Identity is itself, of course, a 'slippery beast': Stuart Hall has carefully described how identities are not unified or singular, but 'fragmented and fractured'.[5] Indeed, objects too are polysemic and can contain several and incongruent meanings as they come into contact with the agendas of different audiences.[6] Igor Kopytoff famously opined that objects are like humans in that they acquire new experiences and are conceptually reinvented in different social and economic circumstances.[7] It is perhaps their palimpsest-like status that makes objects such crucial tools in facilitating the imagining of 'identity' in general. This could also be the reason that material culture has so often been used by outsiders in imagining the Andaman and Nicobar Islands and the identities of their indigenous inhabitants throughout history. The very materiality of the object—its physical presence, its longevity and propensity to travel, the need to care for it and place it *somewhere*, and the possibility of arranging it and juxtaposing it with other objects in specific configurations—also lends a certain potency to the use of material culture in signifying identity and conceptualizing an object's maker and user. Indeed, as I will argue, material culture has always formed a unique platform upon which multiple and various types of audiences have been able to project their perceptions of who the Andamanese and Nicobarese peoples are.

This chapter will examine the changing ways in which the identities of the Andaman and Nicobar islanders have been constructed through material culture, and explore specifically how histories of the islands in the West have been bound up with the interpretation and display of objects. Other scholars have begun the important project of exploring that history from an Andamanese and Nicobarese perspective,[8] but here I seek to examine the capricious histories of the islands as they have been constructed in the West and especially in the UK. I hope to reveal that even the British, hegemonic versions of Andamanese and Nicobarese history are not singular or unchanging manifestations, but rather contested, complex and multifaceted in their ways of seeing. Investigating selected moments from the modern history of British intervention in the Islands, first I will explore how such objects have been used to categorize or fix their makers and users as ethnographic subjects; second, how objects have acted to harness the histories of the islands in order to shed light on European agendas and concerns, and third, how Andamanese and Nicobarese objects have been used to relate the islands' populations to wider entities such as 'Asia', 'India' and the 'Andaman and Nicobar Islands'.

THE ANDAMAN AND NICOBAR ISLANDS IN MUSEUM ANTHROPOLOGY

Tracing the display of the Andaman and Nicobar Islands in UK museums provides rich insight into the various ways in which objects and exhibitions have been implicit in the historicization of these islands and their populations. From the moment of their original appearance in British museums in the second half of the nineteenth century, the Andamanese and Nicobarese have been regularly linked with the enduring image of the 'modern savage'. Despite the diverse interpretations that have been constructed, and the multiple display mechanisms that have been employed, this paradigm has been remarkably persistent. In the nineteenth century, the twentieth century and the present day, the Andamanese and Nicobarese have been subject to the potent ability of the Western museum to cast and classify individuals and regions in historically contingent but repeatedly ethnocentric and often problematic ways.

Nineteenth-Century Imaginings: Evolutionary Hierarchies

In the late nineteenth century, European scientists regularly used samples of material culture to place the Andamanese and Nicobarese on the very lowest rungs of the imagined evolutionary scales that governed scholarship of the time.[9] Key figures such as the collector A.H.L.F. Pitt Rivers (1827–1900) famously argued that objects could be physically arranged according to the perceived 'simplicity' or 'complexity' of their formal or functional qualities; the position of an object in the resulting sequence would indicate the intellectual, economic and cultural capacity of its producer.[10] Through this intellectual exercise, the indigenous populations of the Andaman and Nicobar Islands were often posited as severely lacking in these capacities.

Museums were the most prominent venues for articulating these 'scientific' developments: displays at the British Museum (see Plate 4.1) around the turn of the century, for example, used Nicobarese and Andamanese 'implements and charms of a very primitive character' to 'enable us to understand by what methods man, in his earlier efforts of development towards civilization ... gradually advances towards the cultivation of the industrial and ornamental arts'.[11] Although difficult to identify through the reflective glass, the table case in the immediate foreground of Plate 4.1 seems to display waist belts and bows from the Andaman Islands. Text labels are placed next to each object and, while no longer extant, presumably reiterate the text from the museum guidebook quoted earlier.

PLATE 4.1: Donald Macbeth (photographer), one of the ethnography galleries with table cases from 'Asiatic Islands' and probably objects from the Andaman Islands in the foreground, British Museum, 1908.

Source: Courtesy of trustees of the British Museum.

Elsewhere, at the Horniman Museum in 1910, the Andaman collections were especially separated out from the museum's broader 'typological' arrangements and grouped together geographically in order to help visitors 'in realising the simplicity of the appliances and the fewness of the manufactured objects of the lower races of man'.[12] Up until and in the years immediately after the turn of the century, the Andamanese, in particular, were positioned through the interpretation and display of their material culture as 'modern ancients'. Although they were understood as contemporary subjects, they were chronologically placed as 'early', 'primitive' and 'simple' compared to 'modernizing' European 'civilizations'.

Twentieth-Century Imaginings: Modern Art?

As the twentieth century progressed, scientific thinking also moved on, and assumptions about the viability of evolutionary hierarchies were challenged. Franz Boas, for example, argued for the use of cultural relativism in display practices, and in anthropology more generally, calling for an appreciation of the so-called 'native point of view' on how these objects were used.[13] Elsewhere, the influence of European modern artists such as Picasso and Matisse, with their interest in the apparently primordial and savage 'other', had, by the early years of the twentieth century, created a taxonomic shift, whereby non-Western material culture could be seen as 'art' as well as 'artefact'. For Indian visual and material culture more specifically, a comparable shift also occurred as a result of the efforts of the India Society (established in 1911) and scholars such as Ananda Coomaraswamy and E.B. Havell, who advocated for the recognition of India's fine art traditions.[14]

By and large, however, the material culture of the Andaman and Nicobar Islands seems to have been bypassed by these intellectual developments. The development of new (but pervasively hierarchical) frameworks in museum practice created familiar 'bottom rungs' for both island groups to occupy. In the 1950s, W.G. Archer, the Keeper of the Victoria and Albert Museum's India Section, began his programme of creating 'a true art museum'.[15] To do so, he deaccessioned the institution's ethnographic material (including that from the Andaman and Nicobar Islands) which apparently 'obscured the art objects'.[16] At the British Museum, when two separate departments of 'Oriental Antiquities' and 'Ethnography' were formed in 1945, a 'high culture hierarchism' was similarly applied. As Lissant Bolton describes, the Oriental Antiquities Department was awarded care of the 'palace and temple art', ceramics, paintings and prints of Asia, while the Ethnography Department managed 'objects from the humbler sectors of Asian society'.[17] Given the place of the Andaman and Nicobar Islands in nineteenth-century museum categorizations, collections from the islands came under the remit of the museum's ethnography department in this later period, too. Here, they were valued for their social curiosity at the expense of their artistic merit or (Western) cultural status.

Notably, some individuals and institutions did engage with the productions of the Nicobar Islands in relation to modernist aesthetic ideals: during a trip to the British Museum in 1906, Fauvist painter and sculptor André Derain selected a zoomorphic carved wooden figure of a pig from the Nicobar Islands—known as a *hentakoi* and used in the Nicobars for promoting good health—for inclusion in his artist's book.[18] Much later in the century, Stuart Cary Welch's 1985 blockbuster exhibition at New York's Metropolitan Museum of Art (MET), entitled 'India! Art and Culture 1300–1900', included one, lone Nicobarese carved figure, of a human (a *kareau*, also used in maintaining well-being).[19] However, in line with the complex position that all Indian 'tribal art' held in mid-twentieth century museum practice in Europe and North America,[20] the islands were otherwise excluded from those exhibitions that offered a grudging aesthetic respect to the craftsmanship of other Adivasi artisans in India. Although the Nicobar Islands were included briefly in the MET's 'India!' exhibition, neither the Andamans nor Nicobars appeared in Stella Kramrisch's watershed exhibition of 1968, 'Unknown India: Ritual Art in Tribe and Village' (Philadelphia, San Francisco, and St. Louis).[21] In Kramrisch's remit of selecting exhibits 'as far as they are *works of art*',[22] and in her focus on visual harmony and 'ritual', she prioritized other objects.

Twenty-First-Century Imaginings: Continuing Paradigms

A similar 'disappearing act' has occurred at the British Museum in recent years. In 2002, the departments of 'Oriental Antiquities' and 'Ethnography' were renamed 'Asia' and 'Africa, Oceania and the Americas', and the Asian anthropology collections were transferred from 'Ethnography' to 'Asia'. As a result of this new departmental configuration, the scope to engage with the 'tribal' cultures of Asia has diminished significantly. Today, the main permanent display space for South and South-East Asian cultures at the British Museum is in the Joseph E. Hotung Gallery. This gallery aims to chart the major religious systems of Buddhism, Hinduism, and Jainism as they apply to India, Thailand, Cambodia, Sri Lanka, Tibet, and China, and traces the Chinese civilization chronologically from the Neolithic period to the twentieth century. Small-scale and minority societies that fall outside of these major religions and 'civilizations' have no place in the highly aestheticized galleries that glimmer with precious metals and gems. With the major exception of the Wellcome Trust Gallery, discussed later, the opportunities for the display of objects traditionally excluded from definitions of Asian 'high culture' are non-existent. Indeed, there has been no member of staff dedicated to this material since the departure of the curator for Asian Ethnography in 2009. Perhaps ironically, this institutional reorganization has been seen by some as an attempt to overcome the implicit inequalities (of race, class, and aesthetics) constructed in the previous arrangement.[23] The danger, of course, is that the old hierarchies remain under new guises, and the limited opportunities for display, research or interpretation of 'tribal' objects within the new institutional formulation act to erase places like the Andaman and Nicobar Islands from the museum record entirely.[24]

Indeed, where the Andaman and Nicobar Islands have been displayed in the twentieth and twenty-first centuries, nineteenth-century methods of museum anthropology have largely been retained. In the mid-twentieth century, this was largely because the post-war funding crisis did not allow for radical overhauls of museum displays and interpretation. The British Museum, for example, retained its turn-of-the-century evolutionary displays until the progressive, new Museum of Mankind was established as separate from the main Bloomsbury site in 1970 (here, neither the Andaman nor the Nicobar collections were featured in the Museum of Mankind's pioneering programme of engaged anthropology and post-colonial museology). Conversely, the Pitt Rivers Museum did make alterations to displays of the Andaman Islands during this time, but the typological and hierarchical message remained the same despite the discrediting of these theories in the academy: displays probably arranged by Beatrice Blackwood in 1944 or 1945 compared adzes from 'modern tribal peoples' in Fiji, New Caledonia and the Andamans in order to demonstrate how 'the use of iron had been introduced into their Stone Age cultures by European contacts'.[25] Here, the correlation between ancient European civilizations and contemporary non-European communities was again explicitly drawn, and the European was singled out as the dynamic agent introducing new materials to otherwise 'prehistoric' cultures.

Despite the revolution in museum practice since the 1970s, where Eurocentric ideologies have been critiqued and diverse voices and multiple perspectives on cultural heritage acknowledged, approaches to displaying the Andaman Islands have remained largely static. This is either because the islands, intriguingly, have been repeatedly selected as suitable for inclusion in wider exhibits that engage with the history of museum practice (possibly because they were such a significant part of early museum displays), or because they have been framed in new exhibitions which accidently employ earlier display paradigms. At the Pitt Rivers Museum, for example, Blackwood's 1940s exhibit, complete with historic text labels, is still on display for contemporary audiences to see. The fact that the Pitt Rivers Museum has retained its historic modes of display has made it one of the UK's best-loved museums, but it is nevertheless the case that such text labels continue to evoke the Andamanese as emissaries from a prehistoric past for contemporary audiences largely unaware of the nuances of Andamanese society in past and present. Similarly, at the Horniman Museum, the Andamans is included in the institution's Centenary Gallery which aims to tell the story of the museum's collections over the last hundred years. Andamanese objects are included in a display dedicated to 'personal adornment', and the text panel reveals the exhibit's intention to 'show how later anthropologists explained differences in culture as adaptations to the environment rather than as part of a linear evolution'.[26] Despite this shift in display and interpretation from the nineteenth-century evolutionary paradigm to a focus on the anthropological thought fashionable in the middle years of the twentieth century, it is perhaps still significant that the material culture of the Andamans has been chosen as a tool with which to present British institutional pasts, rather than as providing an insight into a dynamic, contemporary culture.[27] Similarly, in a bid to engage local audiences and explore why collections from the Andaman and Nicobar Islands should be present in a small city on the south coast of England, a recent exhibition at Brighton Museum & Art Gallery considered the objects' assembly by E.H. Man, R.C. Temple and K.S. Tuson in the nineteenth century, rather than their use by indigenous peoples.[28]

The recently remodelled galleries at the National Museum of Scotland, by contrast, were designed with contemporary anthropology and cross-cultural dialogue in mind. Unveiled in July 2011, the new displays include the Andaman Islands by means of a single baby carrier made of bark fibre, dentalium strings and cockle shells (see Plate 4.2). The carrier is incorporated into a display about family and social life in Asia, and is part of a gallery focusing on interactions between people and their possessions. In a subsection entitled 'Taking Care of Baby', the Andamanese baby carrier is juxtaposed with a cane and beadwork baby carrier from Sarawak decorated with three abstract black and red human figures (see Plate 4.3). The text label for the subsection reads: 'Many mothers in Asia carry their babies around with them all day to keep them safe and out of mischief. Whether cocooned in a beautiful basket or held in a simple sling, from the very beginning of life this creates a close bond between mother and baby.'[29]

This description included in the label was no doubt a quirk of the rigorous editing process led by designers and educationalists, and influenced by the difficult text-condensing exercise required in all contemporary gallery developments.[30] However, it is nevertheless startling to see the very

PLATE 4.2: Andamanese infant carrier (1884.39.14) on display at the National Museum of Scotland, 2012.

Source: Courtesy of the author.

PLATE 4.3: Asia Display, Patterns of Life Gallery, National Museum of Scotland, 2012. The Sarawak infant carrier is positioned at the top of the case, above the Andamanese infant carrier.

Source: Courtesy of the author.

vocabulary and similar visual and textual comparisons used by nineteenth-century figures such as A.H.L.F. Pitt Rivers in a contemporary display. The people of Sarawak, of course, would not necessarily have been placed at a particularly high level in Victorian evolutionary hierarchies, but here, as in the nineteenth century, the use of iconic representations of the human figure, that are compatible with Western art histories, seems to help elevate the Sarawak baby carrier above an apparently 'simple' object from the Andaman Islands. The composition of the National Museum of Scotland's Andamanese baby carrier, like all baby carriers produced in the Andaman Islands in the late nineteenth century, is tangible evidence of the constant interactions between the Andamanese and their spirit world: in the Andamanese worldview, spirits, humans and animals are considered to share a common space which must be physically and conceptually negotiated; the entitlement and ability of humans to hunt, reproduce and relocate is carefully determined through cyclical actions of engaging with the spirits in order to gain power, and avoiding the spirits in order to prevent power being exerted over them.[31] The binding involved in creating the bark loop of the carrier, its shell strings and the soft smudges of red clay visible on the bark loop, all act to endow the sling's wearer with a certain status, weight and smell that will attract or repel the spirits as necessary.[32] This is not a 'simple' object, but it is largely cast as such because its complex significance and iconography is not as immediately comprehensible as that of the other objects in the glass *vitrine* around it. Here, the 'Stone Age' character of the Andamanese is not explicitly evoked, but Andamanese design histories continue to be categorized in Eurocentric ways. Similarly, without the display space to reference the contemporary lifestyles and modern material cultures of the Andamanese, a historical fixity, devoid of dynamism, is arguably still evoked.

For more than two centuries then, despite changing ideals of aesthetic value, new hierarchies of humanity, and shifting enthusiasms for particular themes in museum interpretation, there has been a strong *leitmotif* dominating the display of the Andamanese and Nicobarese in museums in the UK and beyond. While the societies allocated places at the highest points of Western orders of art, design and culture have alternated, those on the bottom rungs have remained remarkably static. Analysing the repetition of the 'modern savage' trope provides evidence of the ways in which assumptions formed in the past shape current thinking. Moreover, we see the power of objects to act as attributes of their producers and former owners, apparently providing insight into character and capability. Yet what is clear is that this ambassadorial capacity is not straightforward: the reception of material culture—as the next section will demonstrate—is inevitably subject to the eye of the beholder.

MUSEUM AGENDAS: THE NICOBAR ISLANDS AT THE BRITISH MUSEUM, 2003–8

Despite the persistence with which the Andaman and Nicobar Islands have been harnessed for the purpose of confirming the evolutionary and other hierarchies described earlier, Andamanese and Nicobarese objects have also been subsumed within other display and interpretation agendas constructed by curators, designers and educators. One of the more recent and high profile displays of Nicobarese material culture was at the British Museum between 2003 and 2008. Here, the representation of the Nicobarese became embroiled in a series of contemporary ideological concerns that have recently been at the heart of European and North American museum practice: the objects became vehicles, not only for the presumed identity of their previous owners, but as entities through which to articulate post-colonial museum agendas and a specific perspective in ongoing debates about the validity of the so-called 'Universal Museum'. In this situation, the historicization and identity formation of the Nicobarese through material culture took a complex turn.

The British Museum's Living and Dying Gallery opened in 2003. Explicitly interdisciplinary and international, it draws on geographically diverse collections from Asia, Africa, Oceania and the Americas and aims to consider how communities throughout the world sustain well-being.[33] Largely for conservation reasons, the displays are refreshed every five years, with new themes and objects introduced, but, in the first iteration of the gallery, the Nicobar Islands provided the subject of a central exhibit designed to explore human interactions with the spirit world as a mode of curing sickness (see Plate 4.4). Housed in an enormous glass cube measuring 5 m. high and 6.3 m. in length, the display consisted of a spectacular selection of *kareau*, *hentakoi*, and model houses and boats supported by text panels and small contemporary and historic photographs. Nicobarese culture was subject to the same critical eye as other social groups on display, including the British, who were represented by an art installation designed to shed light on the distinctive approach to well-being taken in the UK; their material culture and cosmology were presented as possessing the same validity as those employed by societies throughout the rest of the world. Yet, here again, the Nicobar Islands, largely represented through material culture, were necessarily harnessed to serve the particular agendas of the museum and other organizations involved. This inevitably had an impact on how the Nicobarese were conceptualized and historicized.

The gallery project was funded by the independent medical research charity, the Wellcome Trust, and the theme of 'well-being' was driven by their medical agenda and public engagement policy.[34] Brian Durrans, one of the museum curators involved, explained how the gallery's explicit

PLATE 4.4: 'Relating to Spirits: Nicobar Islands' display, Living and Dying Gallery, British Museum, 2008.

Source: Courtesy of the trustees of the British Museum.

focus on the present day was also in line with the Trust's desire to give the exhibition a contemporary relevance. Indeed, Durrans described the project as 'a meeting of minds', because new perspectives in museum anthropology already subscribed to by British Museum staff also led to a desire on their part to emphasize the dynamism and contemporaneity of the groups represented and avoid framing the ethnographic 'other' as static, historic and dying.[35] Thus, while nineteenth-century colonial administrators had collected the objects exhibited, the text labels, largely written in the present tense, were employed 'to tell a contemporary story':[36] first drafts for the text panels that stressed the historic use of the objects by their former Nicobarese owners were redrafted to describe their potential use in the present. Although new collecting activity was prohibited by limited access to the islands,[37] the continued use of *hentakoi* and *kareau* in Nicobarese life today was represented by the inclusion of photographs taken in 2000 and 2003 by the human ecologist Simron Jit Singh. In the British Museum's gallery, then, the historic collections were conceptually reframed to align with broader intellectual and external funding agendas.

Their inclusion in the Living and Dying Gallery also ensured that the Nicobarese objects were embroiled in a separate set of heritage debates, more specifically directed by the British Museum. In his foreword to the gallery's guidebook, Director Neil MacGregor argues that the gallery is 'not just about particular cultures' but explores the 'universal' theme of well-being in order to investigate 'common human experience'.[38] Although the use of this rhetoric undoubtedly speaks to the need to acknowledge the funder's agenda, it is difficult not to associate MacGregor's comments with the heated debates that have proliferated since the publication of the 'Declaration on the Importance and Value of Universal Museums' in 2003. The Declaration was a public statement designed to articulate the position held by some of the West's major museums on repatriation and the notion that museums belong to 'the world' rather than specific countries, communities or cultures. As Neil Curtis and Mark O'Neill have separately argued, despite its potential, the premise of the universal museum, perhaps most strongly advocated by the British Museum and MacGregor, tends to rest on a prioritization of Western elite cultural values and Enlightenment assumptions about the value and construction of the 'museum object'. One of the major criticisms of the universal museum's focus on common human experience is that in this process, imperial histories tend to be ignored and erased.[39] Although the Living and Dying Gallery explicitly engages with modes of well-being beyond those prized in by Enlightenment thinking in the West, the charge of sanitizing history can certainly be imposed on the displays in the Living and Dying Gallery (and indeed the British Museum's displays more generally) which, in examining other themes, tend to overlook the complex manufacturing and collecting histories of the objects displayed.

A similar situation can be seen in the current digital exhibition, 'Survival: People and their Land', on display at Kelvingrove Museum in Glasgow. Here the Jarawa of the Andaman Islands are displayed as one of the six featured communities from around the world who have suffered threats to their cultural survival. Although not one of the 'Universal Museums' mentioned earlier (indeed, the critic Mark O'Neill is Head of Glasgow Museums), here again, the institution's aim to draw attention to the common plight of 'indigenous peoples' around the world blurs the complexities underlying the collecting process involved in the display. In order to source the material deemed necessary to depict the theme and engage the target audience, the museum worked closely with the image makers Thierry Falise and Res Gehriger, both of whom are reported to have collected images of the Jarawa illegally through the use of poachers and boatmen, involved in unlawful and harmful tourism on the Jarawa reserves.[40] In her excellent reflexive paper on the process of curating this exhibit, presented at a conference on the material and visual culture of the Andaman and Nicobar Islands in May 2007, Glasgow's World Cultures' Curator Patricia Allan reflected on whether the use of these images and their unsavoury provenance merited the successful engagement of the elusive teenage audience sought by the museum.[41] In the paper and ensuing discussion, no conclusive answer was reached; notably, the images are still on display today.

In a related point, Curtis critiques proponents of the 'universal museum' as emphasizing 'the importance of visual approaches in Western culture' over their social significance to specific communities. He highlights the frequent use of metaphors of 'light' and 'vision' in the Declaration itself and the fact that the majority of signatory institutions are museums of art rather than museums of science, archaeology or anthropology.[42] Indeed, in the case of the Living and Dying Gallery, although key figures such as lead curator Lissant Bolton assert the intention to prioritize theme and context over aesthetics and visual interest, the emphasis is undoubtedly on the spectacular (a fact recognized by Bolton).[43] The Nicobarese objects were explicitly chosen for this purpose: as Durrans recalls, the Nicobar Islands were selected as a case study, not because of his own prior interest or knowledge, but because the objects were accessible during a period of change in the storage arrangements in the museum and because they were large and of an 'arresting appearance'.[44]

All this confirms the familiar argument that museums 'generate representations and attribute value and meaning in line with certain perspectives or classificatory schemas'.[45] Themes formulated in the past can be persistent but museums also tell us about a present state of mind. However, while museums cast an image of their curators and designers and the audiences that use them, in this investigation of the British Museum's Nicobar display, we also see the serendipity inherent in museum work, and that objects have the potential for exercising their own 'agency'.[46] The Nicobarese objects (particularly, the *kareau* and *hentakoi*) possess an inherent physical and visual presence that actively promoted their selection for display in the Living and Dying Gallery. Although, as suggested earlier, Nicobarese material culture has rarely been accepted into the canons of 'high' or 'primitive' art (with some important exceptions), the wooden figures produced in the region do have a certain 'charisma'—perhaps related to their size, colour and anthropomorphic nature—that makes them particularly attractive and suitable for projects requiring objects with a potent physical presence.[47]

The original choice for the gallery's Asian case study had been a selection of masks from Sri Lanka, but the figures and boards from the Nicobar Islands were later chosen as a replacement because they were especially 'visually striking';[48] as Durrans recounted, the Andamanese collections were not considered because they were too small to impact on the architectural space of the gallery.[49] Here, despite the power of contemporary museum and heritage agendas, it was the objects and their skilled makers that facilitated the framing and representation of Nicobarese peoples abroad. Thus, this manifestation of the Nicobar Islands was infused in important ways by actors often seen as silenced and without 'voice'.

OBJECTS AND GEOGRAPHICAL BOUNDARIES

So far the focus has been on how curatorial and design agendas have intervened to frame and fix the Andamanese and Nicobarese peoples as variously 'ancient', 'contemporary', 'savage' and/or 'common'. This section will briefly cast a broader net to examine how wider political and cultural agendas have combined with material culture to formulate discursive frameworks for the history of the islands and their indigenous populations. In colonial histories, the Andaman and Nicobar Islands have often been imagined as conceptually and geographically separate from mainland India; it was, at least in part, their spatial isolation that allowed the British in India to mark the islands out as a locale suitable for the establishment of a penal colony.[50] By contrast, in Indian nationalist histories, the Cellular Jail at Port Blair on the Andamans has been reframed as a major national monument and the region has been integrated into a vision of the independent nation state.[51] But what do the processes of categorization and display of material culture from the Andaman and Nicobar Islands in museums add to our knowledge of these geo-spatial frameworks over time? How have objects been used to designate cultural and state boundaries and to represent the Andamanese and Nicobarese as social, national and imperial subjects?

The annexation of the Andaman Islands (initially in 1793 and more permanently in 1858) and the Nicobar Islands (in 1869) into British India has had a clear impact on the affiliation of the islands' material cultures with specific museum departments. As Aparna Vaidik points out in a different context, colonial map-making helped to supersede earlier maps, charts and navigational texts, which tended to locate the Andamans as a part of South-East Asia in line with Java and Sumatra. By the late eighteenth century, the islands had been 'symbolically replotted . . . on the Imperial map, not as a segment of the Southeast Asian archipelago, but as a frontier outpost of the Empire in India'.[52] Generally speaking, while there are few known donations of Andamanese and Nicobarese objects to British museums before 1858, once sustained contact allowed for more regular collecting, UK museums followed this political trend: the twentieth-century text labels at the Pitt Rivers Museum, for example, explicitly refer to both the Andamans and Nicobars as being part of 'India'. Certainly today, with the domination of standardized electronic collections databases which automatically associate cultural groups with their political boundaries, most UK museums tend to link the islands with 'India' and 'South Asia'.[53] Interestingly, at the British Museum in the nineteenth century, this association was not automatically made, but the link between the islands and the subcontinent has become increasingly cemented over time: in the exhibition guide of 1899, the Andaman and Nicobar Islands were described as being 'adjacent to India', but firmly placed in the 'Asiatic Islands' section of the text and the gallery. They were affiliated with Oceania, Australia and Melanesia.[54] Conversely, in the recent Living and Dying Gallery, a standardized labelling system prioritizing political governance across the museum meant that the provenance of the displayed objects was described as 'Nicobar Islands, Bay of Bengal, India'.[55] The linking of both groups of islands through wider political frameworks by the British and subsequent Indian governments, despite their indigenous inhabitants' distinct cultural differences, seems also to have influenced their conjoining in displays: at the Colonial and Indian Exhibition of 1886, and in the 1920s and 1930s at Brighton Museum & Art Gallery, the Andaman and Nicobar Islands were displayed together.

During the reign of the British Empire and even after its formal demise, imperial constructs seem to have dominated both display and cataloguing practices. Notably, other European countries without this specific imperial history have often incorporated the islands into their 'Insular Southeast Asia' departments: Leiden's Rijksmuseum voor Volkenkunde and Vienna's Museum für Völkerkunde, for example, explicitly differentiate the archipelago's indigenous cultures from the Indian and South Asian collections which are housed in separate departments; Munich's Staatliches Museum für Völkerkunde aligns its Andamanese and Nicobarese collections with Insular South-East Asia, and more generally with Indonesia and Oceania, because 'it is one cultural area'.[56] Conversely, in Indian museums today, it is perhaps unsurprising that the Andaman and Nicobar Islands are incorporated into the rhetoric of India's 'unity through diversity'. This is accomplished through exhibits such as the dioramas of various Indian castes and tribes and their 'Regional Costumes of India' display at Indian Museum in Kolkata (see Plate 4.5). The inclusion of a Nicobar hut in the outdoor 'Village Complex' of the Indian Crafts Museum in New Delhi—a display where craftsmen from fourteen areas of India were commissioned to produce buildings representative of their region's architectural style—acts to incorporate the Nicobarese into a broader nationalist project which

PLATE 4.5: 'Regional Costumes of India' display, Cultural Anthropology Gallery, Indian Museum, Kolkata. The Andamanese are represented at the bottom right, between the two visitors; the Nicobarese are obscured by one of the visitors.

Source: Courtesy of the author.

'co-opts and then tries to smooth out India's vast regional and local artisanal variations'.[57]

Material culture has been central to wider projects of categorizing, fixing and imagining the peoples and sites of the Andaman and Nicobar Islands across the nineteenth, twentieth and twenty-first centuries. The advent of British colonization was not the first time that objects and images were used in this way. However, the 'British period' does provide rich material for an investigation into the processes through which outsiders have been influenced by the materiality of the object when describing the identity and formulating the status of the Andamanese and Nicobarese peoples. This is not least because material culture has been invested with such significance throughout the modern era.[58] The objects produced and used by their makers in the Bay of Bengal and collected by outsiders can be seen as ambassadors of their former owners. Yet, it is clear that the intended or original meanings rarely persist over time. While the physical entity often survives, meanings are regularly adapted to fit the agendas of their new owners; new histories are constructed through material 'evidence'.

What we see is both the changing nature of these histories, but also the regularity with which certain themes persist once established. Nineteenth-century categorizations of the Andamanese and Nicobarese as 'stone age', 'primitive' and 'simple' emerge through material culture in unlikely and otherwise 'post-colonial' settings; colonial constructions of place and nation continue to be framed through collecting and display practices, even today. Despite the object's fixed physical construction, perhaps its beguiling nature is centred in its mirror-like capacity to present us with ourselves. Material culture inevitably acts upon us and challenges our assumptions of humanity,[59] but it also has a role in bolstering specific views of history and the present. As we have seen, not least in British museums, these are contested interpretations, and contested forms of history.

NOTES

1. Claire Wintle, *Colonial Collecting and Display: Encounters with Material Culture from the Andaman and Nicobar Islands*, Oxford: Berghahn, 2013, pp. 139–47.
2. Ibid., pp. 79–80.
3. Fred Davis, *Fashion, Culture and Identity*, Chicago: University of Chicago Press, 1992.
4. Vishvajit Pandya in an interview with the author, 26 September 2008.
5. Stuart Hall, 'Who Needs Identity?' in *Identity: A Reader*, ed. Paul du Gay, Jessica Evans and Peter Redman, London: Sage, 2000, p. 17.
6. Eilean Hooper-Greenhill, *Museums and the Interpretation of Visual Culture*, London: Routledge, p. 51.
7. Igor Kopytoff, 'The Cultural Biography of Things: Commoditization as Process', in *The Social Life of Things: Commodities in Cultural Perspective*, ed. Arjun Appadurai, Cambridge: Cambridge University Press, 1986.
8. Vishvajit Pandya, *Above the Forest: A Study of Andamanese Ethnoanemology, Cosmology, and the Power of Ritual*, Delhi: Oxford University Press, 1993; idem, *In the Forest: Visual and Material Worlds of Andamanese History (1858–2006)*, Lanham, MA: University Press of America, 2009; Simron J. Singh, *In the Sea of Influence: A World System of Perspective of the Nicobar Islands*, Lund: Lund University Press, 2003.
9. For example, David Tomas, 'Tools of the Trade: The Production of Ethnographic Observations on the Andaman Islands, 1858-1922', in *Colonial Situations: Essays on the Contextualization of Ethnographic Knowledge*, ed. George W. Stocking, Madison: University of Wisconsin Press, 1991; Wintle, *Colonial Collecting and Display*, p. 61.
10. David Van Keuren, 'Cabinets and Culture: Victorian Anthropology and the Museum Context', *Journal of the History of the Behavioral Sciences*, vol. 25, 1989, p. 31.
11. British Museum, *A Guide to the Exhibition Galleries of the British Museum (Bloomsbury), with Plans*, London, 1899, pp. 98–9.

12. Horniman Museum and Library, *A Handbook to the Cases Illustrating the Stages in the Evolution of the Domestic Arts*, Part I, London: London Country Council, 1910.
13. David Jenkins, 'Object Lessons and Ethnographic Displays: Museum Exhibitions and the Making of American Anthropology', *Comparative Studies in Society and History*, vol. 36, no. 1, 1994, pp. 262–3.
14. R. Skelton, 'The Indian Collections, 1798–1978', *Burlington Magazine*, vol. CXX, no. 902, 1978, p. 303.
15. Partha Mitter, 'The Imperial Collections: Indian Art', in *A Grand Design: The Art of the Victoria and Albert Museum*, ed. Malcolm Baker and Brenda Richardson, New York: Harry N. Abrams, 1997, p. 228.
16. Ibid.
17. Lissant Bolton, 'Living and Dying: Ethnography, Class, and Aesthetics in the British Museum', in *Museums and Difference*, ed. D.J. Sherman, Bloomington: Indiana University Press, 2008, p. 338.
18. The sketch was made in 1906 and reproduced in Remi Labrusse and Jacqueline Munck Derain, *Matisse-Derain: La Verité Du Fauvisme*, Paris: Hazan, 2005, p. 165. I thank Brian Durrans for sharing this find with me.
19. Stuart C. Welch, *India: Art and Culture 1300-1900*, New York: Metropolitan Museum of Art, 1985, p. 100.
20. Katherine F. Hacker, 'Displaying a Tribal Imaginary: Known and Unknown India', *Museum Anthropology*, vol. 23, no. 3, 2000, pp. 5–25.
21. Stella Kramrisch, *Unknown India: Ritual Art in Tribe and Village*, Philadelphia: Philadelphia Museum of Art, 1968.
22. Letter from Stella Kramrisch to Evan H. Turner, 13 April 1965, Philadelphia Museum of Art Archives, cited in Hacker, 'Displaying a Tribal Imaginary', p. 14. Emphasis as in the original.
23. Bolton, 'Living and Dying', p. 351.
24. Notably, this situation is now greatly improved as a result of the increasing sophistication of the museum's publicly available online collections database. The majority of the Andamanese and Nicobarese objects are now digitized, which in itself forms an important form of (and catalyst to further) interpretation.
25. Text labels currently attached to the adze displays at the Pitt Rivers Museum. Report of the Curator of the Pitt Rivers Museum (Department of Ethnology) for the year ending 31 July 1945. I am grateful to Alison Petch, Pitt Rivers Museum, for bringing the museum's annual report from this year to my attention.
26. Text label, exhibition curated in 2002, cited in E. Poulter, 'New "Ways of Seeing": A Re-Examination of Anthropological and Museological Representations of the People of the Andaman Islands', M.A. thesis, University of Manchester, 2004, pp. 48–9.
27. Ibid.
28. 'Temple, Man and Tuson: Collecting the Andaman and Nicobar Islands', curated by Claire Wintle and Helen Mears, exhibited at the Royal Pavilion & Museums, Brighton & Hove, between March 2005 and September 2007.

29. National Museum of Scotland, text label, Patterns of Life Gallery, National Museum of Scotland, 2012.
30. Chantal Knowles, Principal Curator, Department of World Cultures, National Museums, in an interview with the author, 30 May 2013.
31. Pandya, *Above the Forest*, p. xiii.
32. Ibid., pp. 65, 93, 255, 267.
33. Bolton, 'Living and Dying', p. 333.
34. 'Wellcome Trust Gallery Content Group Meeting', 12 February 2003, British Museum Exhibition Planning Files, Centre for Anthropology, British Museum.
35. Brian Durrans, former Deputy Keeper of Asia, British Museum, in an interview with the author, 30 April 2013. On post-colonial approaches in museums, see Christina Kreps, 'Changing the Rules of the Road: Post-colonialism and the New Ethics of Museum Anthropology', in *The Routledge Companion to Museum Ethics: Redefining Ethics for the Twentieth-century Museum*, ed. Janet Marstine, London: Routledge, 2011.
36. Brian Durrans, former Deputy Keeper of Asia, British Museum, in an interview with the author, 30 April 2013.
37. Ibid.
38. Neil MacGregor, 'Foreword', *Wellcome Trust Gallery: Living and Dying* [pamphlet], London: British Museum, 2002, p. 5.
39. Neil Curtis, 'Universal Museums, Museum Objects and Repatriation: The Tangled Stories of Things', *Museum Management and Curatorship*, vol. 21, no. 2, 2006, pp. 121, 123, 125; Mark O'Neill, 'Enlightenment Museums: Universal or Merely Global?' *Museum and Society*, vol. 2, no. 3, 2004, pp. 191, 199.
40. For a discussion of the politics of contact and the implications for the Jarawa, see Vishvajit Pandya, 'Jarwas of Andaman Islands: Their Social and Historical Reconstruction', *Economic & Political Weekly*, vol. 37, no. 37, 2002, pp. 3830–4.
41. *Objects, Images, Imaginings: New Perspectives on the Material and Visual Culture of the Andaman and Nicobar Islands*, Royal Pavilion & Museums, Brighton & Hove and University of Sussex, May 2007. See Claire Wintle, 'Objects, Images, Imaginings: New Perspectives on the Material and Visual Culture of the Andaman and Nicobar Islands', *Journal of Museum Ethnography*, vol. 20, 2008, pp. 145–52, for details.
42. Curtis, 'Universal Museums, Museum Objects and Repatriation', pp. 119–20.
43. Bolton, 'Living and Dying', pp. 349–51.
44. Brian Durrans, former Deputy Keeper of Asia, British Museum, in an interview with the author, 30 April 2013.
45. Henrietta Lidchi, 'The Poetics and Politics of Exhibiting Other Cultures', in *Representation*, 2nd edn., ed. Stuart Hall, Jessica Evans, and Sean Nixon, London: Sage and the Open University, 2013, p. 127.
46. On the broader question of material culture and agency, see Alfred Gell, *Art and Agency: An Anthropological Theory*, Oxford: Clarendon Press, 1998.
47. On the charismatic object, see Chris Wingfield, 'Touching the Buddha: Encounters with a Charismatic Object', in *Museum Materialities: Objects, Engagements, Interpretations*, ed. Sandra Dudley, London: Routledge, 2010.

48. 'The Wellcome Trust Gallery Project Brief', 8 May 2002, British Museum Exhibition Planning Files, Centre for Anthropology, British Museum.
49. Brian Durrans, former Deputy Keeper of Asia, British Museum, in an interview with the author, 30 April 2013.
50. Clare Anderson, *The Indian Uprising of 1857-8: Prisons, Prisoners and Rebellion*, London: Anthem, 2007, pp. 129–34.
51. Aparna Vaidik, *Imperial Andamans: Colonial Encounter and Island History*, Basingstoke: Palgrave Macmillan, 2010, p. 2.
52. Ibid., p. 13.
53. See, for example, Brighton Museum & Art Gallery, and Manchester Museum.
54. British Museum, *A Guide to the Exhibition Galleries*, pp. 98–9.
55. Brian Durrans, former Deputy Keeper of Asia, British Museum, in an interview with the author, 30 April 2013.
56. Personal communication with Dr Michaela Appel, Head of the Indonesia and Oceania Section, Staatliches Museum für Völkerkunde, München, 21 May 2013.
57. Paul Greenough, 'Nation, Economy, Tradition Displayed: The Indian Crafts Museum, New Delhi', in *Consuming Modernity: Public Culture in a South Asian World*, ed. Carol Appadurai Breckenridge, Minneapolis: University of Minnesota Press, 1995, pp. 220, 226–7.
58. Susan Pearce, *On Collecting: An Investigation into Collecting in the European Tradition*, London: Routledge, 1995.
59. Chris Tilley, 'Objectification', in *Handbook of Material Culture*, ed. Chris Tilley, Webb Keane, Susanne Küchler, Mike Rowlands and Patricia Spyer, London: Sage, 2006.

5

Race, Aboriginality, and the Adivasi

Some Implications for the Andaman Islanders

SATADRU SEN

The aboriginal population of the Andaman Islands is popularly believed to be on the verge of extinction, with barely 600 Jarawa, Onge, Great Andamanese and Sentinelese remaining alive.[1] Since the later part of the nineteenth century, that remarkably resilient assumption has shaped not only official policy towards the islanders, but also the dominant discourse of where so-called 'primitive tribes' might be located in the realities and fantasies of the modern. Because this continues to have significant ramifications for the Andamanese themselves, it may be useful—as polemic and as policy—to consider some aspects of aboriginality, citizenship, and racial death in India. I want to suggest, against the weight of the information on how many Onge and Jarawa are still around, that the death of the native in the islands is by no means inevitable.[2] The Andamanese are dying by and large because they have been consigned and limited to an ethnological domain that is inconsistent with the basic principles of the life of the citizen.

In a national-ideological setting where natives have their own natives, and where the fractures and gradations within that lower level of nativeness must be negotiated continuously, the non-viability of the aboriginal citizen has been determined by the historical and ideological realities of articulating the national self, and by the political and ethical imperatives of insulating the exotic. It is not that the ideological devices for accommodating aborigines within Indian nationhood do not exist; there is, in fact, a highly evolved niche for the aborigine in Indian anti-colonial discourse. This niche has been withheld from the Andamanese, and continues to be withheld from them, by a competing Romanticism that is deeply invested in 'primitive' possessions, and that has recuperated some of the most disagreeable racial attitudes of the colonial era.

It is not necessary here to recapitulate the dense history of the Andaman Islands as a site of racial contact.[3] It is sufficient to outline some general patterns in how the 'civilized' have dealt with the 'savages' of these islands. In the first stage, which might be identified with the first British-Indian colony in the archipelago in the 1790s through the first decade of the second colony, the Andamanese were identified as ethnological subjects, and made the transition from being quasi-mythical creatures to ordinary savages of the era of Pacific exploration. In the second stage, lasting from the 1860s until the 1880s, they existed on the margins of the penal settlement as experiments in the partial incorporation of aborigines into the governance of an island colony: this was the relatively confident period of the Andaman Homes, the 'conquest' of Little Andaman, and of the use of 'tame' islanders in hunting runaway convicts and recalcitrant Jarawas. In both stages, they faced the violence of the colonizers: shooting, kidnapping, forced labour, and exhibition.[4] Following this came a decadently morbid stewardship, beginning with severe outbreaks of measles, influenza, and syphilis.[5] It was now conceded that the Andamanese were dying, albeit under the loving gaze of anthropologists, photographers, and solicitous governors. That funereal vision has persisted into the fourth stage, marked by the accelerated settlement of the islands by migrants from the Indian mainland after 1947, the political mobilization of these settlers, intensified pressure on the forests, land and other resources available to the indigenous population, the building of the Andaman Trunk Road (ATR), and the delinquent place allotted to the 'savages' in the tourist industry in the Andamans.[6]

When we think about indigenous or aboriginal populations in the context of the modern state, we tend to slip into a mode of analysis that is borrowed largely from settler-colonial situations. In the settler colony, Patrick Wolfe has observed, the indigene is superfluous to the social, political and economic order, and a logic of elimination informs the modalities of governance and culture.[7] The consequences can be genocidal.[8] But when it comes to post-imperial, self-avowedly democratic nation states like India, the settler-colonial model has obvious limitations. This does not invalidate or eliminate the relevance of categories like aborigine and indigenous, but it shifts their meanings and their political purposes. The larger society and its political institutions adapt to these new meanings, and certain expectations are formulated regarding the place of the aborigine in the national body and the state. When this shifted, or recast, discourse of indigeneity encounters a more conventional settler-colonial model of aboriginality, as in the Andamans, we have an impasse, for which no resolution has yet emerged. Even without genocidal violence, the logic of elimination continues to apply: the Andamanese can be imagined only as vanishing primitives.

After Indian Independence in 1947, several things have happened in tandem to make the Andamanese situation more settler-colonial than before. One is, of course, migration from the mainland. Unlike convicts, the migrants have become a politically mobilized demographic, able to approach the state with their claims on local resources. The peculiar status of the tribal population, in which they are normatively limited to a shrinking patch of jungle instead of being located in a wider society and geography, has only encouraged settlers to regard them as superfluous people taking up space. The other is that the administration has remained in the hands of people invested in the primitive, and the activists who seek to influence the administration have grounded themselves in the same primitivist assumptions. This investment is itself partly an inheritance of colonial discourses of race, and partly an organic response to the particular political and professional opportunities present in the combination of managerialism and democracy, in which some people are managed and others demand representation.

The continuing 'primitive' status of the islanders reflects the unsettled relationship between the Andamans and India: these are islands in India, and the Andamanese are islands within Indianness. Indeed, the Andamanese have become progressively insular, as growing numbers of Indians have become infected by the primitivist vision of the state-affiliated managers of the tribal population. Whereas tribal people on the mainland have lost their status as objects of ethnography, the Andamanese have become reified in their ethnographic condition. Middle class, urban Indians no longer fantasize about going into the jungle to see Santals, although there was a historical and cultural moment when they did.[9] This is partly because eastern Bihar, where modern Bengalis once went to see 'tribals', is now a tribal state, with a tribal chief minister: a part of the prosaic mainland of Indian politics. Indians seeking delinquent thrills must now enter the delinquent space of the Jarawa reserve, to see (and even touch) the last primitives in the national zoo.

BENOY KUMAR SARKAR AND INDIAN ABORIGINALITY

The present-day Andamanese predicament cannot be assessed in isolation from the mainland as a sort of quaint insular drama, or a free-floating history left over from a defunct empire. The calamity of the Andamanese is very much a part of modern Indian history and its peculiar resolutions of inclusion and exclusion; it is in the premises and innovations of that history that correctives must be sought. Aboriginality is not external to Indianness in the same sense in which it is external to American or Australian nationhood. Indian national narratives have relied upon it from the outset as a constitutive and nurturing element, and not just as a foil against which the self might be defined. Yet when we come to the Andamanese, that construction of the relationship between the nation and the aborigine has proved to be grossly inadequate. The principle delineators of Indian nationhood have resisted accommodating the islanders within the category of the Adivasi, which is the main portal through which aborigines have historically entered Indian polity.[10]

In the middle of the nineteenth century, thanks to Orientalist linguistic scholarship, the class of people who identified themselves as 'Indians' also accepted that some Indians were more 'indigenous' than others. The meaningful divide in indigenousness in their time, however, was between Aryan and Dravidian, and there was a broad consensus that the emergent national community included both Aryans and Dravidians.[11] We have in this relatively early discourse a false settler-colonial vision: false, because the settlement was seen as having taken place so long ago that it was no longer meaningful in a politics of exclusion. Aryan and Dravidian were not fully racialized at this stage, and aboriginality is, after all, reliant upon racialized articulations of hierarchy and political membership.

There was a shift in the discourse in the early twentieth century during the Dravidian nationalist politics of Periyar, but it did not directly affect the content of Indian aboriginality.[12] Original people are not necessarily aborigines. The more meaningful shift had come earlier, when what Dirks called ethnographic colonialism evolved beyond questions of ritual status and language and came to see caste as race, and race as a measurable and gradable quality of the body.[13] Simultaneously, thanks to Gobineau, race became closely tied to the viability of nations.[14] In this context, the nationalist classes could evade neither the importance of identifying an Indian race, nor the difficulty of its apparent unevenness. That unevenness had to be ordered, if not ironed out, within the framework of nationhood. Thus, when middle-class Indians at the turn of the century looked at groups like Santals and Gonds, or the so-called 'tribal people' of the Indian mainland, they saw a racial anomaly. Such tribes were difficult to fit into the nation, not only because they were an anomaly of civilization defined in terms of class, caste, and geography, but also because they were explicitly the objects of anthropology, rather than the subjects of history.

The Romantic aspect of Indian nationalism produced a solution to the problem. From Bankimchandra Chatterjee onward, the search for universal and positivist markers within Indianness were accompanied, usually in the same individuals, with an obsessive search for what was distinctive, different from what was declared to be universal but tacitly understood to be European.[15] These compulsions and desires led to a particular ideological development, which is not only the invention of the Adivasi, but also the location of the Adivasi partially within the explicitly national category of the folk.[16] The aborigine as Adivasi was both subject and object, and as such, a useful fantasy of the deracinated native looking for indigenous pedigrees, and half-men looking for wholeness.

One such native was Benoy Kumar Sarkar, perhaps the most prominent Indian sociologist in the period between the two World Wars. A brilliant young graduate drawn into nationalist activism after the partition of Bengal in 1905, Sarkar soon became an educational pioneer, interested not only in creating nationalist alternatives to colonial pedagogy, but in a wider project of re-educating Indians to be citizens of the modern state and subjects in an unevenly modern world.[17] He read Herder, spent much of the 1920s and 1930s studying and teaching in Germany and Italy, and became a little too sympathetic towards fascism.[18] In general, however, Sarkar held out a model of locating the aboriginal within the national that was both right wing and democratic, if not consistently liberal.[19] He retained from the German Romantics an abiding interest in the folk as a vital but submerged reserve of national history. The folk was the past, the nation was the present, and the state was the future, Sarkar held, and the nation could have multiple folks. But nationhood—especially in the decolonizing world, where the national vanguard was overtly Europeanized and history tainted by Orientalism—required the folk if it were to have any indigenous roots at all.

Travelling in Japan, China, and America during the First World War, Sarkar began a concerted attempt to identify an Indian race. His definition of race was emphatically political: race was a political predicament, such as being colonized, or being dominant in the world. But it was also biological, in the sense that it was subject to eugenics, medicine, and sanitation. He wrote extensively about what he called the 'parianization' of Indianness.[20] He used the term to mean the opposite of Aryanization, i.e. movement towards a classical brahmanical culture and an Aryan race. He sought, instead, to identify Indians—biologically and civilizationally—with what could be described as folk and tribe. His objectives were both descriptive and prescriptive: not only did Indian identity have its roots in the tribe and the folk, it should be embraced as such. Just as pertinently, there was no sharp line between tribe and folk. It was with this grey area between tribe and folk, between the forest, the village and the small town, that he became fascinated. Tribes shaded into multiple folks, and functioned as a soil from which the modern national community grew. Anthropology became a legitimate and alternative national history, and a basis for the regeneration of a degenerate Indianness.

By emphasizing degeneracy and regeneration, Sarkar articulated a vision of race as population. Population, however, is a generic concept, based on the universality of delinquency, criminality and sexual deviance, and the universal relevance of governmentality. It offers no ready answers to what implicates a particular degenerate race in a particular national identity. Geography was not enough; Sarkar had gone out of his way to stress the similar predicaments of the human body in Calcutta, Berlin, and Tokyo.[21] A solution lay in highlighting the 'deep history' of the population by pointing to the indigenous roots of governmentality, articulating a romance of national culture (that might be excavated by the national vanguard), and revisiting the political functions of racial identity. An Indian race—and at the same time, component races that were also political alternatives—could be demonstrated to exist, and to have existed historically, under the surface of a universality derived from metropolitan discourses.

Sarkar's interest in national culture was not identical to the quest that Andrew Sartori has outlined for Bengal between the 1880s and 1947. Sartori argues that in concept and content, 'Bengali culture' was a reaction—in both senses of the word—to the political impasse of liberal nationalism.[22] Both he and Joya Chatterjee have emphasized the Hindu (specifically, Vedantic), authoritarian and anti-Muslim core of this culture.[23] Sarkar was not a paid-up member of this cultural nation, not least because of his investment in a democratic culture of 'parianization'. He represents a way of thinking about race that is undoubtedly elitist but also inclusive, determined to look beyond—and below—the colony to find the post-colonial nation.

We must, at this point, recall Sarkar's persistent Romanticism: that yearning for something intimate and essential lost in history. His construction of early India reflects a particular conception of wholeness, i.e. an embodied spirituality or a moral physicality that had been dismissed by the Orientalist vision of the Orient. He understood that the 'Oriental' of European discourse tended to be either all-spirit or all-body; wholeness was the preserve of Europe. Rejecting the implicit dehumanization, he made a direct intervention in the discourse of race: the defining preoccupations of a people became the stuff of bodies as much as they were the stuff of poetry.[24] The assertion of a pro-sex, pro-love Indian culture became an implicit critique of Europe: a regeneration as well as a defiant assertion of wholeness, and the revival of an 'optimism' that enables change, politics and history.[25]

This investment in physicality took Sarkar beyond the urban culture of Brahmo-influenced *bhadrata*, with its stifling emphasis on restraint, to the rustic world of folk and tribe.[26] He praised Rajani Kanta Sen, the collector of folk music, for having 'given a fresh lease of life to the traditional folk-melodies by exploiting them as medium for modern emotions'.[27] Sarkar's comments on Sen and folk music show, first, his outlook on folk culture: it was necessarily part of the nation, but it was also an externally located asset that must be identified and nationalized. The folk element, in other words, had value only when it was brought into the service of 'modern emotions'. Second, in spite of Sarkar's concern (shaped by reading Pareto) with the state-influenced circulation of elites in the urban milieu, he was quite aware of his location within a wider Hindu race that had itself seen centuries of internal 'circulation', and in which the 'Aryan' elements had constantly been infiltrated by the obscure and the wild.[28] The ideas of purity and mongrelism, equality and superiority, coexisted within this construction of Hinduness. Sarkar was happy to embrace the mongrel aspects of his Hindu identity, but it was a jittery happiness, secure only as long as the right sort of Hindus were in charge of the boundaries of the community. The 'right sort', however, could come from unexpected places, such as the margins of the folk world. They could be both agents and objects of the pedagogical processes that Sarkar called 'sociation', and were both a part of and apart from the modern Indian Self.[29]

Sarkar's analysis of rural Bengal would unfold over a number of years. In the early 1910s, he became increasingly interested in the collection of folklore and folk music, as these were understood by the *bhadralok*. Here, he was well within the elite project of the construction and expansion of Bengaliness by giving the metropolis its cultural hinterland, which Calcutta-based intellectuals like the Tagores (and pioneers of Bengali children's literature in particular) initiated in the late nineteenth century.[30] The project had become more intensive and politically charged in the Swadeshi years, when rural Bengal was reimagined to give urban children privileged access to a Romantic extra-colonial world that adults could not inhabit convincingly.[31] But urban intellectuals did not work alone; they were often patrons of relatively obscure enthusiasts based in mofussil towns. These men were marginal in more ways than one, but for that reason, they were positioned to function as intermediaries of folk culture, and indeed, of racial identity on the frontier between modern Bengaliness and something primordial.

Sarkar's long collaboration with Haridas Palit should be seen in that context. As Sumit Sarkar has noted, Palit came from a very poor, Namasudra background, which he advertised along with his rise to respectability as a politician and cultural expert. He was active in the National Education movement and the creation of rural night schools.[32] His humble origins on the margins of Bengali society became an asset in the formulation of his subsequent social status: it gave him access to knowledge that the born respectable did not have. Whereas Benoy Sarkar had left provincial Malda for Calcutta and Leipzig, Palit had remained on this inner frontier of Bengaliness, facilitating an inward-directed cosmopolitanism. Like other contemporary collectors of folk culture, he cultivated a reputation as a wanderer in places dislocated in time, a collector of lost histories.[33] He introduced Sarkar to his specific interests, such as the Gambhira and Gajan festivals of rural and small town life. These quickly became Sarkar's own areas of investigation, a 'dazzling' field of inquiry.[34] While it can be argued that Sarkar usurped Palit's work, it would be fair to say that Sarkar became the next level of collection and mediation, presenting Palit to an outer world of scholarship, analysis, and race-making.

Rituals like the Gambhira and Gajan appealed to Sarkar and Palit because they offered glimpses of a true—or alternative—racial self, political community and form of knowledge. Significantly, the researchers were located outside the educational-institutional framework of the colonial state and committed to alternative pedagogical projects. Neither was detached from the world of modern, European knowledge: Palit's descriptions of his work are indistinguishable from European narratives of Romantic 'collection' and folk-making.[35] But their construction of an Indian Volk was an anti-colonial, counter-institutional project, conducted by people whose provinciality and marginality to the colonial order placed them at the centre of the Volk nation.[36] Writing down the obscure ritual and intellectual lives of unremarkable people in backwaters like Malda, finding it 'dazzling', and interpreting it as 'history', was part of the recovery of nation and race outside colonial curricular preoccupations, and apparently free of colonial imaginaries of the peoplehood. Because the primitive precedes modern political identities and politically frozen boundaries, stilled migrations and disrupted contacts, the folk could function at the level of an ancient cosmopolitanism, pointing towards the mingled prehistory of the races of the world.[37] What had been locked into a hinterland or wilderness could become a means of 'travelling'. Similarly, the folk produced new links between Indians of various types, proving that 'notwithstanding the narrow provincial spirit of the modern educated Indians, due to the growth of habits and sentiments in watertight administrative compartments, the soul of India is really one'.[38]

By seeing a national 'soul' in the folk, Sarkar echoed Herder, but they were not on the same page. Sarkar's folk was more diverse than Herder's, and diversity was valuable within a unified national project. At Gambhira festivals, Sarkar wrote, the ethnologist would find not only peasants and tribal people, but also ordinary Bengalis dressed as 'Santhals and other aboriginal tribes', dancing with a decidedly *abhadra* lack of restraint, their bodies pierced by burning arrowheads.[39] Sarkar's Gambhira was not only overtly physical, it was also an occasion of racial confusion and rearticulation: located on the zone between the peasant and the tribal, and provocatively fusing those worlds. Sarkar's alertness to songs about Shiva becoming a cultivator[40] shows his awareness of the processes of peasant-making and Hindu-making—i.e. simultaneous race-making and culture-making—among aboriginal people on what Eaton would call the 'Bengal frontier'.[41] The interest in the Dionysian is reminiscent of Frazer, and reflects a similar search for a submerged primitive.[42] In each case, there is an unstated desire to merge with the primitive.[43] But whereas the savage of European primitivism was a decadent tropical hallucination,[44] Sarkar's interest in an Indian primitive was also recuperative: he was the native in search of racial wholeness. Not surprisingly, he focused on elements that had been ejected or marginalized by the British and modern Indians alike. This was not a search for racial purity; it was, rather, the deliberate searching out of 'impurities' as the new substance of race, or a reconstitution of race in the colony, which had lost its bridges to the world. The folk in its varieties and convergences provided a way of getting around the ossified, derelict political compartments of the present time. This was the opposite of the insularity to which the Andamanese have been relegated since the brief moment when they were imagined, by colonial observers, to be present in India, Australia, and even Europe.[45]

In Sarkar's early explorations of rural Bengal, we find him insisting that 'Hinduism'—understood as pure religion—was an Orientalist red herring; what mattered was the 'Hindu race', which, being subject to discovery and ascription, was endlessly expansive. The worldly bases of this community were most readily visible in tribal culture. Sarkar's vision of the racial community is marked by its openness, and the folk was the level at which this openness is most evident. Not only were there multiple folk, each folk was historically hybrid.[46] Just before his foreign travels and the Great War, he engaged with the foundational questions of ethnographic nationalism in India: the reality (or otherwise) of an Aryan race, its origins, and its relationship to non-Aryans. The idea of distinct peoples converging in a common geography and history—a 'melting pot' nationhood—suited Sarkar's disinterest in racial purity. Race develops historically, he suggested, through the accumulation of 'impurities' and the development of political purpose. He was, ultimately, uninterested in fetishizing Aryans as the exclusive insider-race in India. There were multiple insiders, and he wanted them all as his ancestors. That anthropological diversity was a discovery—or at least the claim—of unexplored nooks of ancestry and origin, which was exciting to a man invested in a *world* of exploration.

The fluidity of racial mixture and ethnic interpenetration was highly desirable to Sarkar also because it reflected the operation of political power—the ebb and flow of warriors—without which India would be reduced to unworldly impotence and irrelevance. The compulsively miscegenating, politically alive folk could be mined for the masculinity and militarism the elites desperately wanted.[47] The tribes of the forest secreted 'national volunteers' who made up the armies of ancient India, Sarkar insisted.[48] It was of vital importance to him that the folk constitute not only a racial root, but also an alternative bedrock of the Indian state. While he foreshadowed Dirks by positing his own ethnographic state, his agenda was different from that of Dirks' ethnographer-administrators.[49] Whereas the latter—alongside people like Portman in the Andamans and the 'protectors' of aborigines in Australia—constructed a menagerie to possess, manage and enjoy, Sarkar was proposing a counter-state *of* the menagerie, in which primitive rituals demonstrate the repossession of the state by the racialized.[50]

Sarkar's state was itself managerial. What he saw as the 'militarism' of the folk also formed the basis of its criminality; what made the state viable was precisely what the state must manage constantly through punishment and education.[51] Folk festivals function in Sarkar's narrative as an ancient national pedagogy, explicitly described as being both moral and political.[52] These lessons, he suggested, complemented the shastric literature on 'polity, warfare, town-planning, administrative machinery and financial management, arts and crafts, sex, hygiene, sanitation, eugenics, etc.'[53] Democracy and civic life were the secret history of the folk: 'The Pala dynasty owed its ... legitimacy to "election" by the Folk, and it was the Folk that dominated the age in matters of faith.'[54] The folk were diverse but unifying, equipped with mechanisms of reconciliation that could function across the enmities and oppressions of caste and the Hindu-Muslim relationship.[55]

The democratic nature of tribal society was not a new idea, but Sarkar brought it to bear on the wider community of Indians through the mechanism of the folk. Once again, we find the folk restoring a wholeness that had been damaged or denied by colonialism. We also find education taking on a democratic appearance: it was not just a top-down process of the urban elite teaching the rabble, but of the rabble teaching themselves and others, even if the lessons appear to be borrowed from modern textbooks. In the Bengali context, moreover, education not only produced culture, it was culture itself.[56] In Sarkar, we see the extension of that elite understanding of education to the folk. Folk pedagogy generated the self-governing political community with recognizably modern processes of surveillance and the 'publication' of 'annual reports'.[57] 'The hidden offences and secret vices of individuals are exposed by them, and thus very valuable services are rendered to morals,' Sarkar observed approvingly about Gambhiras.[58] As a quasi-state, the folk provided a way of reconciling the individual and the community within the purposeful and 'healthy' political structure.[59]

Folk festivals also revealed to Sarkar the existence of submerged indigenous elites who were a point of recognition and inspiration.[60] These tribal elites were not only natural objects of sociation and incorporation into the new national vanguard, they existed unnoticed on the edge of the colonial metropolis.[61] Sarkar was driving at connections that were both obvious and complex, suggesting that folk traditions serve as multiple bridges, connecting the *bhadralok* world with the peasant world, the world of peasants with that of tribal people, and the culture of the present with the distant past.[62] This connectedness filled out the national community, reducing the gap between those who value culture and those who constitute culture. At heart, therefore, the university-educated, upper caste *bhadralok* were also part of the folk.

Sarkar remained invested in the primitiveness of his rustics, which was analogous to the primitiveness of the European folk; Europe was too useful to ignore. He knew, also, that he was dealing in ascribed identities and utilities, and did not seriously imagine that elite ascribed identities could be seized by the marginal and remade into insurgent national identities.[63] But just as the European folk could function as a bedrock foreshadowing European modernity, the Indian folk was a thrilling vision of the modern in the primitive and the primitive in the modern, akin to seeing a ghost. As in any Romantic project of recovering the folk, that ghostly element was reinforced by an anxiety—both sharp and decadent—that the folk were dying out, destroyed inexorably by a vulgar modernity that could not be disavowed.

Awareness of that death, ironically, could be racially invigorating. Sarkar quoted the poet Baradacharan Mitra as saying, 'We should, all of us, do our best to see that ancient festivities of Bengal like those of the Gambhira do not die out.'[64] Gas and kerosene lighting had infiltrated the Gambhira, Sarkar noted wryly, and Ravi Varma was replacing older styles of decoration to make the proceedings 'look grand and glorious . . . in the eyes of modernists.'[65] It was by becoming aware of such loss that modern Indians could realize their race as a new political truth. Sarkar's attention to the details of lighting and decoration, and the conversion of obscure festivals into rituals of tourism, indicates an internalization and also an aesthetic mobilization of the Gobineau-inspired notion of racial death, and the wider discourse of the death of the savage. But unlike in the Andamans, where the death of the savage or *adeem janajati* (literally, 'primitive population') is the regrettable disappearance of an irreconcilable other, the prospect of losing the folk was, for him, also a loss of the national self.

TOWARDS A POLITICS OF CITIZENSHIP IN THE ANDAMANS

We have in Sarkar the construction of an indigeneity that is simultaneously internal and external to the national self, and this is a basic aspect of the Adivasi as a paradigm of indigeneity. Because it has something useful to offer to the model of nationally identified citizenship, the concept generates obvious possibilities for tribal self-assertion. I am referring not to the *hools* and rebellions beloved to subaltern historians, but to the work of politicians like Jaipal Singh, which brought Adivasis into active and participatory roles in the national mainstream.[66] They entered wearing primitiveness like a contextual badge of identity that was not essentially different from other modern identities. It was, however imperfectly, a self-directed, negotiated and modern union with Indianness, premised more on similarity and equality than on difference and inferiority. It provides, in fact, a model of self-representation that has undergirded aboriginal mobilization and activism in every liberal democracy since the Second World War.[67]

For the non-tribal Indian, the aboriginality of the Adivasi promises a receptacle—temporal, spatial and racial—for that part of the modern self which is at odds with the generic, liberal framework of the democratic state. It holds a part of the self in abeyance from a subjecthood with roots in colonialism. That is precisely why it is democratic: it permits, in theory and to some extent in practice, a two-way movement between generic citizenship and aboriginality. It is, in theory, a rather elegant resolution of modern India's problem with the primitive, updating rather than replacing older, extra-colonial notions of the porous boundary between wilderness and civilization. Within this resolution, extreme forms of violence and exploitation have persisted, but that is arguably because the boundary has been poorly managed by the state.

The debates that occurred in India in the 1950s around Verrier Elwin and national policy towards tribal people were more about management than about the framework itself.[68] Few disagreed with the premise that tribals represented a primitive *Indianness*, although Elwin himself seemed to hedge. In the present day, that framework has been consolidated on the mainland: it is not difficult to see that the problems that affect Adivasis are not significantly different from the problems of poor peasants. That framework, however, collapses when we look at the Andamans, because it becomes clear that not all aborigines are Adivasis. Here, considerations of racial peculiarity pose intractable problems, the primitive apparently has nothing to offer the citizen except illicit pleasures and pride of possession, and democratic resolutions of aboriginality within the nation become elusive. Sarkar, who did not hesitate to identify himself with the Adivasi, could call for 'colonization' of the Andamans without a trace of irony.[69] Nationalist discourse generally holds the islands apart from a mainland and a mainstream. Apart from the episode of the penal colony, there is no convincing link between the two spaces in the Indian historical narrative.[70]

That dislocation has been most acute when it comes to the indigenous islanders, who entered Indian discourse very differently from the Adivasis of the mainland. Santals did not have to wait for the British in order to become familiar to Indians. Risley and his colleagues added an important facet to the knowledge, but they had no monopoly on the processes of knowing.[71] The Andamanese, on the other hand, came to Indians almost entirely through British mediation. Even the chatter of convict society was only semi-autonomous of colonial narratives and power structures.[72] Under the circumstances, the Andamanese that Indians conceived remained fundamentally alien: accidental discoveries unsupported by indigenous discourses of familiarity and kinship. They entered India not through the semi-open category of the Adivasi, but the closed category of the *adeem janajati*.

Not surprisingly, the Indian national encounter with the Andamanese has been colonial on at least four interconnected levels. One is the straightforward business of expropriation: the various kinds of crowding out, hemming in and encroachment, enabled and justified by the total displacement of one set of ideas about land, space and ownership by another.[73] At another is a vulgar museological outlook: Jarawa dolls for sale in Port Blair shops (see Plate 5.1), tourism entrepreneurs getting aborigines to strip or dance for the cameras of visitors from the mainland (the museological modality is vulgar in all historical settings—there is no 'proper variety' to set off against the Third World derivation).[74] The third

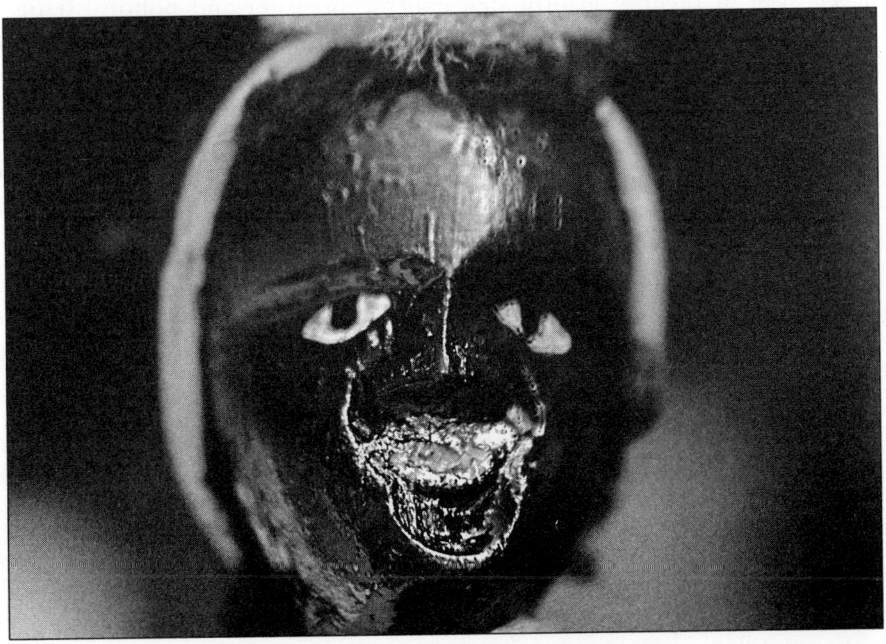

PLATE 5.1: Jarawa figure sold at Port Blair.
Source: Courtesy of the author.

is the issue of ethnocide. The fourth is political exclusion, which enables all of the others. Linking and symbolizing these predicaments is a familiar question of coming and going. At the heart of what Elwin and others debated in the 1950s were the questions: can non-Adivasis 'go to' Adivasis, and can Adivasis 'come to' the nation state? Because Adivasis were acknowledged as Indians, both questions were ultimately answered in the affirmative, although coming and going would not be on equal terms.

But *adeem janajati* are not unquestionably Indians: excluded from nation and folk, they are exotics, out of time as well as out of place. The great imbalance of coming and going in the Andamans has corresponded to this exclusion. Outsiders can go to the Andamans: the very existence of the place is an invitation to colonization, tourism and various kinds of aesthetic and erotic experience. More pertinently, the Andamanese cannot come out. We will not soon see a situation in which the Jarawa, let alone the Onge, are encouraged to fly to Delhi or Munich. Those who try to keep *adeem janajati* in their proper habitat believe either that they have no desire to travel, or that they should have no such desire. Desire must depend on cultural transfers that the 'protectors' of the Andamanese themselves control fully. Portman, who for the most part also wanted to protect the Andamanese, would have understood and approved.

Why can the Andamanese not come out, and what exactly must they remain within? Why can they not even want to cross what has become a *kala pani* in reverse: a forbidden expanse of water and political status? The answer is race: the *adeem janajati* is encapsulated in somebody else's vision of race, with no way out except death. This is where we come to the issue of ethnocide.[75] We must be extremely careful about using terms like ethnocide when it comes to the Andamans. There would seem to be no question that the Andamanese are 'dying out' because the Indian nation has 'gone' to them. The death, however, is an ideological construct. There is no longer a deliberate policy of killing the Andamanese, or even a quasi-Australian, quasi-American or quasi-Afrikaner tolerance of casual murder.[76] Yet unlike Australian and American aborigines, who have acquired considerable control over the boundaries of their ethnic identity and are no longer required to 'look', 'live', think or reproduce a certain way in order to be considered racially alive, the Andamanese are imprisoned—by powerful outsiders—within quaint standards of genealogy, phenotype and lifestyle. The entire debate about their survival has been framed as the 'protection' and visibility of racial purity, in a way that would be unthinkable with, say, Germans or Bengalis. When we categorize the Andamanese predicament as ethnocide, we produce ethnicity as a fragile fossil. An identity that privileges racial purity is inevitably 'vulnerable': it is, Wolfe points out, the consignment of the aborigine to an 'ever-dwindling category'.[77]

At the conference about the Andamans at which the preliminary version of this chapter was presented, no Andamanese were present. The organizers cannot be singled out for blame: the situation is no different at conferences held in India, even in Port Blair. The presence of primitives at such conferences would be unthinkable. Everybody knows that there are no Jarawa anthropologists or Onge activists. Nearly seventy years after the decolonization of India, the idea that a Jarawa or an Onge might appear at a conference on their own initiative, to speak as their own agents, remains a cause for nervous laughter. The quaintness of the prospect is not very different from Victorian skepticism about native people with Ph.D.(s). It signifies a colonial residue that has been recuperated by the Indian state and civil society in a margin of the world of rights and citizenship. In this margin, which is a recognizable form of what Giorgio Agamben called a 'state of exception' or pocket of normative abnormality, the Andamanese are still produced as a cultural commodity for consumption by the 'civilized' administrators, activists and academics who claim to represent them.[78] Their peculiar 'primitiveness' and 'vulnerability' have remained valuable bases of careers and reputations.

Because the Adivasi politics of the mainland did not cross over to the Andamans, the Andamanese have been consigned to a protected innocence—life without politics—that deprives them of agency, representation and life itself. Enforced primitiveness will, however, continue to fail as a policy, because the modern genie cannot be put back in the bottle: the activists and administrators who seek to insulate the islanders cannot undo the history of the past 225 years. They cannot even close the ATR. And indeed, they are yet to make a convincing case that the ATR *should* be closed, because they have not demonstrated that the Jarawa, through whose territorial reserve the road runs, want it to be closed. It is the historical norm that people will move about and interact, even if the interaction is not on equal terms. It is segregation that is coercive and extraordinary, and it does not work.

To begin to imagine what might work, we have to decide what 'work' means in this context. If it means clinging to a romantic preservationism, i.e. fetishizing an inflexible, anti-historical idea of what it means to be an aborigine or a 'primitive tribe', then that work will amount to little more than an extended funeral. Yet that is the work that marks the activist posture in the Andamans. The activists who claim to speak for the Andamanese are, for the most part, English speaking, college educated and middle class, more at ease with the Indian left than with the right. They are, however, remarkably reminiscent of Victorians in their responses to the savage. One activist has described her delight when a naked Jarawa man felt her breasts and spread her legs in the jungle; the same person has expressed her horror at the prospect that the Jarawa may be downloading pornography on their mobile phones.[79] They are rather comfortable with the idea of 'primitive tribes' as children, whose lives must be simultaneously 'protected' and controlled by enlightened well-wishers. It is as if the debates on race, rights, and citizenship that have driven the politics of aboriginality in other democracies—Australia, New Zealand, Canada, and the United States—since the Second World War have never happened.[80] And indeed, they have not happened in India.

We are, thus, left with an activism in which race is biologically inherent, identity is beyond politics, some people are trustees, and others are held in trust. In this perspective, the 'primitiveness' and 'vulnerability' of some people so defines who they are that if they were no longer primitive and vulnerable, they would no longer be people at all. So they must be 'protected' from change at all costs, protected from contact with outsiders, from germs, from information, alcohol and pornography, and protected also from adaptation to the modern world of politics, money and rights, because adaptation suggests agency, which children cannot possess. *Ador kore shikey tule rakhbo tomay ratri-din* ('Tenderly I'll hide you in the larder, where you'll be safe and sound') as the satirist Sukumar Ray might have said.[81] They must be insulated in a bubble of jungle as a middle class fantasy (explicitly, a 'dream')[82] of pre-capitalist purity and innocence, cocooned in somebody else's hope that capitalist society will not find them out. Because that hope is known to be false and the insulated are a kind of living dead, the enterprise is shrouded in a vocabulary of imminent extinction and a sentimental, masochistic anguish that allows activists to weep at the podium at conferences.

Since that posture is both bizarre and oppressive, 'work' in the Andamans will have to mean a form of assimilationism. One cannot live in a modern state and reject assimilation altogether without normalizing terrible disadvantages. It is only the assimilated who can resist effectively, and who can re-articulate their identity. But assimilationism can mean many things. It can mean, for instance, the total deregulation of contact. Under those circumstances, it is possible that the Andamanese would quickly lose their land and be absorbed into a labouring underclass. That would be a 'bad thing' in the sense that economic exploitation is bad, but the exploitation of the Jarawa would not be a worse thing than the exploitation of the Santal, or of the non-tribal poor, for that matter. To assume that it would be a bigger tragedy is to fall into the primitivist trap, taking the Andamanese along.

Total deregulation, however, is not the only available form of assimilationism. The most reasonable approach may very well be a minimalist one that protects the tribal reserve, guaranteeing the exclusive ownership of its land to the tribal group. What the members of the tribe do on that land would be absolutely up to them. If they want to meet tourists or film-makers, that would be their business. If they want to leave, return, start a business, marry a Tamil, drink themselves to death, or download pornography on their phones, that would—and should—be their business. Beyond ensuring their ownership of the reserve, the state and civil society organizations should make certain options available to them: schools, dispensaries, access to the economy in the form of jobs and microfinance, access to the courts, access to forums that provide redress against exploitation and harassment by employers and policemen, access to information, voting rights, civil rights, the ability to travel, the ability to become unrecognizable to those who are invested in the primitive. Information must be a two-way flow: not only must 'we' learn about the tribes, but the tribes must know what options are available to them through the Indian state and society.

By way of an ideological framework, it is useful to recall two observations Partha Chatterjee made about society and politics in independent India. One is that the Indian state has, from the outset, been pulled between a discourse of rights, centred on the agency and entitlements of the rights-bearing citizen, and a discourse of policy, focused on populations that pose problems of governance and must be treated as the objects of state action.[83] The latter is a patently undemocratic and violent inheritance of colonially-incubated modernity, and the 'primitive tribe' in the care of middle class managers is its ultimate manifestation. The other observation is a point Chatterjee made about the Muslim Civil Code. The individual member of the minority group, he wrote, must have the option of functioning as a generic rights-bearing citizen, without giving up his or her minority identity.[84] The state must protect both options: the generic as well as the particular. It might be argued that the Jarawa and Onge are not like Muslims or even Adivasis, that they are extraordinarily vulnerable. It is, however, precisely this perception of extraordinariness that is the problem. The so-called primitive groups must be allowed to be ordinary. It is ordinariness—not 'dreams'—that must be facilitated by well-wishers of the Andamanese: ordinary resources, ordinary identities, ordinary constitutional status.

That facilitation need not be an abstract or exotic concept. It can follow the standard model of Indian federalism, in which there is no contradiction between a particular identity (like being Bengali) and the generic identity (being Indian). The state can take unremarkable, practical steps to make this possible, such as teaching Andamanese languages in the local schools—to *all* children, tribal and non-tribal—in addition to Hindi and English, teaching the history of the islands in addition to Indian history, employing the Andamanese as teachers, and enforcing the Scheduled

Tribe quotas in employment and education. Revision of the educational curriculum in the islands is a particularly important part of a democratic approach to assimilation, because it can ensure a measure of mutuality in assimilation: not only must aborigines learn the culture of the mainstream, the mainstream should incorporate aboriginal culture into its own everyday texts. That is precisely the intervention that Sarkar made in the politics of Indian aboriginality.

Whether we like it or not, primitives—by definition—live in the modern world, subject to relations of unequal power. Whether we like it or not, our perceptions and policies impact upon them, and have already impacted upon them. The urge to insulate them from the world, or to place them under the guardianship of a few wise brown parents who are entirely fallible, is a part of that unequal power, and as much a form of objectification as any colonial art, scholarship or governance. It prevents them from responding to the impact of modernity, and perpetuates the injustices of their situation. The only effective defence of the primitives we wish to protect lies in giving them the means of understanding *our* understanding of primitiveness, giving them access to *our* means of power. They would then at least have a chance to reformulate their ethnicity and their political relationship with others. They may no longer be Jarawas or Onges, and perhaps that would be a real loss. But it is more damaging, and unacceptably colonial, to think of it as a loss to some well-intentioned and proprietary understanding of a civilized world.

NOTES

1. K.S. Singh, ed., *People of India: Andaman and Nicobar Islands*, Madras: Anthropological Survey of India (hereafter ASI), 1994, pp. 1–29.
2. K. Mukhopadhyay, R.K. Bhattacharya and B.N. Sarkar, eds., *Jarawa Contact: Ours with Them and Theirs with Us*, Calcutta: ASI, 2002.
3. Satadru Sen, *Savagery and Colonialism in the Indian Ocean: Power, Pleasure and the Andaman Islanders*, New York: Routledge, 2010; M.V. Portman, *A History of Our Relations with the Andamanese*, Calcutta: Office of the Superintendent of Government Printing, 1899.
4. Sen, *Savagery and Colonialism in the Indian Ocean*, pp. 17–20, 53; idem, 'On the Beach in the Andaman Islands: Post-Mortem of a Failed Colony', *Economic and Political Weekly*, vol. 46, no. 26, 2011, pp. 177–86.
5. Satadru Sen, 'Medical Colonialism and the Andamanese', in *Adivasis in Colonial India*, ed. Biswamoy Pati, Hyderabad: Orient BlackSwan, 2011, pp. 269–92.
6. Meena Menon, 'Petition Against Jarawa Tourism in the Andamans', *The Hindu*, 17 July 2014.
7. Patrick Wolfe, *Settler Colonialism and the Transformation of Anthropology*, London: Cassell, 1999, pp. 2–3.

8. Even in colonies where indigenous labour was a rational requirement, Michael Taussig has suggested, primitivism has generated irrational excesses of violence and terror. Michael Taussig, *Shamanism, Colonialism, and the Wild Man: A Study in Terror and Healing*, Chicago: University of Chicago Press, 1987, pp. 50–73.
9. Satyajit Ray's 1970 film *Aranyer Din Ratri* is a case in point.
10. Biswamoy Pati, *Adivasis in Colonial India*, pp. 1–30.
11. Romila Thapar, *The Aryan: Recasting Constructs*, Gurgaon: Three Essays, 2008, pp. 25–64.
12. Sumathi Ramaswamy, *Passions of the Tongue*, Berkeley: University of California Press, 1997, pp. 62–76.
13. Nicholas Dirks, *Castes of Mind*, Princeton: Princeton University Press, 2001, pp. 43–60.
14. A.C. de Gobineau, *The Inequality of the Human Races*, London: Ostara, 2013, pp. 1–35.
15. Sudipta Kaviraj, *The Unhappy Consciousness*, Delhi: Oxford University Press, 1998, pp. 1–26; Dipesh Chakrabarty, *Provincializing Europe: Postcolonial Thought and Historical Difference*, Princeton: Princeton University Press, 2000, pp. 3–11.
16. Partha Mitter, *The Triumph of Modernism*, London: Reaktion Books, 2007, p. 29.
17. Satadru Sen, *Benoy Kumar Sarkar: Restoring the Nation to the World*, London: Routledge, 2015.
18. Satadru Sen, 'Wars of the Emasculated', *Economic and Political Weekly*, vol. 48, no. 16, November 2013, pp. 45–6; Benjamin Zachariah, 'Rethinking the Absence of Fascism in India', in *Cosmopolitan Thought Zones: South Asia and the Global Circulation of Ideas*, ed. Sugata Bose and Kris Manjapra, New York: Palgrave, 2010, p. 185.
19. Benoy Kumar Sarkar, *Dominion India in World Perspectives*, Calcutta: Chuckervertty, 1949, pp. 166–8; H.S. Hughes, *Consciousness and Society: The Reorientation of European Social Thought 1890–1930*, New York: Vintage, 1977, pp. 215–22.
20. Benoy Kumar Sarkar, *Villages and Towns as Social Patterns*, Calcutta: Chuckervertty, 1941, p. 187.
21. Sarkar, *Villages and Towns*, pp. 33–4; idem, *The Futurism of Young Asia*, Berlin: Julius Springer, 1922, pp. 250–6.
22. Andrew Sartori, *Bengal in Global Concept History*, Chicago: University of Chicago Press, 2008, pp. 68–108.
23. Joya Chatterji, *Bengal Divided: Hindu Communalism and Partition, 1932–1947*, Cambridge: Cambridge University Press, 2002, pp. 150–90.
24. Sarkar, *The Futurism of Young Asia*, p. 267.
25. Benoy Kumar Sarkar, *Love in Hindu Literature*, Tokyo: Maruzen, 1916, p. 52.
26. On restraint and *bhadrata*, see Satadru Sen, *Traces of Empire*, Delhi: Primus Books, 2014, pp. 58–74.

27. Sarkar, *The Futurism of Young Asia*, p. 312.
28. Hughes, *Consciousness and Society*, pp. 78–82, 249–77.
29. Sarkar, *Villages and Towns*, pp. 241–2.
30. Satadru Sen, *Disciplined Natives: Race, Freedom and Confinement in Colonial India*, Delhi: Primus Books, 2012, pp. 42–68.
31. Ibid.
32. Sumit Sarkar, *Beyond Nationalist Frames*, Bloomington: Indiana University Press, 2002, pp. 69–71.
33. Benoy Kumar Sarkar, *The Folk Element in Hindu Culture*, London: Longmans, Green & Co., 1917, pp. ix–x.
34. Ibid.
35. Ibid.
36. Ibid.
37. Ibid., p. 7.
38. Ibid., pp. 23–4.
39. Ibid., p. 53.
40. Ibid., pp. 82, 108.
41. Richard Eaton, *The Rise of Islam and the Bengal Frontier*, Berkeley: University of California Press, 1993.
42. Henrika Kuklick, *The Savage Within: The Social History of British Anthropology*, Cambridge: Cambridge University Press, 1991, pp. 8–17.
43. Taussig, *Shamanism, Colonialism, and the Wild Man*, pp. 10, 51–73.
44. Sen, *Traces of Empire*, pp. 19–36; Taussig, *Shamanism, Colonialism, and the Wild Man*, pp. 74–92.
45. Sen, *Savagery and Colonialism in the Indian Ocean*, pp. 25–52.
46. Benoy Kumar Sarkar, *The Positive Basis of Hindu Sociology*, Allahabad: Panini, 1914, pp. 52–7.
47. Indira Chowdhury, *Gender and the Politics of Culture in Colonial Bengal*, Delhi: Oxford University Press, 2001, pp. 40–65.
48. Sarkar, *The Positive Basis of Hindu Sociology*, p. 52.
49. Dirks, *Castes of Mind*, pp. 43–60.
50. Sen, *Savagery and Colonialism in the Indian Ocean*, pp. 1–24.
51. Sarkar, *The Folk Element in Hindu Culture*, p. 108.
52. Ibid., pp. 114–15.
53. Ibid.
54. Ibid., p. 169.
55. Ibid., pp. 133–4.
56. Tithi Bhattacharya, *Sentinels of Culture: Class, Education and the Colonial Intellectual in Bengal 1848–85*, Delhi: Oxford University Press, 2005.
57. Sarkar, *The Folk Element in Hindu Culture*, pp. 19–21.
58. Ibid.
59. Ibid.
60. Ibid., p. 74.
61. Ibid., p. 16.
62. Ibid., p. 127.
63. Sarkar, *The Positive Basis of Hindu Sociology*, p. 53.

64. Sarkar, *The Folk Element in Hindu Culture*, p. 16.
65. Ibid., p. 65.
66. Ranajit Guha, *Elementary Aspects of Peasant Insurgency in Colonial India*, Delhi: Oxford University Press, 1983, pp. 1–17; Ramachandra Guha, *India After Gandhi*, New York: Harper, 2008, pp. 272–5.
67. James Carson, 'Mastering Language: Liberty, Slavery, and Native Resistance in the Early Nineteenth-Century South', in *Native Diasporas: Indigenous Identities and Settler Colonialism in the Americas*, ed. Gregory Smithers and Brooke N. Newman, Lincoln: University of Nebraska Press, 2014, p. 209; Duane Champagne, 'Tribal Institution Building in the Twentieth Century', in *Native Diasporas*, ed. Smithers and Newman, p. 349.
68. Ramachandra Guha, *Savaging the Civilized: Verrier Elwin, His Tribals, and India*, Delhi: Oxford University Press, 1999, pp. 261–77.
69. Sarkar, *Dominion India in World Perspectives*, p. 134.
70. Sen, *Disciplining Punishment*, p. 1.
71. Dirks, *Castes of Mind*, pp. 212–24.
72. Sen, *Savagery and Colonialism in the Indian Ocean*, pp. 157–80.
73. Vishvajit Pandya, 'Movement and Space: An Andamanese Cartography', *American Ethnologist*, vol. 17, no. 4, 1990, pp. 775–97.
74. Bernard Cohn, *Colonialism and its Forms of Knowledge*, Delhi: Oxford University Press, 1997, pp. 9–10.
75. Sita Venkateshwar, *Development and Ethnocide: Colonial Practices in the Andaman Islands*, London: International Work Group Indigenous Affairs, 2005.
76. Taussig, *Shamanism, Colonialism, and the Wild Man*, pp. 1–36.
77. Wolfe, *Settler Colonialism and the Transformation of Anthropology*, p. 176.
78. Giorgio Agamben, *State of Exception*, Chicago: University of Chicago Press, 2005, pp. 1–31.
79. Madhusree Mukherjee, *The Land of Naked People: Encounters With Stone Age Islanders*, London: Houghton Mifflin Harcourt, 2003, pp. 183–5.
80. Champagne, 'Tribal Institution Building in the Twentieth Century', p. 349.
81. Sukumar Ray, 'Bhoy Peyona', *Samagra Shishusahitya*, Calcutta: Ananda Publishers, 1976, p. 9.
82. Mukherjee, *The Land of Naked People*, p. 185.
83. Partha Chatterjee, *Wages of Freedom: Fifty Years of the Indian Nation State*, Delhi: Oxford University Press, 1988, pp. 1–20.
84. Partha Chatterjee, *A Possible India: Essays in Political Criticism*, Delhi: Oxford University Press, 1997, pp. 228–62.

6

Spatial Dimensions in Narratives of History

Sri Lankan Repatriates on Katchal and Little Andaman

FRANK HEIDEMANN

A MISNOMER AND ITS OBJECTS

When Hugh Tinker published his seminal monograph, *A New System of Slavery: The Export of Indian Labour Overseas 1830–1920*, in 1974, he wrote about the past.[1] In the same year, Sri Lankan repatriates reached Katchal, and a few years later Little Andaman. They were not sold like slaves in marketplaces in the eighteenth century, nor recruited as indentured labourers in the nineteenth century; but they were brought to remote islands with little choice and little information. Today, these Sri Lankan repatriates have the right to vote and can leave and travel to any destination in India that they wish. However, they have no political representative, no place to go and no means of travel. Most of them stay where the state machinery run by the Director of Rehabilitation brought them. Their 'repatriation' was as legal as the slave trade and the indentured labour system.

On Katchal, forty-eight families were settled between 1972 and 1976 on rubber plantations. Over the past four decades, their numbers have grown and marriages outside of the repatriate community have taken place. Each family was promised two secure positions on the plantation, which—in theory—could be passed on to the next generation. Recently, they learned that the land, which was given to them after their arrival to build houses and a kitchen garden, could not be sold or inherited, since it is tribal land. They founded their own associations, wrote petitions and went on a hunger strike to achieve a transfer to another island, along with proper land rights. In contrast, on Little Andaman, forty-three families of Sri Lankan repatriates were given five acres each of agricultural land. About half of them sold their land and moved to other places. They did not found their own association, but joined political parties and started to fight for their rights. Labour migration, which Tinker describes in *A New System of Slavery*, is not a past history but an ongoing process. The repatriation of stateless Tamils from Sri Lanka moved more than half a million people from the upcountry of that island to the plains of south India, to small villages, to suburban slums or to hill stations. Those relocated to the Andaman and Nicobar Islands had the longest passage of all repatriates. They were settled without being consulted in an alien environment, a fact still largely unrecognized by politicians, administrators and human rights activists on the mainland.

In this chapter, I engage with the history of the Sri Lankan repatriates, which offers various possibilities for interpretation. Their history is—like other histories—complex and contested, in the past and in the present. But the general understanding of how repatriates evaluate their past has changed over time. History was transformed in the late 1980s and early 1990s. Before the Singhalese–Tamil conflict became violent, the place of origin, Sri Lanka, was praised as a good place to live, but after the open violence spread all over the island, it was seen as a troubled state. Rather than writing an encyclopaedic account of their history, I prefer to write about the process of repatriation as it is remembered today and the encounter between Sri Lankan repatriates and other migrants on the Andaman and Nicobar Islands.[2]

In 2011 and 2013, I conducted interviews with repatriated individuals. When I met them, I introduced myself as a researcher from a German university who had worked more than three decades ago on an aid project in upcountry Sri Lanka and later conducted fieldwork among other Sri Lankan repatriates in south India. Since I knew about places, trade unions, politicians and major events in Sri Lanka and repatriate settlements in Tamil Nadu, my interlocutors understood my sincere interest in their life. Their interest in speaking to me involved their desire to speak of their pain and problems, to hear about Sri Lankan settlements on the mainland, or to inform the general public about their struggle through the writings of a professional scholar. Our talks were equally influenced by my interest in subaltern studies, political anthropology, the concept of the state, and—broadly speaking—I wanted to see what had happened to the people, those who had to leave Sri Lanka when I worked there as a young volunteer. The theoretical focus of this chapter emerged through my conversations with these repatriates. These face-to-face encounters are the impetus and key source for this chapter.

Richard Burghart argued in *The Condition of Listening* that we should reject the model of an active speaker and a passive listener: 'By listening, I mean an act that acknowledges and in some measure transforms the speaker.'[3] Speaking and listening creates a social field in which both speaker and listener find new roles and new positions. The question is not whether the subaltern can speak, but if those who exercise power over symbolic and material resources hear them. In this case, Sri Lankan repatriates speak among themselves, often in council meetings, and their representatives address government representatives and occasionally have meetings with the chief secretary.[4] When they speak with an anthropologist, the agenda changes. What they said and how they phrased it, the way they presented their homes, fields, photo albums, passports, letters, and their feelings while remembering the past, all these moments did not exist before, but during our encounters. The basis of my writing are those moments of intersubjective truth—according to Jürgen Habermas, the ideal communicative act.[5] I tried to speak to people of all ages, but the most intimate talks I had were with almost a dozen men of about my own age (mid-fifties), who left Sri Lanka in the late 1970s. Some were politically active or had had economic success and a few men had enjoyed a relatively good education in Sri Lanka. When I listened to those men, I experienced intensive moments of sympathy and respect for their life, but at the same time, felt angered about the effects of history that tore apart families and displaced hundreds of thousands of stateless labourers. The conditions of listening were the context of their speaking.

At the outset, it must be noted that the term 'Sri Lankan repatriate' is a tricky misnomer.[6] In the second half of the nineteenth and in the beginning of the twentieth century, the forefathers of the 'repatriates' were recruited from the Tamil-speaking south Indian coastal districts to coffee and later tea plantations in Ceylon. After Ceylon Independence in 1948, citizenship was granted on the basis of origin and not birth. In spite of their long residence in the upcountry, the Ceylon government considered the Tamil labourers as Indian migrant workers. Since the Indian government was not prepared to grant citizenship to those indentured labourers in Ceylon, Malaysia, Fiji, and the Caribbean, the Tamils became stateless. Later, two agreements were made to resolve their unclear status. The Sirimavo-Shastri Agreement of 1964 and the Amendment, the Sirimavo-Indira Gandhi Pact of 1974, stipulated the 'repatriation' of 6,00,000 persons to India and that 3,75,000 should be granted Ceylon (after 1972, Sri Lanka) citizenship.[7] In both cases, the numbers were to include the addition of 'natural increase'. The repatriation process, the state-organized rehabilitation and the settlement of this destitute labour force brought them to unknown places.

Most of the 1,15,000 families who were repatriated to India between 1968 and 1986 did not settle in or near their ancestral homes and lands, but instead sojourned in south India. The highest concentration can be found in the Nilgiris District, which is as far away from their ancestral home as Sri Lanka.[8] To repatriate means to send people back to their own country, but the Sri Lankan upcountry Tamils did not consider themselves Indians. Moreover, their final destination did not turn out to be their ancestral homelands. To call the Tamil relocation from Sri Lanka 'repatriation', therefore, is both illogical and imprecise. Officially, the Indian Government offered a rehabilitation scheme for each family who came to India under the Indo-Sri Lanka agreements of 1964 and 1974. For those families sent under one of the state-run schemes to the Andamans, the term has a bitter aftertaste. They became part of the long list of migrants who came as convicts from various places in colonial India, as indentured 'Ranchi' labourers from what later became Chhattisgarh and Jharkhand, as Tamil refugees from Burma, as settlers from Bengal and as traders and entrepreneurs from Tamil Nadu and Kerala. They are known in public by a term created by the state. Though 'Pre-42' identifies people and communities settled in the Andamans according to the period in which they immigrated to the islands, the terms 'Sri Lankan repatriates'—and similarly 'Ranchis'—indicate the region of origin and implicitly identify their social status as unskilled labourers. A further aspect of the inappropriateness of the term 'repatriates' is buried in a collective historical consciousness. This requires a detailed explanation.

I argue that the Sri Lankan repatriates' shared idea of history places the stress on space and movement rather than time and the course of events. The supposedly descriptive term 'repatriates' swallows up a temporal dimension. It ignores the context of past events. It is a commonplace that interpretation of the past is created in the present. But here, in this context, the *present* state of places overshadows features of *past* places. Therefore, the semantic field of contemporary Sri Lanka is taken as a fact of the past. History, as a complex process linking past and present, maximizes movement and migration but minimizes structural transformation. I claim that in the contemporary understanding of history among the repatriates, among their neighbours and among representatives of the 'every-day state',[9] it is place and space that explain their history, rather than a succession of events. Among the repatriates, their place of residence is the main indicator of their identification within the group. It matters whether a family lives in Katchal and works on a rubber plantation, in Little Andaman as a settler who owns five acres of land, or in the urban area around Port Blair. The exact place of origin in Sri Lanka, time of arrival in the islands and caste affiliation do not create major distinctions. In my view, the strongest manifestation of their individual histories is the settlement pattern of the present. The omnipresent expression of their collective history is the name they give themselves: 'Sri Lankan repatriates in Katchal' (or elsewhere) represents a condensed form of history and identity; it links their origin and destination with the cause of their movement and relocation.

The history of Sri Lankan repatriates, as it appears in a few scholarly texts, is interwoven in a colonial and post-colonial history.[10] Their own narratives are embedded in local contexts and localities along their migration routes. Unlike in urban Port Blair, where monuments in public places are materialized forms of, or claims to, the past, their settlements on the islands show no visible objects of historical reference. It might appear as a matter of surprise that Sri Lankan repatriates, a group defined by their history, have no great narrative, no cultural hero or trans-regional political leader, no common temple and no shared agenda. In each conversation I had with repatriate individuals, it was the family and the specific migration line that mattered. Listening to repatriates, the notion of injustice done to them emerges as a dominant topic. My interlocutors identified themselves as members of an amorphous group with a shared destiny.

When I tried to locate Sri Lankan repatriates around Port Blair and on Little Andaman, I was surprised by their social invisibility. In many places, they were either unknown to neighbours, were confused with Tamil repatriates from Burma, or simply taken for Tamils from the mainland. Looking back, one of the possible explanations might be that the former Sri Lankans were newcomers and that differences in language and appearance were not obvious to outsiders. In each place of residence, Sri Lanka repatriates built minimal social systems and associations were formed on two islands. These bodies use the official designation with the place name and add 'welfare association'. Their activities take the community out of anonymity; they organize meetings and public protest, inform the press and write letters to government agents or petitions to higher authorities.

From the point of view of the government the strongest manifestation of the presence of the Sri Lankan Tamil repatriates are thick office files with correspondence and minutes. In the Andaman and Nicobar Archives, the correspondence with the repatriate associations is kept in a voluminous file titled 'Resettlement of Sri Lankan Tamils from Katchal'.[11] At regular intervals, they document their problems and call for a new settlement location. The file contains the minutes of several meetings with high officials and their promise to consider their case. Looking back, the file establishes a sharp contrast to the public invisibility of the Sri Lankan repatriates. In comparison to other subaltern groups, the small number of Sri Lankan repatriates gained much more attention within government circles than other groups like Ranchis or Burma repatriates. There seem to be two main reasons for the extensive production of petitions and memorandums. First, in upcountry Sri Lanka, a massive labour movement commenced in the 1930s and has remained influential up to the present day. This indicates that the Sri Lankan repatriates were experienced in organizing themselves politically and effectively, expressing their position and needs in writing. Second, my collection of life histories suggests that—in comparison with Tamil Nadu—a higher degree of trade unionists, former supervisors or members of *kangany* families[12] opted to come to the Andaman and Nicobar Islands rather than other repatriation destinations. Therefore, a relatively high proportion of the Sri Lankan repatriates were leaders experienced in advocating for the interests of themselves and their workforce.

One further point of comparison with the mainland should be noted. Repatriation of Tamil people from the tea plantation region of Sri Lanka resulted in a harsh and often shocking confrontation with an everyday caste system in Indian villages, small towns and slums of larger cities. This did not happen in the Andaman and Nicobar Islands, where the concepts of ritual purity and hierarchy based on birth are less effectual.[13]

Before I embark on their *history*—or, on *their* history—I need to refer to an omnipresent confusion. Even among well-informed respondents in the Andamans, I found many who subsumed repatriates from Sri Lanka under the large but confusing category 'Tamils in Sri Lanka'. Historically and politically, at least two groups must be differentiated: the upcountry Tamils, the subject of this discussion, are called 'Indian Tamils' in Sri Lanka and are geographically located in the central highlands;[14] they are separate from the 'Ceylon Tamils', a pre-colonial people settled in the north and in the east of the island since time immemorial. The Ceylon Tamils fought for a separate Tamil state and did not agree with inclusion in the political entity of the Sri Lankan state. The Indian Tamils, on the other hand, are stateless contemporaries and seek integration into the Sri Lankan state as citizens.[15] The two groups have never shared a leadership, political force, or vision for the future. In spite of these facts, the two groups are frequently conflated and taken as a single entity, 'Tamils in Sri Lanka'. In mainland India, especially in Tamil Nadu, repatriates have become confused with Tamil refugees from Sri Lanka.[16] While the former left their work and their families behind and relocated at the invitation of the Indian government, the latter crossed the border because their physical existence was endangered. On the Andaman and Nicobar Islands, the political agenda of the Sri Lankan upcountry Tamils, i.e. a peaceful coexistence with the Singhalese Sri Lankan majority, is not known. The press reports exclusively on the struggle for an independent state fought by the Ceylon Tamils. As will be shown later, this confusion has also affected the settlement of Sri Lankan repatriates on the Andaman and Nicobar Islands.

THE PASSAGE TO THE ANDAMAN AND NICOBAR ISLANDS: MOMENTS IN A LIFE HISTORY

Mr R. Perumal is the head of one of the forty-eight families who were repatriated to Katchal between 1972 and 1976. I found his name in one of the records kept in the Andaman and Nicobar Archives.[17] When I had this file in hand, I was impressed by the voluminous paperwork. Several hundred pages documented in detail the political and administrative process initiated by a few dozen plantation-labourers in their quest to be resettled. The name 'Mr. Perumal' appeared on a personalized document to prove the settlers' history. The name was entered into a form used by the Assistant High Commission of India in Kandy, Sri Lanka. The form contains an enormous amount of detail about the process of repatriation; one and a half pages tell how families and their luggage were to be brought from Sri Lanka to Port Blair. Besides Mr Perumal's name, there are five more handwritten entries: the name of the head of the family is followed by the number of family members, the passport number, the date of shipping, the officer's signature and the date. This is the document for his family of six, and was signed on 24 February 1975. They were to be sent from Sri Lanka to India one week later, on 3 March 1975. This document was created by the Andaman administration to regulate responsibilities for the passage through Mandpam Camp in the Ramanathapuram District, Cummunipundi Camp in the Chingleput District and Madras to Port Blair. It mentions the granting of cash dole, medical treatments including vaccinations and the name of the shipping agent in charge of the luggage. The state machinery appears to be well organized; it takes care of people and luggage, and treats both with almost equal paternalistic, efficient care.

Later, when I met Mr Perumal in his house near Port Blair, I learned that the passage took more than one year. His family stayed thirteen months at Cummunipundi, waiting for an order to move on. They were used to a cool and often chilly climate in upcountry Sri Lanka, but in India they were exposed to temperatures above 40 °C. While staying in the camp, Mr Perumal's sons went to school and worked in tea shops, his wife delivered a child, and he worked as a casual labourer in the rice fields of the neighbouring villages. In all those months, they had no information about how long the stay in Cummunipundi might last. These uncertainties and fears are not represented in the document but they are central to his memories. Later he learned about the reasons for the long stay in the camp: the rubber plantation on Katchal was not yet in need of labourers and the accommodation had not yet been constructed.

Mr Perumal remembers 24 February 1975, the day he signed the document arranging the relocation of his family. He had taken a crucial decision based on rather limited information. In his case, he opted for Indian citizenship and was in the privileged position of being able to choose a particular rehabilitation scheme. Others were not asked at all. Most of the repatriates (79 per cent) were lumped into the category receiving a 'business loan', that is, a one-time cash payout amounting to between Rs.1,000 and Rs.5,000. Their tracks vanish somewhere in south India, their life histories remain untold here.

Mr Perumal was better informed than others. Mr P. Doraisamy, a good friend he knew from his plantation, the Lindula Estate, wrote long letters from Little Andaman. Mr Doraisamy and his eldest sons had themselves been informed about life in the Andamans by Rengasamy, the son of Marudai, one of the first three repatriate families on Katchal. These and all other letters from the 1970s have been lost, the last ones during the 2004 tsunami. They are remembered as a mixture of enthusiastic statements about the good government support, the freedom they enjoyed in the Andamans (in contrast to the political situation in Sri Lanka) and reports of hardship and isolation. A few of my informants felt that the letters were written by lonely settlers in enthusiastic terms in order to motivate friends and relatives to come. Mr Ramasamy, the son of Mr P. Doraisamy, took the trouble to write to the Deputy Commissioner of Rehabilitation in the Andamans and received a detailed answer. Others had heard radio spots about the Andamans and asked no further questions. Looking back, they described their choice of going to the Andaman and Nicobar Islands as a naive, adventurous decision.

After 'opting'[18] for a particular rehabilitation scheme, Mr Perumal and his family increasingly became the objects of an administrative procedure. They continued their work on the tea plantations and waited for the order to move to come. In many cases, there was less than a week's time between notification and departure, leaving little time to pack up all one's belongings and board a lorry with the boxes to be carried to the next railway station. In the late 1970s, when I worked on a development project on a tea plantation close to Ragala, I witnessed the dramatic scenes of farewell. Families were split up und physically separated, often forever. They became objects of the state and were transported to the jetty like cattle to the slaughter. Before their departure, documents were checked; repatriates remember a compulsory vaccination, and rather chaotic moments of lost luggage or missing family members. One man from Little Andaman told me that a fraud who appeared to be most helpful stole all their cash under the pretext of changing it into Indian currency.

The first stop for the Perumal family was on the principal route of all repatriates coming from Sri Lanka. They stayed in the Mandapam Camp, where their forefathers were accommodated or put under quarantine on their way to Ceylon so many years before. In independent India, the colonial recruitment site was turned into a repatriation camp. The length of people's stay in Madapam varied, as do their memories of those days. Some families stayed a few days, others more than a year. The camp became a transit lounge for some and a detention camp for others. Those who came at a relatively young age with high hopes and good spirits and arrived in the comparatively cooler months of December, January or February remember a busy and exciting place where they met old acquaintances and new people from various districts in Sri Lanka. Older people and those who came from the cool upcountry climate in Sri Lanka to India in the hot months of April or May often fell ill and suffered enormous physical and mental hardship. All repatriates scheduled for the Andaman and Nicobar Islands were sent to the Cummunipundi Camp, north of Madras (today Chennai).

Mr Perumal remembers his long stay in Cummunipundi with mixed feelings. In all, eight families had joined together in Sri Lanka to opt for the same scheme: Mr Perumal's brothers Kuppusamy and Periasamy; his wife's brother Thulasidar with his three brothers Subbiah, Krishnasamy, and Vishudas; and their sister (married to Swaminathan). They were to become the biggest family cluster among the Sri Lankan repatriates on the islands. The unity of his co-travellers and his expectations of finding new work and their own property on a beautiful island made him happy—at least in the first weeks. But Mr Perumal's extended family was not united at all: some close relatives stayed back in Sri Lanka and Mr Perumal's brother moved to his wife's native region south of Madras. Like most repatriates in south India, his family maintains a loose network; they write letters or make phone calls on special occasions.

In April 1976, eighteen families were taken from Cummunipundi to Madras and embarked on a ship, the *Hariyana*. After a six-day sail, they reached Port Blair, where they were received by officials and disembarked on the same day for the 430 km. trip to Katchal. After their final arrival, all were exhausted, many weakened from seasickness, but there was somehow a positive spirit of having reached their goal. Mr Perumal and his wife worked on the rubber plantation up to their retirement. In the years following their arrival, their children were among the few individuals who left the island for a better education. Supported by the quota system, they were able to enter higher educational institutions and got government jobs in Port Blair and Tamil Nadu. Today, the parents, their two married children and their grandchildren live together in a house close to Port Blair. They constitute an exceptional case: they freed themselves from the isolation of Katchal and from dependency on the goodwill of the state. Mr Perumal, his wife and his son were the only members of the family to visit Sri Lanka again. They experienced moving moments in the houses of close relatives and deep disappointment in a post-war state. On 16 March 2013, Mr Perumal and his wife celebrated their fiftieth wedding anniversary. They are a remarkable couple and have maintained their confidence, faith and dignity in spite of many hardships and sufferings. I enjoyed their hospitality and learned a great deal about Katchal, a place I had known only from photographs, narratives, maps, letters and a few videos I was able to see in the homes of other researchers in Port Blair.[19]

RUBBER PLANTATIONS IN KATCHAL: THE 'BEAUTY OF DEMOCRACY' AND LIVING IN A 'HOTEL ROOM'

When the first repatriates arrived at Katchal, they entered a new world. They experienced a whole new ecosystem and encountered unknown people. Basic facilities were minimal or non-existent. There was no electricity and no running water, but a doctor visited the plantation occasionally. The local school was staffed with a single teacher and classes ran from the first to the fifth year, and Tamil was the language of instruction. The repatriates were given temporary accommodation and half an acre of land for a kitchen garden. The spirit, settlers (which was the new legal status of those repatriates) told me, was most positive. After the troublesome journey and the first months of hardship, 'we experienced the beauty of democracy. We became citizens of India, got work and a piece of land.'[20] On the plantations, supervisors came from Kerala and basic communication was possible. But there was hardly any contact beyond the group of repatriates.

The classification of land became a major issue and one of the reasons for the separate file in the Andaman and Nicobar Archives mentioned earlier. When one of the settlers wanted to register the land of the kitchen garden and of the house site in his son's name, he was met with shocking news: the land which had been promised and given to him was tribal land. It could be used by his family, but not sold or inherited. As one man put it: 'A certain bitterness came up. We all felt cheated, because the land given to us turned out not to be ours. We could use the land like you use a hotel room. But we were promised land, which means to us, land which you own.' Indeed, a closer look at the documents made clear that no permanent construction was permitted on the half-acre of land, and that it was meant to be used only as a kitchen garden. Moreover, keeping cows and chickens was not officially permitted because they might harm the rubber production. The realization of the legal status of their land raised a major political issue in Katchal, one that remains a matter of dispute today.

Right from the beginning of the settlement, repatriates wrote letters to the tahsildar and other local authorities to express their grievances and to seek improvement in governmental facilities. One of the complaints was about the lack of educational facilities. For teaching in Tamil, there was just one teacher who taught all repatriate children in one room simultaneously up to the fifth year. They were glad when a second teacher came, but this had an unexpected result. In the first years a few children, all boys, went to Port Blair to continue their education beyond the fifth year, but this stopped when schooling was offered locally up to the tenth standard. The boys who went to Port Blair entered colleges or government service. I met most of them in the course of fieldwork. It must be noted that their rise up the career ladder was encouraged or even made possible by the quota system, which enabled children of 'settlers', a distinct and supported category, to improve their economic position. Ironically, the improvement of local schooling had the unintended result of excluding the next generation of pupils in Katchal from higher education and white-collar jobs.

The Sri Lankan repatriates of Katchal organized themselves and formed the Katchal Settlers' Welfare Association in 1990, headed by K. Kalaiselvam, M.A., and S. Chandrasekeran. For a quarter of a century, their main problem has been the legal status of their land. Since they live and plant on tribal land, they have asked to be resettled on a different island with the same rights and subsidies, and land titles for five acres of agricultural land per family. A proposal to settle them in Campbell Bay was rejected. The Home Ministry in Delhi argued that in the light of the present political situation (i.e. the Tamil struggle for an independent state in Sri Lanka), it was not advisable to settle Sri Lanka Tamils in Campbell Bay. The confusion of Ceylon Tamils with Indian Tamils appeared in the words of a government servant in New Delhi and had a direct impact on government policy. One of the repatriate delegates from Katchal told me that once at an official meeting the Lt. Governor asked him the question: 'Why did you go there [i.e. to Katchal]?'—displaying a striking ignorance of the repatriation scheme and the migration history of the Sri Lankan repatriates.

In the view of the Katchal Settlers' Welfare Association, the government made 'a terrible mistake' (as expressed in several interviews with repatriates in Port Blair once settled in Katchal) in settling repatriates on tribal land. The attempts of administrators from one department to solve this problem were foiled by those from other departments, since tribal land cannot be converted into settler land. Once the association wrote to the government asking for the repatriates to be declared tribes, but the Home Ministry in Delhi replied that they 'cannot create another tribe' on the Andaman and Nicobar Islands. At least one official letter per annum is sent by the association and they feel that time is running out, since they are desperately trying to find a solution before the first generation of settlers die. In 1999, the settlers agreed to be settled separately on different islands, and the administration began to search for smaller units of resettlement on various islands. The settlers feel that they are being abandoned in remote locations and ignored by the Indian Government. On one occasion, they made a drastic move to draw attention to their situation and handcuffed the local Member of Parliament (MP) on his visit to the island in 1992, sparking a joint action by the police and the navy to rescue him.

On another occasion, they attempted to secure land by going into the forest and felling trees to open up new agricultural lands, but after negotiations, they ended this action. On 23 October 2009, the association organized a one-day hunger strike in Katchal and in Port Blair with the support of the Tamizhar Sangam. They attracted some public attention, but were unable to secure solutions to their pressing problems.[21]

In March 2013, I had the opportunity to talk to Mr Kalaiselvam, the only graduate from the first batch of students in Port Blair who moved back to Katchal. He works as an agent for the Life Insurance Corporation of India (LIC) and looks after his clients on Katchal and the neighbouring islands. Thanks to his work, he makes frequent visits to Port Blair, where we met. Besides the major problems of land titles, he mentioned several day-to-day problems with the administration. According to Kalaiselvam, the local administration is not cooperative in several ways. Recently, he wanted to register a Katchal youth association, but it was refused. In January 2013, the Katchal Settlers' Welfare Association was registered after many years of discussion about whether a settlers' association could be registered on tribal land. In his view, the last forty years on Katchal have been an ongoing struggle for recognition, for land rights and for an appropriate legal status. The main problem, however, is the loss of settler status, which repatriates enjoyed in the past and, critically, which opened access to schools and government jobs. But this status has been rejected in recent years.

According to Mr Kalaiselvam, the local population on Katchal are Nicobarese who number between approximately 2,500 and 3,000. Their economic basis is fishing and copra production. Most of them are Christians and they are settled in places close to the shore. Several hundred of them lost their lives in the 2004 tsunami and a great portion of their land was flooded. As a result of the earthquake, their land lost elevation and is covered by saltwater. This led to internal migration and many Nicobarese moved to higher elevations where rubber is planted and where the repatriates are settled. The two populations—indigenous and immigrated—moved closer together in a spatial, but not a social sense. Besides linguistic barriers, there are different views on the status quo: Nicobarese consider the islands as their property and migrants as invaders; repatriates see themselves as a hard-working labour force sent by the Indian Government, with fewer privileges and rights. Therefore, it is no surprise that the Lt. Governor wrote in his letter to the Home Ministry that a resettlement of repatriates to other islands would be advisable to avoid tension and conflict on Katchal.

The settlers of Katchal replicate certain social forms which I found in the mainland and which have their cognitive roots in late Indian colonial history. In the first half of the twentieth century, the former *kangany* system of recruitment and supervision was at first an object of British colonial control and later made way for a growing trade union movement in the 1930s. The parents of the heads of families who came to India as repatriates were strongly influenced by a social system controlled by trade union leaders. The latter replaced the old paternalistic *kanganies* and served in the place of political party leaders for the stateless upcountry Tamils. Matters of social and legal concern became written objections; the appropriate way to complain or protest was in letters. As such, social status and leadership required literacy and writing skills. This kind of habitual and embodied performance was practised in Tamil Nadu and on the Andaman and Nicobar Islands. On the mainland, however, repatriates enjoyed more freedom of movement and mobility, because travel was not restricted as on the Andaman and Nicobars and public transport was always available. They followed job opportunities and in the Nilgiris they occupied government land and received land titles before election time. Their letters were stored in local politicians' steel cabinets and became untraceable. On the Andaman and Nicobar Islands, they could not move freely from island to island and could not encroach land. Their letters were kept in government offices and compiled in the archives. I am not aware of any place on the mainland where a few dozen families remained in the same location, as they did on Katchal. For most of the island settlers there, repatriation turned out to be a one-way ticket to a 'dead end street'.

A second layer of replication becomes visible if we take a closer look at the form or style of the protests performed by Katchal settlers. Copies of their correspondence with the government were sent to the local press and to the Tamizhar Sangam. In order to claim a mandate to speak for a clearly demarcated group, they register associations and print letterheads. They organize public hunger strikes to attract attention. Officials visiting the island are given a formal, highly respectable reception. To prove their claims, the association conducted a house-to-house survey among all repatriate families. They are, therefore, able to show evidence that the number of repatriate families grew to 173 in 2012. In short, the settlers of Katchal replicate modes of performance of the state and appear as a well-organized social entity with legal claims and well-developed communication skills. They seek proximity and maximal communication with the state. This, however, constitutes a sharp contrast to other communities such as the Ranchis, whose majority seek more distance from the government and use isolation as a strategy to avoid government interference.[22]

The sociological situation on Katchal offers a most interesting aspect with regard to how repatriates see their neighbourhood. The main issue in the settlers' struggle is the land, which belongs to the Nicobarese and is claimed by repatriates. However, the dispute is not between the two communities residing in the island, but between settlers and the government. This struggle, like most contestations involving state property or resources, opens up a field of competition in which competitors' proximity to or recognition by the state counts. It is not like a fistfight or a hundred-metre run, where the competitor is next to you, but like a contest in which the referee is not among the competitors.[23] The structure of the scenario is not specific to the region discussed here. In comparison with mainland India, on the Andaman and Nicobar Islands, there are less powerful local caste panchayats, there are fewer conflicts between landlords and labourers, less bargaining between producers and traders, but more government resources that could be subject to contestation and altercation. A second difference which must be noted is the democratic representation of the citizen. There is no local government, no legislative assembly, no MLA (Member of Legislative Assembly) and less influence of political parties on administrative procedures.[24] Taken together, I would assume that the sociology of small islands, even in faraway places, is overshadowed by a state which is not just 'imagined'[25] but omnipresent.

LAND COLONIZATION IN LITTLE ANDAMAN: SETTLERS AMONG STRANGERS

The history of those repatriate families who were settled on Little Andaman Island was in a way very similar to that of their fellow repatriates on Katchal. They left their homes in Sri Lanka and were sent to a most distant place in an unknown land. They lost track of family members on their long trek through camps and institutions; they underwent hardship and built a new life. But there was and is a major difference: the settlers of Little Andaman did not receive employment or proper housing, and in the first years of settlement, their experience—at least in my reading of their life histories—involved more constraints and hardship. However, they were given five acres of land and other forms of material and institutional support to build up a livelihood of their own.

Little Andaman, like Katchal, was inhabited exclusively by tribal people before the Ministry of Rehabilitation decided to use the land for their own projects. According to government plans, 10,000 people were to be settled, but a much smaller number was integrated in the land colonization scheme.[26] In 1965, Ranchi labourers were brought to the island by the Rehabilitation and Reclamation Organization (RRO) to clear the jungle. They began their work in Hut Bay, and this place name became synonymous with Little Andaman in local usage. The distance from the jetty served as the principal identifier for the villages that developed along the only road leading north. Repatriates from Sri Lanka live at 22 km. and at 28 km., the better-known names for Rabindra Nagar and Vivekanandapuram.

In December 2011, I spoke to almost all Sri Lankan repatriate families and conducted eight interviews with settlers of the first or second generation.[27] They remember their journey from Sri Lanka to Port Blair, just like those who went to Katchal. In their first days in Little Andaman, they stayed in Hut Bay, in a camp behind the present Consumer Cooperative Society, which is still called 'Ceylon Basti'. Then, they were shifted to a bigger camp at 28 km., Vivekanandapuram, and from there they walked to their assigned lands. The government agencies (in interviews often referred to as the agricultural department) told them how to cultivate the land and distributed seeds, manure, pesticides and water pipes. Loans were given for cows and goats, others kept hens or ducks. Other departments supplied mosquito spray and basic medical aid. Up to the first harvest, each family was entitled to a rice ration and a minimum of other foodstuffs. After two years, tin sheets for roofing were brought to Vivekanandapuram and the settlers built their own houses. However, there was no electricity or running water, and hardly any transport facilities. The Tamil schools went up to the eighth year and the Tamil community—Sri Lanka and Burma repatriates—built their first temples. Today, each community possesses at least one Hindu temple, but both congregations claim to have worshippers from both groups.

Hardship in those first years is a central element in all eight interviews. Some remember those days with visions of adventurism and heroic deeds, while others speak of despair and fear, of failed harvests and illness. The 'beauty of democracy' of Katchal was conspicuous by its absence. On Little Andaman, repatriates compared their situation with Sri Lanka and with their Bengali neighbours: 'In Sri Lanka, all documents were in Sinhala, English and Tamil, while here [in Little Andaman] all was in Hindi or Bengali.'[28] Bengali speakers outnumbered the Tamil speakers and one of my informants put it this way: 'Bengalis got the status as an OBC [Other Backward Classes] without any reason. On the [Indian] mainland you get a quota for your caste, here you get it for your majority.' When the Sri Lankan settlers explained the situation to me, they stressed the point that they are not—like Bengalis—refugees who knocked on India's door, but repatriates who were brought here on the initiative of the Indian Government. They were called and they should be treated at least on equal terms to the Bengali refugees. Hardship, which was in the beginning a physical experience, became a socio-cultural and political predicament. One respondent identified this situation—being in a linguistic and political minority—as the main reason for emigration from Little Andaman and concluded, 'If I die there are hardly six men to carry my body to the funeral ground.'

Among all families, the settlers of Katchal included, there is one case marked by significant economic success. The head of the family, born in

1949 on a Sri Lankan rubber estate, worked as an assistant manager and storekeeper before repatriation. He rejected an offer to become a bus driver in Chennai or to join the rubber plantation in Katchal. Instead, he went out to get his own land in Little Andaman and succeeded. With his extended family, he cultivated paddies in the first five years after his arrival and then planted betel nut trees and worked as a casual driver. His economic success began with the production of cement bricks and the investment of his profit in commercial vehicles. Today, he owns five trucks (of which two were damaged by the tsunami), one Caterpillar and one rickshaw. Among his employees for brick production and for his small lorry fleet are men from all communities settled in the area. His sons and daughters work and live in Port Blair and he can rely on a well-organized personal network. His name is associated with the local Hindu temple as he is the main donor. He also arranged for the idol to be transported from Tamil Nadu to Little Andaman and he also pays the pujari.

The other few families who can be considered well-settled achieved progress and success due to education, government jobs and the state quota system. One family at Vivekanandapuram came to India with seven children, of which the eldest had finished school in Sri Lanka. A medical officer who visited their camp was looking for medical assistants and the two eldest sons in the family became helpers, then assistants, and later received training in medical skills in Tamil Nadu. They became medical officers and their brothers found jobs as drivers or in the fire brigade. The sister got married and moved to Port Blair, where most of the siblings live today, either in service or retired. A second family, most of whose children found work in the public sector, came from Katchal. Three brothers work in the public service, including one with a career in the Indian Army, far away from the Andaman and Nicobar Islands. Besides these two families, there are a small number of individuals in permanent white-collar positions. What they have in common is that they were classified as settlers and entered the public sector with this designation. Their children, however, were refused this status, even if their father and mother, paternal grandfather and grandmother fell into this category. The evidence from the life histories speaks clearly: upward social mobility only became possible for a few and in all cases, except the entrepreneur mentioned earlier, the quota system turned out to be the crucial factor. A second observation is that among those who worked in permanent jobs or in government offices, there is a significant tendency to develop a second source of income such as owning small houses for rent, opening little shops at roadsides or partnering in microenterprises.

Unlike Katchal, there was no repatriate association on Little Andaman. My respondents pointed out that there were individual, but not collective claims and that there was no off-duty time like in Katchal when everyone could meet. In their memory, they all worked on their individual fields and collaborated only if necessity arose. For funerals, they joined together and later they built temples. The evidence in the archive, however, tells of occasions when the settlers handed over petitions to visiting government representatives and political parties found it difficult to create a reliable vote bank. Two people, however, became public figures at the time of election and stood for a political party. One of them won the post of ward member in local elections and the other was instrumental to the founding of the Tamil Settlers Welfare Association of Vivekanandapuram and Rabindra Nagar in 2012. This association brings together Burma and Sri Lankan repatriates, and their main demand is to be recognized as OBC. In Katchal, there was a sociologically well-defined group with a common history that joined hands and formed an association, but in Little Andaman the founding initiative grew out of a demand common to the Tamil-speaking settlers in two locations. The trend of communicating beyond the group boundaries can also be seen in marriage patterns. In Katchal, but more significantly in Little Andaman and even more explicitly in the area around Port Blair, there is a growing tendency for the Sri Lankan repatriates to marry Tamil partners, either from the Indian mainland or (Tamil-speaking) Burma repatriates.

LIFE HISTORIES OF MIGRANTS: THE PREDOMINANCE OF SPACE

Most life histories are narrated orally and only a small fraction find their way into a written form. More often than not, it is not the narrator who writes, and it is not the first recorded account, but one following several stages of rewriting that becomes 'history'. The transformation from event to memory to narration to textual codification is not just a change of genre and a modification of the content, but also includes social interactions. The speaker and the listener may not share the same ideas about abstract concepts like space, time, change, structure and agency. When I spoke with people of Sri Lankan origin on the Andaman Islands, it took us a while to get used to each other's concept of history. Our common understanding was that history is the narrative or idea of the genesis of the present. But I had studied their history from the nineteenth century to the present using archival materials and organizing my data on a timeline, while they and their forefathers had experienced a series of migration processes and organized memory by places. They did not know whether their forefathers were recruited from south India to the British colony Ceylon in the 1880s or 1920s, but they could certainly tell the name of the village they came from. In their own life history, what mattered was the migration journey and the places where they lived. Their succession of places has a reference to my concept of timelines, but since their turning points and transformations coincided with the movement to a new place, their emphasis stressed the departures from old and their arrival at new locales.[29]

The few dates that Sri Lanka repatriates in the Andamans remember were the days on which movement and journeys took place, in most cases the dates of departure or arrival of the vessel that brought them to the islands. There was one exception when a moment of change or transformation did not coincide with movement: the tsunami on 26 December 2004 caused devastation, hunger and death for many people in the Indian Ocean and became a key temporal marker. Again, after this date, migration followed. Families were brought to rescue camps and the Nicobarese on Katchal moved from their lower territories toward the repatriate quarters at a higher elevation. Though few calendar dates were remembered by my interlocutors, I argue that the spatial dimensions in their narratives of history are the main markers of change in the lives of Sri Lanka repatriates in the Andaman and Nicobar Islands.

In all interviews, the process of migration from Sri Lanka to India was qualified clearly in either positive or negative terms. The positive qualifiers referred to citizenship and land ownership in India and to the absence of ethnic discrimination. Some praise Indira Gandhi (and not Lal Bahadur Shastri) for signing the Indo-Sri Lankan agreements. Those who experienced greater suffering complain about the status quo, about the dominance of Bengali speakers, about the uncertainty of agriculture, and about the loss of family bonds. Their measurement of the quality of past processes is a subjective evaluation based on their feelings about being in the here and now. The comparison, however, rarely considers any process over time. They compare places in a timeless framework: Sri Lanka with Tamil Nadu or with Little Andaman; Little Andaman with Katchal or with Port Blair. Considering the lack of access to information and the emotional power of past events, this strategy comes as no surprise. A clear but rather unexpected parallel appeared when I talked to senior citizens or officials in Port Blair from north India. Their general knowledge of Sri Lanka derives from press reports that describe a country troubled by ethnic conflicts. They explain the process of migration in the light of a war that happened *after* repatriates came to India. History, as a tool to explain the present based on the past, works first in spatial and then in temporal terms. In all narratives, the same places appear with different qualifiers and without much of a chronological order. This multiple reading of history—'multistory'—is about the quality of place and space.

RAJU'S UPCOMING IN LIFE: FROM STRUCTURE TO AGENCY

The life stories of elderly people appear to be structured by the enforced migration from Sri Lanka to India and by a struggle for survival. The passage of Mr Perumal contains moments of state power and administrative decisions. The date of his departure from Sri Lanka and the duration of his stay in Cummunipundi Camp, the date of his sailing to the Andamans and his work and life in Katchal were by and large not decided by him. In a similar way, the settlers on Little Andaman speak of the movement from Ceylon Basti to Vivekanandapuram, the advice by the Forest Department about what and how to plant, the delivery of roof-sheets for their houses and the allotment of land. The younger generation, which grew up after the migration, tell their life with a stronger emphasis on their own agency. They stress their own decisions, their failure or success in school, their attempts to find work, to move to new places, or to find a marriage partner. The following life story is a shortened version of a taped interview of more than two hours recorded in December 2011 in Port Blair.

Raju grew up in Sri Lanka in a southern plantation district and attended school for his early years near the plantation.[30] His grandfather's village was not far from Madras, and he recruited labourers as a *kangany* from there. In those days, it was very easy to move from Ceylon to the Tamil districts in India, many boats made the journey regularly.[31] In the plantation, his grandfather was a supervisor and in charge of a workforce of about fifty persons. His father, one of seven children, became a soldier and was stationed for about ten years in Singapore. After his return to Ceylon, he got married and tried various jobs after Independence, and finally moved further south to an area where most people were Singhalese. Raju was born there and attended a Singhalese school, where he experienced various forms of discrimination. After his father's intervention, and on the headmaster's advice, Raju's name was changed into a Singhalese name, but the harassment did not end. The three Tamil students in the class had to sit on the ground, while others sat on benches. In the break, the tea was served in cups, but the three Tamils got coconut shells. Another problem was that there were no Hindu temples close by. When the Indo-Ceylon agreement was signed and when the Tamils in Sri Lanka learned that most of them had to leave for India, his father took the opportunity to register for a land colonization scheme. However, Raju's elder brother had already married a Tamil girl in Sri Lanka and her family did not want to leave for India. So, the family was separated.

At the age of eight, Raju left Sri Lanka with his family for good. He never saw his relatives, again but learned through letters about the birth of his brother's children. Lorries took him and his family to the next railway station and by train they went to Talaimannar and from there, they took the ferry to Rameshwaram. Raju remembered the atmosphere as depressed and frightening and that there was little assistance. They met one man who offered his help and gave comfort to them. He warned them about the dangers of vaccination and took them to the ship without going through the medical procedures. After they passed emigration a new topic arose: how to exchange Sri Lankan rupees into Indian currency? The man offered to arrange the money exchange but vanished with the cash on the other side of the customs clearance. The family reached India without any savings. They were accommodated in camps in Rameshwaram and then in Cummunipundi, where Raju worked in tea shops and looked after the sheep of local farmers. He did not enrol in school, since they expected to depart at any moment. More than one year passed with no means of income and in a state of permanent uncertainty.

On 13 July 1975, along with a group of nineteen repatriate families, they reached Katchal. They were shipped from Madras to Port Blair, where they were welcomed by officials and treated well. But they had no place, nor time to rest. After four days of seasickness at Port Blair, all the families continued and made a two-day trip to Katchal beginning that same day. While his parents worked on the rubber plantation, Raju went to school and had to learn the Tamil script, because his first schooling was in Sinhalese. On the island, there was one teacher for Tamil instruction who came from Kerala, like most of the foremen on the plantation. He was a nice person, taught without teaching materials and without physical punishment but with a lot of encouragement. All repatriate children joined the school and stayed up to the fifth standard. After passing this stage, Raju, at the age of 15, wanted to continue his studies. He learned that there were schools in Port Blair, but his father would not allow him to continue his studies because the family had no means. One day, when the ship from Port Blair was expected, he made a bundle with two shirts, two pairs of trousers and his school documents and hid it behind a bush. Later he stole Rs.300 from his father's box. Under a pretext, he left his house and sneaked off to the ship. In the last moment before departing, he entered the vessel. When the conductor found him, he convinced the man to take him without a ticket. On the ship he met a nice man, who took him to his home in Port Blair and introduced him to the Christian School. Supported by a government stipend, he studied up to the twelfth standard.

Later, Raju told me, that the year he left Katchal was within a small window of opportunity. Two years after he left, the school in Katchal was extended up to the tenth standard, and nobody left the island for higher education. Raju called it a contradiction, or an irony of development, that the improvement of a school hindered further education. In total, four boys from Katchal studied in Port Blair in those days. One of his peers continued his studies in Chennai, the others were able to find government jobs. Raju used to work in his school holidays, became acquainted with a few officials and entered a government department directly after school. His father, with whom he made peace as his schooling progressed, was proud of him. As a government servant, he made a few trips to the Indian mainland. Once he accompanied his superior on his transfer to Delhi. He was in charge of his luggage, which became a challenge when the train derailed; many passengers were injured and taken to hospitals. But Raju stayed back and protected his superior's luggage. For his loyalty and effort, he was granted one month paid leave. This was his second window of opportunity and he used it well. He visited his grandfather's village near Chennai, introduced himself and found a remote cross cousin for a marriage alliance. One year later, the marriage took place and the couple bought a small house in Port Blair where their children now attend school. Raju is grateful to god because life was good to him. On the last day we met, he presented me with a copy of *Tirukkural* of Tiruvallur. Raju is one of the most outstanding personalities I met in these last years.

CONCLUSION

The state of India created the administrative category 'Sri Lankan repatriates'. The Sirimavo-Shastri Pact (1964) and its Amendment formed the judicial basis for the resettlement of more than 4,27,000 people from Sri Lanka to India between 1969 and 1987. The state machinery organized the transfer and the rehabilitation of these individuals and families. Through them, the blueprint of rehabilitation was converted into a physical form. Today, Tamils from the former Ceylon who came under this pact all live in south Indian states, mainly in Tamil Nadu, and also in the union territories Pondicherry and the Andaman and Nicobar Islands. Apart from their country of birth, speaking Tamil, and the experience of being uprooted and brought to India as repatriates with few means, they have little in common. There can be small doubt that ill-informed and mostly illiterate people became the objects of a massive state project. They were uprooted, resettled and renamed as a group. In south India, repatriates demonstrated a high degree of mobility, but in the Andaman and Nicobar Islands, they stayed by and large on the islands where they were settled. Like their forefathers, who were recruited from south India to pick tea in Sri Lanka and produce that critical export, repatriates were moved to an unknown and remote place, like those who worked on a rubber estate on Katchal and cultivated cash crops on Little Andaman.

In contrast to the Ranchis and other subaltern groups in the Andaman and Nicobar Islands, Sri Lankan repatriates display a pronounced class consciousness. In order to achieve their goals, repatriates organized themselves and founded or joined welfare associations on both islands. These associations replicate institutional and symbolic forms of the state. They seek legal registration, create offices such as president, secretary and treasurer and write minutes of their meetings. They design letterheads and write official letters to high state representatives adopting a language used by the state. On Katchal, the settlers conducted a survey[32]—a census in miniature—following a format used by governments in South Asia in colonial and post-colonial times. The ultimate form of protest—a hunger strike—used by the Indian National Congress and the Gandhian movement in the struggle for independence was also adopted to express grievances. Central demands relate to resources, which the state has created: land titles and reservations. The dialectical relationship of the state and its citizens is illustrated in this microcosm. On Katchal, repatriates compete with Nicobarese over land rights, and on Little Andaman repatriates from Burma and Sri Lanka have joined together to struggle for inclusion in the OBC list. From a historical perspective, the state created the category 'repatriate' which exists today as an organized social group. Repatriates are defined by their origins and their history, expressed neither in their collective history, nor in statues, heroic figures or in ritual forms. They exist as a group because they had to create a public face to address the state. In short, a category created by the state continues to exist in the presence of its creator.

On small islands, however, this process has an enormous impact on the coexistence of local groups. Competition for resources does not occur between neighbours but is shifted to an extended arena. The state has the monopoly of power, over land and reserved categories. The state is the referee in most local rivalries. The two sides of the coin are the monopoly of power and the obligation to solve problems. The self-identification of social groups is, therefore, not just a matter of how they differ from other groups but also a matter of their affinity to the state. Repatriates' reminders about the terms of the Sirimavo-Shastri Pact have a double message: we all share the same history and it is the state that has created and invited us; the state is the procreator and host and has paternal duties and obligations. The role and the presence of the state differ from its form on the mainland. Besides obvious facts such as the geostrategic importance of the Islands, massive financial support from the central government and an economy centred on state institutions, movement and land issues are subject to a higher degree of state control and regulation. In short, the state owns and controls most of the vital resources and, therefore, enters competitive fields as a key actor. Local leadership requires a high degree of administrative knowledge and formal skills to address the state.

But can repatriates speak to the state? They speak to politicians, to public servants and also to journalists. They repeat their arguments for betterment, but there is little achievement. Each context creates specific 'Conditions of Listening'.[33] My interlocutors made clear that they do not trust local politicians and that there is no hope, because they are numerically too small to constitute a vote bank. When they speak to public servants, their talks extend over a longer time span; repatriates sense a kind of understanding on a personal level and in the best case, they feel acknowledged. After talking to lower level administrators they are encouraged to write letters, petitions and memorandums, which I found in the Andaman and Nicobar Archives. There is no doubt that repatriates command the language of the state and their texts are forwarded to higher authorities. I also have no doubt that these texts are read by many public servants. But after talking to the authors of these documents, I came to a tragic conclusion. The genre, which is required to express grievances in a written form requires a distinct style and rhetoric. The deep disappointment and despair of the people concerned is kept out of the texts. If subaltern people want to speak to the state, they cannot say what is at stake. Suffering and pain are squeezed into phrases and become incognizable. The contrast of spoken and written averments suggests that the language of the state mutes the voices of distress and agony.

One way forward is to talk indirectly to the state. Public protest, rallies and hunger strikes are occasions where grievances can be expressed. But such expressions are relegated to a public domain far from offices and ministries. It seems to be a ubiquitous phenomenon that fundamental and emotional (outdoor) protest is transformed into a formalized and structured (indoor) form when protestors cross the doorstep of the state.[34] This is taught at schools when class representatives speak to the headmaster and turns into embodied knowledge. Authorities like teachers, police, judges, administrators, etc., create an aura that minimizes emotionalized expression and allows critical statements only in a formalized expression. Public protest, however, is less restricted and permits many forms. On such days, journalists appear and listen. They acknowledge the speaker in their presence and use their own genre to report about them. The paper cuttings of such events reach the state and are kept in the same file along with letters and petitions. Spivak's programmatic question, whether the subaltern can speak, leads us to consider the conditions of listening, which in this case shows a fundamental contrast between public spaces and state offices.

History on the Andamans is both about time and about space, about the succession of events, and about movement. In this large territory, clearly marked with coastlines and huge distances, there is no pre-eminence in the trajectories of time and space. In places where identity and status is linked to migration, historical time cannot overshadow geographical movement. Settlement patterns constitute spatial orders and draw historical lines. But talking to settlers and sailing from one island to another, I felt that the sea swallows both time and space. Among settlers, it was the mother tongue and the region of origin that overshadowed caste, religion and moment of arrival.[35] I am aware of the contrast to the time-bound category 'Pre-42' and I clearly oppose the idea of generalizing my conclusion on social plurality in the Andaman and Nicobars. Instead, I prefer to support the view of 'multistory' or multiple views on history as a concept. For the settlers whom I met, I suggest that space overshadows time: what matters to them are their places of origin and residence. In any attempt to understand their process of identification, a temporally dominated view of the genesis of the present—or a Euro-American concept of history—prevents an emic understanding of settlers' lives.

NOTES

1. Hugh Tinker, *A New System of Slavery: The Export of Indian Labour Overseas 1830–1920*, London: Oxford University Press, 1974.
2. For a general overview on the state-controlled migration process to the Andamans, see Swapan K. Biswas, *Colonization and Rehabilitation in Andaman and Nicobar Islands*, Delhi: Abhijeet Publications, 2009. A short note on p. 101 refers to the Sri Lankan Repatriates on Katchal.
3. Richard Burghart, *The Conditions of Listening: Essays on Religion, History and Politics in South Asia*, ed. C.J. Fuller and Jonathan Spencer, Delhi: Oxford University Press, 1996, p. 300.
4. The minutes of these talks are kept in the Andaman and Nicobar Archives in the folder 'Resettlement of Sri Lankan Repatriates on Katchal'. Repatriates seek higher wages, better housing, more medical care, investment in education, and—most importantly—proper land rights.
5. Jürgen Habermas, *The Theory of Communicative Action: Reason and the Rationalization of Society*, vol. 1, Boston: Beacon Press, 1984; idem, *The Theory of Communicative Action: Lifeworld and System—A Critique of Functionalist Reason*, vol. 2, Boston: Beacon Press, 1987, cited from Burghart, *The Conditions of Listening*, p. 301.
6. Historically, 'Sri Lankan Repatriates' is an inappropriate term. For readability, I choose not to use inverted commas. Among the few publications on Sri Lanka repatriates in India, see V. Suryanarayan, M. Vamadevan, and R.R. Sivalingam, *Rehabilitation of Sri Lankan Repatriates: A Critical Appraisal*, Madras: University of Madras Press, 1986; M. Vamadevan, *Sri Lankan Repatriates in Tamil Nadu: Rehabilitation and Integration*, Madras: Zen Publishers, 1989.
7. Urmila Phadnis and Lalit Kumar, 'The Sirimavo-Shastri Pact of 1964: Problems and Prospects of Implementation', *India Quarterly*, vol. 31, no. 3, 1975, pp. 249–69.

8. Frank Heidemann, *Die Hochland-Tamilen in Sri Lanka und ihre Repatriierung nach Indien*, Göttingen: Edition Re, 1989; Centre For Research on New International Order (CNRS), *A Report on the Survey on Repatriates from Sri Lanka*, 2nd edn., Madras, 1983.
9. Christopher J. Fuller and Véronique Bénéï, eds., *The Everyday State and Society in Modern India*, London: Hurst & Company, 2001.
10. Daniel Bass, *Everyday Ethnicity in Sri Lanka: Up-country Tamil Identity Politics*, New York: Routledge, 2013; Valli Kanapathipillai, *Citizenship and Statelessness in Sri Lanka: The Case of the Tamil Estate Workers*, Delhi: Anthem Press, 2009.
11. A great part of the correspondence relates to the claim of *patta* (land titles), because Katchal land is classified as 'tribal territory' and land cannot be registered as individual property. The administration was actively but unsuccessful engaged in searching for alternative islands for a resettlement.
12. *Kanganies* (Tamil: *kan* = eye) are foremen on plantations in Sri Lanka and Malaysia who recruited landless labourers from Tamil villages in the nineteenth and twentieth centuries.
13. For the process of repatriation to Tamil Nadu, see Yvonne Fries and Thomas Bibbin, *The Undesirables: The Expatriation of Tamil People of 'Recent Indian Origin' from the Plantations of Sri Lanka to India*, Calcutta: K.P. Bagchi Publishers, 1984; Frank Heidemann, 'Immigration Labourers and Local Networks in the Nilgiris', in *Blue Mountains Revisited: Cultural Studies on the Nilgiri Hills*, ed. Paul Hockings, Delhi: Oxford University Press, 1997, pp. 148–63.
14. Haraprasad Chattopadhyaya, *Indians in Sri Lanka: A Historical Study*, Calcutta: O.P.S. Publishers, 1979.
15. K.M. de Silva, *A History of Sri Lanka*, Delhi: Oxford University Press, 1984.
16. Abhijit Dasgupta, 'Repatriation of Sri Lankan Refugees: Unfinished Tasks', *Economic and Political Weekly*, vol. 38, no. 24, 2003, pp. 2365–7.
17. The sheet on which his name is written is in the file titled 'Resettlement of Sri Lankan Tamils from Katchal'.
18. The term 'option' confuses the fact that 79 per cent of all families were not integrated into an employment or land colonization scheme but given a 'loan' to start their own 'business'. However, the small number (0.20 per cent) of all repatriates who enjoyed a land colonization scheme talk about their own option (Director of Rehabilitation, Madras, statistical information 1987).
19. I would like to thank Mukeshwar Lall for sharing visual images of Katchal.
20. The unattributed quotations in this section are from three group interviews with Sri Lanka repatriates settled in Port Blair, recorded in February and March 2013.
21. The representatives of Sri Lanka repatriates wrote several letters to local newspapers, but only a few appeared. In the *Andaman Herald* (29 July 1999), it was stated that they wrote ten petitions regarding their struggle between 30 August 1990 and 3 November 1995. 'But till date no favourable action were taken in favour of them. So, the Sri Lankan Settlers decided not to

poll their votes incoming parliamentary election, if their problem remain unsolved soon.'

22. On the recent history of the Ranchi community, see Philipp Zehmisch's 'The Invisible Architects of Andaman: Manifestations of Aboriginal Migration from Ranchi' (Chapter 7) in this volume.
23. Not on the Andaman Islands, but on the mainland I noted a statement by a local leader about his struggle with the local administration over contested land rights: 'The beauty queen has impressed the jury, not the other girls.'
24. The union territory is represented by one Member of Parliament in New Delhi, and the ministries in the capital and the Indian Army have a greater impact on everyday life in the islands.
25. Benedict Anderson, *Imagined Communities: Reflections on the Origin and Spread of Nationalism*, London: Verso, 1980.
26. Biswas, *Colonization and Rehabilitation*, p. 100.
27. The quotations in this section are paraphrased from my notes taken after the interviews. No personal names are mentioned to guarantee anonymity.
28. All quotes stem from Tamil informants and were collected during my fieldwork on Little Andaman and in Port Blair in 2011 and 2013.
29. The phenomenon to put an emphasis on place was not new to me. In Munich, I found the same tendency among students of social anthropology, who grew up in expatriate families. In the other life histories I came across in professional environments, it was places-cum-degrees or job assignments that were the main markers in their narratives. The movement from one place to another ignores the age of each family member but bundles the collective experience into a collective moment.
30. To guarantee anonymity, the name will be a pseudonym and certain details like his place or residence or his workplace will be omitted or remain vague.
31. The concept of *kala pani* as a danger of ritual pollution did not apply for Tamil plantation labourers.
32. I would like to thank the Katchal Settlers' Welfare Association for a copy of the survey on 'Details of Family Settled Under Shastri-Sirimavo Pact, 1964 at Katchal Island' which surveyed a total of 544 individuals.
33. Burghart, *The Conditions of Listening*.
34. For an ethnographic description, see Frank Heidemann, 'Objectification and Social Aesthetics: Memoranda and the Celebration of "Badaga Day"', *Asian Ethnology*, vol. 73, nos. 1–2, 2014, pp. 91–110.
35. This appears in clear contrast to Tamil Nadu, where most people speak the same tongue and it matters who came first. Society is based on property, purity, and origin, but the latter was spatially often unknown and perceived in relative order to the advent of others. Moreover, hierarchy finds its expression in the temporal course of events.

7

The Invisible Architects of Andaman

Manifestations of Aboriginal Migration from Ranchi

PHILIPP ZEHMISCH

To work with an axe is a pure pleasure for a Ranchi.

This local proverb vividly portrays the entangled history of 'coolie' migration and the colonization of space in the Andamans from 1918 onward. The so-called Ranchis'[1] 'pleasure to work with an axe' is a stereotypical allusion to the particular function assigned to these contracted aboriginal labourers from the Chotanagpur region in central India:[2] Ranchi labour cleared the Andaman forests and erected infrastructure that prepared the ground for the settlement of rehabilitated settlers and other migrants. These territorial expansions into the forest went along with large-scale timber extraction, which remained the islands' major export until the beginning of the new millennium.

However, after transporting thousands of Chotanagpuris to the islands when they were required to create a labour force in the Andamans, the authorities denied a subject position to many of those who wished to stay on. It appears that officials expected them to silently and invisibly return to their homelands after completing the tasks assigned to them. When labour contracts expired or when private companies left the islands—especially after the demise of the timber industry—they were left to fend for themselves as homeless and landless individuals.[3] Many Ranchis turned to daily wage labour, leased or bought land from settlers or worked as dependent sharecroppers. A significant number of former contract labourers encroached

* This chapter includes some paragraphs from my yet unpublished Ph.D. thesis (Philipp Zehmisch, 'Mini-India: The Politics of Migration and Subalternity in the Andaman Islands', Department of Social and Cultural Anthropology, Ludwig-Maximilians-University, Munich, 2015).

forestland to construct houses and cultivate gardens and paddy fields—often near the spaces they had previously cleared for timber companies or the Forest Department.

When the anthropologist L.P. Vidyarthi surveyed the Andamans as member of a team of the Home Ministry in the 1970s, he probably anticipated that the rapid rise of encroachments all over Andaman was going to become a major legal and social problem in the following decades. Calling the Ranchis the 'builders of the modern Andaman',[4] he proposed that the administration should provide those Ranchis willing to settle in the islands with suitable land.[5] Vidyarthi's proposal was turned down by the administration because some local communities and politicians strongly opposed it.[6] Instead, in 1984, reserved and protected forests were demarcated and those former labourers who lived in these forests were officially declared squatters.[7] Because encroachment villages were technically illegal, the reach of state welfare was severely limited in these locations.

As a result of their alienation from the means of production, very few of the 50,000–60,000 Ranchis in the Andamans today have experienced or achieved social mobility. This stands in stark contrast to individuals from Pre-42, settler, and other migrant communities. Consequently, this third-largest community in the Andamans lacks influential political leaders and spokespersons to effectively demand access to the state-dominated system of development. Asking local civil society members, social workers, politicians and government servants about their opinions on the reasons for the Ranchis' meagre socio-economic success, they responded that they were 'backward' because of their 'primordial' way of life.[8] They described the Ranchis as 'simple', 'hard-working' and 'submissive', with no ambition or aspiration to become 'modern'. It was broadly assumed that they were 'tribals, and quite happy in the forest'.[9]

Rejecting such hegemonic assumptions, this chapter aims to deconstruct contemporary stereotypes by analysing the historical production of 'Ranchi-ness' as a persistent by-product of the colonization of the Andamans in the twentieth century. I seek to demonstrate that the particular character of the Ranchis' socio-economic disenfranchisement and their political silence needs to be regarded as a yet untold manifestation of Andaman history. This particular form of subaltern history[10] will be embedded and contextualized by drawing analogies to the emigration of Adivasis from Chotanagpur since the nineteenth century with a particular focus on discourses of aboriginality.[11] Drawing parallels between this larger framework and the history of Chotanagpuri migration to the Andamans since 1918, I discuss the ways in which colonial relations of power and knowledge and their legacy conditioned the Ranchis' recruitment as well as their social position in the penal colony and the post-colonial island society.

COLONIAL EMIGRATIONS FROM CHOTANAGPUR

The contemporary stereotype that Ranchi Adivasis 'enjoy' working in the forests developed as a result of the trajectory of colonial classifications which constructed 'the primitive as both exotic tribal and everyday manual labourer'.[12] The colonial category of the 'hill coolie' emerged in the nineteenth century, among others, along with large-scale Adivasi emigrations from Chotanagpur that were caused by population growth, forest clearance, environmental degradation, famines, and seasonal variations in the region.[13] Furthermore, the colonial state had introduced a system of forest reservation, agrarian transformations, and administrative changes in the land tenure system which restricted common access to forest resources, dispossessed peasants and forced them into debt.[14] As a result, thousands of impoverished Adivasi peasants searching for wage labour were systematically recruited by contractors and sent to overseas destinations and across British India—especially to Bengal, Assam, Bihar, and Orissa where they worked on indigo and tea plantations and constructed railways and roads.[15]

Accompanying this process, Adivasis were attributed with racial stereotypes in order to justify the utility and 'natural' order of unequal relations of production. In nineteenth-century Bengal, the hill peoples of Chotanagpur and Santal Parganas were termed 'Dhangar' (originally a nomadic, herding group from Maharashtra) and 'Boonahs (wild men), Junglis (of the jungle), or Kols [the name of an ethnic group from central India used as synonym for 'savage' labourers]'.[16] The term 'Dhangar', then, stood for primitivism and a lack of caste status and civilization.[17] Colonial representations of Dhangar labourers, written in 1837 and 1840, are—unfortunately—reminiscent of contemporary stereotypes: 'The Dhangurs are always spoken of as more akin to the monkey than the man. They have no religion, no education, and in their present states no wants beyond eating, drinking and sleeping: and to procure, which they are willing to labour.'[18]

In the course of the nineteenth century, Dhangar came to be replaced by the term 'aborigine'. The new language of aboriginality categorized certain sections of the subcontinental population as plantation labourers and became an indicator of the coolies' racial fitness.[19] Different degrees of aboriginality, measured in terms of the regional origin of labourers, determined a hierarchy of first-, second- and third-class coolies.[20] As 'primitive' *junglees*, who came from the forests, the British classified 'pure aborigines' from Chotanagpur as 'first-class coolies', because they were assumed to be docile, hard-working and sufficiently racially fit to endure adverse climatic and ecological conditions.[21] The transformation of Chotanagpuri Adivasis into a 'coolie nation' thus builds on a 'modernist discourse of the primitive'[22] that enabled their ideological and material exploitation.

RANCHI MIGRATIONS TO THE ANDAMANS, 1918–46

Since the second decade of the twentieth century, contract labourers from Ranchi replaced Andaman convicts, taking over the specialized tasks of forest clearance and infrastructure development.[23] The shift from convict to coolie labour, i.e. from forced labour to the market-based model of privatized labour exploitation, aimed to enhance the economic productivity of industrial timber exports.[24] There was a growing demand for Andaman timber and at the same time, a decrease in suitable forest labour.[25] The British were concerned about the general unsuitability of convict labour to extract and transport timber.[26] They assumed that aboriginal forest dwellers from Chotanagpur would cope better with the harsh Andaman environment.[27] Further, the British aimed to expand the boundaries of the Andaman penal colony. The replacing of convicts with specialized forest labourers enabled the colonizers to increase the number of convict settlers, whom they rehabilitated on cleared plots of forestland.

The recruitment and transportation of the Ranchis was organized by the Catholic Labour Bureau at Ranchi. At the end of 1918, 400 Oraon and Munda labourers from different villages had been contracted for a duration of six months.[28] After their selection at Ranchi, they had been sent to Kolkata, then shipped to Port Blair. Most of these labourers were 'first generation Catholics'.[29] In May 1919, a priest from Ranchi visited this first batch of transported labourers to get to know their situation and to prepare for the reception of the next group. He met them on Curlow Island in North Andaman where they were clearing forests, putting up huts and building roads. Most of them were eager to be engaged to work for another six months.[30]

The contracting system was called *sardar* (recruiter) *chalaan. Chalaan* can be translated as 'clearance (of a ship), despatching of goods, an invoice for goods, bringing before the magistrate'.[31] This sterile and technical vocabulary speaks to the reality of this system—that humans were designated as resources or goods to be shipped and used. Because of the role foreign missionaries played in their transportation, most labourers used the term 'father' or 'mission *chalaan*' to refer to these organizers. Jesuits from Ranchi came regularly to the islands as representatives of the Catholic Labour Bureau and acted as spokespersons of labourers who complained about hardships inflicted by forest camp officers. There is one known record of Jesuits submitting a critical report, which led to the dismissal of a camp officer for mistreating a labourer.[32] However, the main function of the Jesuits in this context was to provide their 'tribal children' with spiritual services at forest camps. The labourers entrusted their earnings to the fathers, who passed them on to their kin on the mainland through the

Chotanagpur Mission Catholic Cooperative Credit Society, popularly known as 'Mission Bank'.[33]

The Ranchis' positionality as an aboriginal and subaltern 'coolie race' has come to efficaciously influence their subsequent exploitation, discrimination and marginalization. Particular to the Andamans was the local setting of the penal colony: they migrated into an established system defined by specific conditions of labour, discipline, law, speech, environmental relations, and encounters with the Andamanese. Further, the emplacement of the Ranchis in the Andaman forests by the colonial administration was linked to local conceptualizations of space. As Kanchan Mukhopadhyay points out in Chapter 8 of this volume, 'Space and Identity in Pre-42 Communities of the Andaman Islands', space in colonial Andaman was divided into three categories: *bajar* (marketplace) i.e. the zone of Port Blair; *basti,* which applied to villages within a forty-kilometre radius of the town; and *jangal* (wilderness) located beyond this frontier. Each place was associated with a different status. Both town dwellers and villagers regarded those who lived beyond the frontier, such as the Ranchis and the Karen, as inhabitants of *jangal.*

It is safe to argue that the Ranchis were not accidentally placed in the ecological transitory zones of Andaman frontier regions. Opaque and 'wild' jungles were associated with 'savagery' and earmarked for logging in order to yield profits and create a transparent and 'tamed' landscape of ordered settlements populated by governable subjects. The British seemed to consider these aboriginal forest dwellers, nominal agriculturalists who hunted and gathered,[34] as suitable 'architects' of the ecological and social transformation of the *jangal* they intended to effect through forest clearance. Further, if colonial ideas about the evolutionary order of humankind[35] were applied in the Andaman context, then the Ranchis fitted conceptually into the racial 'niche' between the more 'primitive' Andamanese 'Negritos' and the majority of caste convicts. Chotanagpuri aboriginal people, thus have to be understood as another —albeit quite invisible—human force in the space of encounter between the British, the Indian convicts and settlers and the Andaman islanders, which Satadru Sen, borrowing Heidegger's notion of the *Lichtung*, has called 'the clearing'.[36] One among many possible sites of this encounter might have been Sound Island where some Great Andamanese lived near the Ranchi labourers of a forest camp.[37]

From 1923 onwards, Ranchi labourers were allowed to stay in the Andamans after their six-month contracts had ended.[38] Seeking to ensure the social reproduction of the labour force, they were even offered permission to stay permanently.[39] As baptized Catholics and an established coolie race, they were regarded as potentially pioneering residents of the colony's periphery. When I interviewed the Ranchi community leader

Agapit Kujur,[40] he commented on this process: 'You see here in Andaman, the people craved for Ranchis because our people were jungle men.' Corroborating existing stereotypes, he emphasized that these labourers were satisfied with their work and the jungle environment: 'Of course, they liked it, they also enjoyed it! In the jungle, they got pigs, deer, fish, crabs and other things. They were very happy to work!'

Nonetheless, most of these early migrants refused to settle on Andaman. Kujur told me that most preferred to circulate seasonally between their homelands and places of migrant work. The recruitment of young male Catholics from Ranchi continued until 1942, when the Japanese occupied the islands and the British left. Out of 900 Ranchis who stayed during the occupation, 123 died[41] likely due to starvation or execution as suspected 'spies'. Majid, the first Indian Chief Commissioner, offered the surviving Chotanagpuri labourers free land as an incentive to stay. Nonetheless, few chose to remain.[42] However, Kujur highlighted that until December 1946, the reinstalled British administration recruited 1,300 new Ranchis because of labour scarcity.

CHOTANAGPURI MIGRATIONS SINCE 1947

After Independence, the colonial framework for settling 'socially deviant' groups on indigenous lands was continued. The Indian administration constructed the sparsely populated Andamans as an 'empty' space that could be colonized and commercially exploited.[43] Rehabilitation and colonization schemes served to 'fill' supposedly unproductive spaces by installing an Indian settler population in the islands that visibly underlined the national claim on the overseas territory. As on the mainland, refugees were settled on cleared tracts of forest inhabited by indigenous peoples.[44] The transfer of disadvantaged groups into those areas and the proposed economic exploitation of forest resources renewed the demand for specialized labour forces.[45]

As a result of the general scarcity of labour as well as positive experiences in the past, the administration started to revive the contracting of Chotanagpuris.[46] Between 1946 and 1956, more than 12,000 Ranchi labourers were recruited.[47] The community leader and researcher Agapit Kujur highlighted that, in the decades after Independence, the authorities exclusively recruited illiterate labourers. This practice demonstrates that the exploitation of labourers relied specifically on the engaging of subalterns who lacked the technologies (such as literacy) necessary to effectively campaign for or claim labour rights. Kujur noted, however, that he had come across some individuals who had subverted this demand by simply not revealing that they knew how to read and write. Based on personal memories, the late Govinda Raju, a local journalist, described in a newspaper article how he had perceived the Ranchis' arrival at Port Blair:

> Scantily clad in dhoti and a worn-out, discoloured kurta or just a vest to cover the trunk, Ranchiwallahs could be seen disembarking from SS Maharaja and walking along the edge of the road like an army of ants carrying their possession in a sanga [carrying stick] containing their belongings. A silent procession of human beings from another world; without a word uttered! That was late 1940s and 50s.[48]

As in colonial times, Chotanagpuri labourers were contracted by middlemen of the Catholic Labour Bureau at Ranchi. The bureau's monopoly on transportation was terminated in 1954 when the Belgian Father Verelst, who acted as spokesperson for the Ranchis, was expelled by the administration. He had complained that a Forest Department official had been illegally deducting Rs.10 per month from Catholic labourers' salary for the construction of a Hindu temple.[49] After two to three years, the *father chalaan* recruitment was revived under the aegis of Indian priests. In the meantime, private contractors entered the field. The new recruiting system bore the name of contractors, such as Ozman *chalaan*, Zel *chalaan*, Saif *chalaan*, Suleyman *chalaan* and Dipu *chalaan*. The shift of contracting policies also impacted the religious structure of the Ranchi community: church agents transported a vast majority of Catholics, but private contractors tended to recruit Hindus, Lutheran Catholics, some Muslims and so-called 'animists', who, in later years, have come to identify themselves as Sarna or worshippers of spirits residing at sacred groves. In spite of these other migrants, Catholics have remained by far the largest religious group among the Ranchis.

The majority of labourers were employed by various government agencies like the Forest Department, the Public Works Department, Andaman Harbour Works, the MES (Military Engineer Services), the GREF (General Reserve Engineer Force), the BRO (Border Roads Organisation), and the RRO (Rehabilitation Reclamation Organisation).[50] Apart from clearing forests for settlements, Chotanagpuri labourers expanded the airports at Port Blair and Car Nicobar and they built numerous other roads as well as buildings, jetties and breakwaters all over the islands.[51] Parallel to public employment, they were also given jobs by private companies that processed timber, such as Albion Plywood at Long Island, Jayshree Timber Industries at Bakultala, Andaman Timber Industries (ATI) at Bambooflat, Western India Match Company (WIMCO) and P.C. Ray & Co. from Kolkata which had leased North Andaman from the administration in the 1950s for the purpose of large-scale extraction.[52]

In 1956, 9,900 Ranchi labourers were already on the payroll of the Forest Department.[53] The largest numbers, however, came in the late 1960s.[54] Around 1970, there were approximately 15,000 Chotanagpuri labourers in the islands.[55] During that time, they composed about one-third of the working population.[56] Some of my interlocutors told me that they came repeatedly on different contracts. Apart from those who were recruited and brought by contractors, I came across a good number of Ranchis, who had arrived on their own in order to seek employment or to find a place to start a new life. Most labourers who stayed permanently were eventually joined by their families, relatives, and friends from the mainland.

The Andaman authorities envisioned the positionality of the Ranchis quite differently than that of Bengali refugees, who were cast as agricultural pioneers.[57] The few instances in which Ranchis were allotted land by the administration can be interpreted as being inspired by the idea to settle 'pioneers' of forestry and infrastructure development at the frontier. Between 1952 and 1954, fifteen Forest Department labourers and their families were settled at Borhem Valley and Foster Valley in Middle Andaman and twelve families at Long Island. They were allotted five acres each under a 'forest village scheme'.[58] Forest villages on the mainland aimed to 'emplace' labourers on reserved forestlands in order to enhance the reproduction of labour and to put them under the complete control of the Forest Department.[59] Interlocutors on Long Island, who had been settled under the forest village scheme, told me that their tenancy right on this land has remained insecure.

Reminiscent of the forest village scheme,[60] altogether 341 Ranchi Forest Department labourers and their families were allotted land under the colonization scheme.[61] Starting in 1959, within three years, 197 families were settled on cleared plots of forest on Baratang Island.[62] What is more, in the following years, the administration settled Ranchi families in Hanspuri, Bajota, Ram Nagar, Rampur, and Smith Island. As far as I know—numbers given by interlocutors sometimes varied—each family received five acres of hilly and five acres of paddy land, but no additional concessions were awarded as it was the case with other settler groups.[63]

The establishment of Adivasi settlements in marginal zones apparently suited the policy of strategic colonization. It aimed to extend the space of 'civilization' against the 'wilderness' of the forests. Baratang, for example, was a central location for timber extraction.[64] Its proximity to the Jarawa reserve made it imperative to settle able-bodied labourers as colonizing peasants. As a result of this policy, Baratang has transformed into a place with a Ranchi majority. Beyond that, the decision of the administration to allot land to a larger number of Ranchi labourers was also influenced by local politics.[65]

DISCURSIVE MANIFESTATIONS OF ABORIGINALITY

The stereotype attached to the Ranchis' aboriginality has continued to haunt the post-colonial condition. The anthropologist O.P. Verma, for example, wrote in the 1970s that previously the islands had not been suited for human settlement because they were 'filled with forests and hostile tribals'.[66] For him, the Ranchis were the main agents of territorial expansion, because they 'were ready to settle and work in deep forests'.[67] The community leader Agapit Kujur and other interlocutors told me that, while at work and while living in the forests—which included engaging in hunting and gathering activities—these labourers frequently encountered indigenous islanders. Many Ranchi labourers were killed by the Jarawa. Apart from such violent encounters, 'friendly' contact, barter and other forms of exchange took place, too. For example, the social adaptation of some Ranchis to the Great Andamanese on Baratang Islands was described as a success. Accordingly, they adjusted 'themselves [to the] native men of Baratang ... whereas the refugees of East Bengal feel it difficult to adjust with the changed situation'.[68] The anthropologist Vidyarthi proposed that it 'would be fascinating to study how they [the Ranchis] managed to establish affinity with the Andamanese and how one of them even led family life with an Andamanese woman.'[69] Romanticizing indigenous human-environment relations, Verma reasoned that Chotanagpur and Baratang were both 'hilly area[s] filled with forests and tribal peoples' and thus 'may be both compared as mother and child'.[70] Referring to the omnipresent notion of Mini-India, Verma declared the Ranchi microcosm of forest camps and settlements in Baratang as 'Mini-Chotanagpur'.[71] Creating a literal analogy to their homelands, I heard Ranchis on Baratang call the Jarawa 'Birhor', a term which refers to a group of hunter-gatherers in Chotanagpur.

Linked to the notion of aboriginality, the colonial stereotype of the Ranchis' docility has also persisted to the present day. Verma wrote, for example, in the 1970s: 'The main cause of so much employment of Ranchi labourers in forest and P.W.D. departments is that "Ranchiwallah" is the only hard and faithful worker in Andaman and Nicobar Islands.'[72] A retired manager of the Western India Match Company (WIMCO), which produced matches on the islands until 1995, told me that for timber extraction, he had preferred to employ Chotanagpuri Adivasis. 'Ranchis', he explained to me, 'are simple, but they work hard and do not complain.' Furthermore, he assured me that he appreciated that they usually did not organize in unions or demand holidays and lunch breaks. A Forest Department official pointed out that the last time his department employed daily-rated labourers, they 'wanted only Ranchis'. He reasoned:

> Ranchis are hard-working, highly submissive and down-to-earth. That's why already the British chose them. They are good to give orders. Compared to other communities, you can extract more work from them. They won't crib much. If it is raining, they will not demand a raincoat; if it is cold, they will not demand a sweater. Every contractor will love them!

Similarly, the rehabilitation of Ranchis under the colonization scheme was officially framed as a reward for the labourers' 'faithful' behaviour, meaning they were 'unlikely to complain against the Department'.[73] Contemporary self-definitions of Ranchi settlers correspond with the prefabricated image of their 'docility'. For example, when talking about the reasons for their settlement in Baratang, one older settler told me: 'We were selected, because we are *imandar* [faithful, honest] and because we don't cheat and complain.' However, when I asked him why he thought that the administration settled them at this precise location, he answered: 'Because it is in the middle of the jungle and so backward that most people don't like to live here.'

UNEQUAL PROPERTY RELATIONS AND A DESIRE FOR RECOGNITION

Migration and settlement processes have decisively influenced socio-economic stratification processes among the Ranchis and other communities in the Andamans. Large numbers of refugees and repatriates were settled on allotted plots of forestland previously cleared by Ranchi labourers. As a consequence of this cleavage, unequal property and class relations were established between the Ranchis and other communities in the decades that followed. The settlers became landowning farmers with access to social mobility, while the majority of Ranchis remained landless and 'poor'. Exemplifying some of the ethical difficulties of this unequal treatment, the journalist Govinda Raju pointed to the situation of those Ranchis who had been employed by the Border Roads Organisation (BRO) from 1969 until 1970 to prepare the ground for the settlement of ex-servicemen at Campbell Bay in Great Nicobar:

> These Ranchi labourers had not seen anything other than Campbell Bay. They settled there itself on vacant land, forest or otherwise. Yet did not complain, followed their covenant of silence. They kept on pitching their tents close to their places of work. Nobody in the local Administration ever told them that they were illegal squatters on forest or revenue land. In the meantime, much water had

flown down the Galathea and the Kalpong [rivers in Great Nicobar and North Andaman]. Migrants from other parts of the country were plundering the forest with impunity actively aided and abetted by politicians of all hues, and raising settlements in forest land. There was a distinct discriminatory treatment in dealing with the Ranchiwallahs and others. Those who had earned revenue for the islands through [the] forest department, who had created [a] massive infrastructure for Bengali settlers and others, were themselves living in ramshackle jhopdis [huts] in abject poverty, despair and neglect.[74]

The subtext speaks about the ways the political relations of the Ranchis to other settler and migrant communities and the state seem to be negatively shaped by the perception of these unequal policies. Agapit Kujur expressed clearly how many Ranchis feel about such differential treatment by the authorities: 'Before the government settled the Bengalis, our people came and cleared the jungle. The Bengalis just came as guests, but the workers were the Ranchis!'

Expressive of these views, a sensitivity about the meagre rewards for the exploitation of their labour power in processes of colonization has started to enter the popular consciousness of the Ranchi community. Interestingly, Vidyarthi's description of the Ranchis as 'modern builders' of the islands resonates in the articulations of contemporary Ranchi leaders.[75] Congruent to Vidyarthi's formulation, these elite actors claim public recognition of the fact that their community pioneered island development. I encountered such collective means of self-definition when talking to former Chotanagpuri contract labourers themselves: they regularly stressed the importance of their personal and collective contribution to development processes, from which the whole society has benefited. They emphasized that it was they who constructed the infrastructure of the Andamans, such as the wharf at Haddo or the ATR, which are now used by all residents. Many underlined the 'blood and sweat' poured into such projects when they worked without proper medical care, technical equipment or work-specific clothing. My interlocutors were united in their complaint that their efforts have never been appreciated, neither by the government nor by members of other communities. These powerful iterations of subaltern history have, however, not yet been taken up into public discourse. Nonetheless, it indicates that these 'docile aboriginals' are labouring to become visible as Adivasi 'architects' of modern Andaman.

This chapter has revealed that contemporary 'Ranchi-ness' has become manifest as a result of this community's history of migration and labour. Their emigration from Chotanagpur and their transportation to the Andamans were conditioned by relations of power and knowledge in the British Empire that impacted their later post-colonial condition.

The colonial discourse of aboriginality provided an ideological background for Chotanagpuri recruitment and shaped the ways in which their relationships to the state and the Andaman society have been defined and negotiated.

Aboriginal 'hill coolies' were regarded as being suited to working and living in the transitory zone between the 'civilization' of settlements and the 'wilderness' of the Andaman forests. Their suitability has been linked to ascriptions of collective racial characteristics such as docility, submissiveness and physical strength. The hegemonic discourse of their aboriginality was reiterated by the fact that Chotanagpuri migrants have, indeed, adapted well to the social and ecological conditions at the frontier: they have withstood attacks by indigenous islanders and interacted with them, they have endured the inhospitable tropical climate and sustained themselves. Further, the power of stereotypes has conditioned the Ranchis' entrance into local relations of production. Recruiters and employers have appreciated that as a workforce they are easy to control, discipline and exploit. They have had no reason to empower them—vividly illustrated by recruitment policies in the 1950s, which followed the principle of specifically employing illiterate labourers. The pervasive socio-economic and political marginalization of this people—constructed and constrained as voiceless and 'backward' aborigines—has, thus, caused their labour power to remain precarious and largely informal.

However, the rising political consciousness among the Ranchis about their contribution to the colonization of the islands points to their desire to remember the hardships this historical process entailed, while, at the same time, working towards a different form of public recognition. There are strong indications that the contract labourers from Ranchis and their descendants do not want to be identified or discriminated against as 'aboriginal coolies'. Instead, they prefer to be recognized as residents of Mini-India with an Adivasi background. If these counter-hegemonic interpretations of their subaltern past and present will one day be acknowledged at Port Blair, then the invisible architects of Andaman are likely to become visible, respected, fully contemporary citizens of the Andaman society.

NOTES

1. Far from denoting a homogeneous group, 'Ranchi' encompasses members of a large number of tribal groups such as Oraon, Munda, Kharia and smaller numbers of Gond, Nagbansi, Lohra, Chik Baraik, Kawar, Turi, Rautia, Maheli, Gusai, Kumhar, Bhumia, Bokta and some others. Their recruitment by the Catholic Labour Bureau in the town of Ranchi has caused them to be called 'Ranchis' or 'Ranchiwallahs' (Sarit Kumar Mukerji, *Islands of India*,

New Delhi: Publication Division, Ministry of Information and Broadcasting, Government of India, 1992). 'Ranchi', therefore, denotes a place or region from which migrants originated but not necessarily a homogeneous group of people defined by the boundaries of caste, tribe or a vernacular. The descendants of these migrant labourers who grew up in the Andamans merged into a larger unit of identification as Ranchi community and adopted Sadri as *lingua franca*.

2. The Chotanagpur Plateau extends across parts of the present states of Jharkhand, Chhattisgarh, Orissa, Madhya Pradesh, and West Bengal. In this chapter, I do not use the term 'Chotanagpur' as a narrowly defined geographical location but rather as a socio-cultural notion used by the Ranchis to refer to the places they actively remember as their 'homelands'. As such, some references to Chotanagpur may not coincide neatly with the exact geographical boundaries of the region.
3. Govinda Raju, 'Ranchiwallahs: The Pains of Dispossession', *The Light of Andamans*, vol. 35, no. 2, 13 August 2010 [Yahoo Group Message] [https://in.groups.yahoo.com/neo/groups/andamanicobar/conversations/messages/6758], accessed 16 April 2015.
4. L.P. Vidyarthi, 'Development Plans of the Tribes of Andaman and Nicobar Islands: An Action-oriented Report', *Journal of Social Research*, vol. 19, no. 2, 1976, pp. 74–85, see especially p. 8.
5. Ibid., p. 9.
6. The information stems from an anthropologist who prefers to remain unnamed because of possible political consequences.
7. Govinda Raju, 'Ranchiwallahs' Battle Cry', *The Light of Andamans*, vol. 35, no. 2, 13 August 2010 [Yahoo Group Message] [https://in.groups.yahoo.com/neo/groups/andamanicobar/conversations/messages/6757], accessed 16 April 2015.
8. The fieldwork data presented in this chapter was generated from January to June 2009 and January 2011 to January 2012.
9. Cecil J. Saldanha, *Andaman, Nicobar and Lakshadweep: An Environmental Impact Assessment*, New Delhi: Oxford & IBH Publishing Company, 1989, p. 14.
10. Gramsci (Antonio Gramsci, *Gefängnishefte*, Band 9, Hamburg: Argument Verlag, 1999) was the first to use the term 'subaltern' in order to describe social groups like peasants, non-organized labourers and others who had no class consciousness and who were denied access to the means of production controlled by the dominating classes (Bill Ashcroft, Gareth Griffiths, and Helen Tiffin, *Key Concepts in Post-Colonial Studies*, London and New York: Routledge, 1998). The term 'subaltern' has been taken up by the Subaltern Studies collective to conceptualize persons that have been cut off from upward social mobility and the cultural lines that produce the colonial subject in South Asia (Gayatri Chakravorty Spivak, 'The New Subaltern: A Silent Interview', in *Mapping Subaltern Studies and the Postcolonial*, ed. Vinayak Chaturvedi, London and New York: Verso, 2000, pp. 324–45). By focusing on suppressed or silenced accounts of subaltern women, minorities, disadvantaged or dispossessed groups, refugees, exiles, etc., the Subaltern Studies

historians have started to write a South Asian 'history from below' (Ranajit Guha and Gayatri Chakravorty Spivak, *Selected Subaltern Studies*, New York: Oxford University Press, 1988, p. vi).

11. Satadru Sen defines the notion of aboriginality as 'a residue of savagery and a political construction initiated by non-aborigines' (Satadru Sen, *Disciplined Natives: Race, Freedom and Confinement in Colonial India*, Delhi: Primus Books, 2012, p. 338). For a further discussion of the term, see also Satadru Sen's 'Race, Aboriginality, and the Adivasi: Some Implications for the Andaman Islanders' (Chapter 5) in this volume.
12. Kaushik Ghosh, 'A Market for Aboriginality: Primitivism and Race Classification in the Indentured Labour Market of Colonial India', in *Subaltern Studies X: Writings on South Asian History and Society*, ed. G. Bhadra, G. Prakash, and S. Tharu, Delhi: Oxford University Press, 1999, pp. 8–48, see especially p. 10.
13. Crispin Bates, 'Coerced and Migrant Labourers in India: The Colonial Experience', *Edinburgh Papers in South Asian Studies*, no. 13, 2000, pp. 1–33, see especially p. 8; Gyan Prakash, 'Introduction: The History and Historiography of Rural Labourers in Colonial India', in *The World of the Rural Labourer in Colonial India*, ed. Gyan Prakash, Delhi: Oxford University Press, 1992, pp. 1–46, see especially p. 44; Hugh Tinker, *A New System of Slavery: The Export of Indian Labour Overseas, 1830–1920*, London: Oxford University Press, 1974, p. 47.
14. Nandini Sundar, *Subalterns and Sovereigns: An Anthropological History of Bastar, 1854–2006,* 2nd edn., New Delhi: Oxford University Press, 2007, pp. 112–14.
15. Bates, 'Coerced and Migrant Labourers in India', pp. 14–16; Ghosh, 'A Market for Aboriginality', p. 17; Alpa Shah, *In the Shadows of the State: Indigenous Politics, Environmentalism, and Insurgency in Jharkhand, India,* Durham and London: Duke University Press, 2010, p. 54; Tinker, *A New System of Slavery*, pp. 46–9. Considering wider practices of labour transportation across the Indian Ocean, Tinker estimated that between 1840 and 1850, two-fifths to one-half of the indentured labourers at overseas destinations were 'hill coolies' (Tinker, *A New System of Slavery*, p. 49). In addition, approximately 2,50,000 Chotanagpuri tea plantation labourers went to Darjeeling and Assam between 1870 and 1900 (Tinker, *A New System of Slavery*, p. 51). According to the 1891 Census, 3,33,000 persons in Assam and Bengal came from Chotanagpur and the Santal Parganas. This number rose to 7,07,000 in 1911 and 10,00,000 in 1921, amounting to a total of 25 per cent of the population in their homelands (Shashank Kela, *A Rogue and Peasant Slave: Adivasi Resistance, 1800–2000,* New Delhi: Navayana, 2012, p. 259).
16. Ghosh, 'A Market for Aboriginality', p. 17.
17. Ibid., p. 32.
18. John Scoble, *Hill Coolies: A Brief Exposure of the Deplorable Condition of the Hill Coolies in British Guiana and Mauritius*, London, 1840, as quoted in Tinker, *A New System of Slavery*, p. 63.
19. Ghosh, 'A Market for Aboriginality', p. 33.

20. Ghosh, 'A Market for Aboriginality', p. 32.
21. Ibid., pp. 29–32.
22. Ibid., p. 10.
23. Clare Anderson, 'Refugee Resettlement in the Andaman Islands: Colonial Precedents, Post-colonial Predicaments', ESRC End of Award Report, RES-067-27-0001, 2008, p. 6.
24. Taylor C. Sherman, 'From Hell to Paradise? Voluntary Transfer of Convicts to the Andaman Islands, 1921–1940', *Modern Asian Studies*, vol. 43, 2009, pp. 367–88, see especially p. 370.
25. Anderson, 'Refugee Resettlement in the Andaman Islands', p. 6.
26. Ibid. As a consequence of the moist tropical climate, mortality rates of convicts remained comparatively high (Sherman, 'From Hell to Paradise?' p. 371).
27. Raju, 'Ranchiwallahs: The Pains of Dispossession'.
28. Benjamin Barla, 'Lieven's Tribal Catholic in Andaman, Port Blair', 2009, pp. 1–2. Parts of my reconstruction of the history of Ranchi migration stem from Benjamin Barla, a local spokesperson of the Ranchi community. Barla migrated to the Andamans in 1948 and has, therefore, witnessed the entire post-Independence period. Luckily, I was able to obtain a copy of the unpublished paper 'Lieven's Tribal Catholic in Andaman', which Barla had written and distributed among members of the Catholic community.
29. Barla, 'Lieven's Tribal Catholic in Andaman', p. 1.
30. Ibid.
31. Nathaniel Brice, *A Romanized Hindustani and English Dictionary*, New Delhi and Chennai: Asian Educational Services, 2005, p. 37.
32. Barla, 'Lieven's Tribal Catholic in Andaman', p. 2.
33. Ibid., pp. 2–3.
34. Kela, *A Rogue and Peasant Slave*, p. 23.
35. Lewis Henry Morgan, *Ancient Society*, New York, 1877.
36. Satadru Sen, *Savagery and Colonialism in the Indian Ocean: Power, Pleasure and the Andaman Islanders*, New York: Routledge, 2010, pp. 10–11. For Sen, the clearing is both a literal and metaphorical space at the margins of the colony, an experimental space, neither settlement nor jungle, in which self and other were revealed but also productively blurred (p. 10).
37. The information stems from the diary of the German anthropologist Dr Egon von Eickstedt about his Andaman tour in January 1928 (Lydia Icke-Schwalbe, 'Life and Culture of the Aboriginals in the Andaman Islands under Colonial Forestry in 1927–28', presentation delivered at the conference 'Manifestations of History in the Andaman Islands', Ludwig-Maximilians-University Munich, 22 June 2013).
38. Raju, 'Ranchiwallahs: The Pains of Dispossession'.
39. Anderson, 'Refugee Resettlement in the Andaman Islands', p. 6.
40. Kujur researched the history of migration from Chotanagpur to the Andamans working at the archives of the mission at Ranchi. As he has not yet published this research, I quote him here on the basis of two extensive interviews I conducted with him in 2009 and 2011.

41. Barla, 'Lieven's Tribal Catholic in Andaman', pp. 22–3.
42. Ibid.
43. Uditi Sen, 'Dissident Memories: Exploring Bengali Refugee Narratives in the Andaman Islands', in *Refugees and the End of Empire: Imperial Collapse and Forced Migration in the Twentieth Century*, ed. Panikos Panayi and Pippa Virdee, Basingstoke, Hampshire: Palgrave Macmillan, 2011, pp. 219–44, see especially p. 222.
44. Sundar, *Subalterns and Sovereigns*, pp. 196–7.
45. Raju, 'Ranchiwallahs: The Pains of Dispossession'.
46. Kiran Dhingra, *The Andaman and Nicobar Islands in the 20th Century: A Gazetteer*, New Delhi: Oxford University Press, 2005, p. 81.
47. Raju, 'Ranchiwallahs: The Pains of Dispossession'.
48. Ibid.
49. Barla, 'Lieven's Tribal Catholic in Andaman', p. 5.
50. Anstice Justin, 'Ranchi', in *People of India: Andaman and Nicobar Islands*, vol. XII, Anthropological Survey of India, ed. K.S. Singh, Madras, New Delhi, Bangalore, Hyderabad: Affiliated East-West Press, 1994, pp. 172–83, see especially p. 174; Saldanha, 'Andaman, Nicobar and Lakshadweep', p. 14.
51. Barla, 'Lieven's Tribal Catholic in Andaman', p. 10.
52. Ibid., p. 5.
53. Raju, 'Ranchiwallahs: The Pains of Dispossession'.
54. Swapan K. Biswas, *Colonization and Rehabilitations in Andaman and Nicobar Islands,* Delhi: Abhijeet Publications, 2009, p. 11.
55. Vidyarthi, 'Development Plans of the Tribes of Andaman and Nicobar Islands', p. 8.
56. O.P. Verma, 'The Working Composition of the Ranchi Tribal Labourers in Andaman and Nicobar Islands: A Case Study of Baratang Island', *Journal of Social Research*, vol. 19, no. 2, 1976, pp. 114–24, see especially p. 115.
57. Sen, 'Dissident Memories', p. 222.
58. Barla, 'Lieven's Tribal Catholic in Andaman', p. 23.
59. Sundar, *Subalterns and Sovereigns*, pp. 116–17.
60. Dhingra, *The Andaman and Nicobar Islands in the 20th Century*, p. 82.
61. Barla, 'Lieven's Tribal Catholic in Andaman', p. 24.
62. Biswas, *Colonization and Rehabilitations in Andamans and Nicobars,* p. 89.
63. Letter, Deputy Commissioner to Chief Commissioner, 14 October 1963, Rehabilitation, File 4, No. 27/13(7)/7054/63, Port Blair Archives.
64. A popular local narrative relates the name Baratang to the history of forest extraction. Accordingly, a huge tree weighing twelve tons (bara-ton) was felled here. Chandi writes, however, that the name was derived from the Andamanese, who call their camp sites '-tang' and the locally available Talipot Palm (*C. Umbraculifera Linn*) 'Barata'. Baratang is one of the few islands that has retained its name to the present day, since it was mentioned by Ptolemy and Ibn Battuta (Manish Chandi, 'Territory and Landscape Around the Jarawa Reserve', in *The Jarawa Tribal Reserve Dossier: Cultural & Biological Diversities in the Andaman Islands,* ed. Pankaj Sekhsaria and Vishvajit Pandya, Paris: UNESCO, 2010, pp. 30–42, see especially p. 32).

65. The Andaman Indian Association—the successor organization of the Andamanian Association, which had been previously known as Local Born Association and later returned to that name—submitted a memorandum demanding that no more East Bengal refugees be settled. The association argued that increasing numbers of Bengali Hindu settlers would disrupt the 'homogeneous community' of Andaman Indians (Biswas, *Colonization and Rehabilitations in Andaman and Nicobars*, p. 90). Biswas opined that some Local Borns feared that their community might become a minority vis-à-vis the Bengali settlers. It can, thus, be assumed that the settlement of Tamil and Burmese repatriates, Malayalis, four families from Mahé and Ranchi Department labourers also served to appease the Local Borns (Biswas, *Colonization and Rehabilitations in Andaman and Nicobars*, pp. 88–91).
66. Verma, 'The Working Composition of the Ranchi Tribal Labourers', p. 122.
67. Ibid.
68. Ibid., p. 116.
69. Vidyarthi, 'Development Plans of the Tribes of Andaman and Nicobar Islands', p. 8.
70. Ibid.
71. Verma, 'The Working Composition of the Ranchi Tribal Labourers', p. 122.
72. Ibid., p. 116.
73. Dhingra, *The Andaman and Nicobar Islands in the 20th Century*, p. 82.
74. Raju, 'Ranchiwallahs: The Pains of Dispossession'.
75. Vidyarthi, 'Development Plans of the Tribes of Andaman and Nicobar Islands', p. 8.

8

Space and Identity in Pre-42 Communities of the Andaman Islands

KANCHAN MUKHOPADHYAY

The Andaman Islands are located at a distance of little more than 1,000 km. from mainland India. Colonization of the islands began relatively recently, slightly more than one and a half centuries ago. The islands came to accommodate immigrants from mainland India who were unable to return to their homelands; their links to those places remained limited in several ways or at times their connections were completely severed. As a result, they went through processes of new identity formation that often defied the norms of identity construction common in mainland India. Certain universal attributes of multinational as well as multicultural polities, however, were observable in the islands. Temporal dimensions of identity formation remained key here, as elsewhere, as the promoting factors did not remain static. However, this chapter attempts specifically to understand effects of space on the processes of formation and perpetuation of identity among certain communities who were confined to the islands for many years.[1]

SPACE

In the Andaman Islands, both space and time play crucial roles in identity formation of inhabitants. Groups of people identify themselves and others with reference to both factors; the spaces their people came from, where they settled in the islands and the period in which they reached the islands. The history of the islands can be divided into four periods. The pre-colonial period lasted until the islands were colonized permanently in 1858. Although the British Navy established a base on the islands in 1789, it was completely withdrawn in 1796. The second, or penal colony period, began with the reoccupation of the islands in 1856 by British authorities. They established a penal colony within two years and there received deported convicts and also rehabilitated individuals and communities on a large scale. During the third period—Japanese occupation—the islands were occupied by the Japanese military from 1942 to the conclusion of the Second World War in 1945. The fourth period begins with India's Independence in 1947. The way space and time are understood in the Andaman Islands is closely related to how and when the territory was colonized. The process of colonization was not limited to space; groups of people who were engaged in colonization activities became colonized entities, too. There are close similarities visible between the ways different groups of people and different categories of space are identified. It is noteworthy that space is rarely identified according to its inhabitants. On the contrary, people are often identified according to the spaces they inhabit. The following discussion argues that the processes of identity formation among islander communities both in the past and in contemporary times are influenced more by the factor of space than of time. There is no doubt that time is a crucial issue for identifying some of the communities, especially the Pre-42 groups, who were settled by the island authorities before the advent of the Japanese in 1942. When we consider the present-day situation, we can still see that the identity markers used by different communities are primarily constructed on the basis of spatial categories.

Different sections of the Pre-42 communities, who will be discussed in more detail, began reaching the Andamans in 1858. Those who reached the islands in 1858 and those who came half a century, or more, later are bracketed together under the term 'Pre-42'; the precise temporal moment of reaching the Andamans is not nearly as important as are the places their forefathers came from and whether they settled in urban, rural or wild spaces.

Representations of space are largely dependent on an imagined discontinuity of space; the social science discourses on contact, conflict, and contradiction between cultures and societies sometimes rest on a presupposition of natural disjointedness. It has been recognized that the 'assumed isomorphism' of space, place, and culture cannot adequately explain certain real-life conditions. The inhabitants of the borderlands who are not moored to any one side of the dividing line present one such situation. Presence of cultural differences within a given space may give rise to multiculturalism; similarly, subcultures coexisting with a dominant culture within same 'geographical and territorial space' pose another kind of problem. In a post-colonial situation, it becomes difficult to identify a 'new culture' with reference to any specific territory.[2]

In the Andaman Islands, we find a situation that contests the natural disjointedness of space but for different reasons. Before colonization, the Andaman archipelago was exclusively inhabited by hunter-gatherer communities whose impact on the land and water was, in comparison to agricultural or industrialized societies, nearly negligible. The indigenous peoples of the Great Andaman Islands divided themselves into two broad categories on the basis of their relationship with the ecological niche—forest or coast—that was their primary site of inhabitation and resource exploitation. In Aka-Bea-da, a Great Andamanese language, one of the groups was *ar-yoto* (coast dwellers) and the other was *erem-taga* (forest dwellers).[3] The Onge of the Little Andaman Island have four territorially differentiated clans. Within each, there is a two-fold division of *eahambelakwe* (turtle hunters) and *eahansakwe* (pig hunters).[4] Niche has not always been conceived of as an ecological category. Each niche can be described as summation of qualities of the geographical space, of people's historical experiences, and their notions about the space. The combination of these attributes makes one niche distinguishable from another, even though they share similar ecological characters.

During the colonial period, space was categorized depending on how it was colonized. The settler populations of this period were instrumental in colonizing the land. However, as a subservient labour force, they were not in control of the change they enacted. So, spaces like urban centres or rural settlements were not considered to be the creation of the captive workforce, for them different categories of space were given factors. But the inhabitants came to be identified according to specific types of niche. From the perspective of immediate occupiers of space or niche in the Andaman Islands, it can be said that in both the pre-colonial and colonial period, space was accorded a primary position and people were identified by their spatial relationships and location. There was, however, a major difference between two sets of people: the indigenous islanders who identified themselves through local ecosystems were ecosystem people; the people deported to the penal settlement were displaced persons adjusting to ecosystems created by the authorities of the colony. As proposed by Bourdieu, the relation of both the groups of people to the space they inhabit can be equated with the relative position of power among them and those relations are demonstrated in varied ways.[5] It has been noted by Guha that Bourdieu's approach approximates a static account of power and status.[6] The power relations of the Pre-42 communities with others and their mutual status have changed due to factors that were often beyond their control.

Taking a broad sweep of anthropological studies of space and place, Low and Lawrence-Zuniga identified six thematic categories on the basis of how people enter into meaningful relationships with the locales they occupy, how they attach meaning to space, and transform 'space' into 'place' by the attachment of qualities such as sacredness. They noted how experience is embedded in place and how space holds memories that are connected to the people and events.[7]

The argument that the social identity of a people is related to the space or more specifically to the niche they inhabit is particularly significant for the Pre-42 communities. Seldom did the consciousness of those people alter the space they were made to inhabit; rather the space often fashioned their consciousness. The situation closely approximates the 'multiple drafts' model of consciousness proposed by Dennett; following his proposition, the process of construction of 'self' can be described as involving content fixation in any of the several semi-independent agencies in the human brain, which is propagated to other components, and one single content is built.[8] Both identity and space have been considered as parts of collective consciousness and expressed through the worldview of a people in the sense that consciousness has a discernible influence on the ways they interpret the world around them and decide how to interact with it.

IDENTITY

To delineate the boundaries created and maintained between different communities of the Andaman Islands, they have been conceived of as ethnic groups. In this chapter, I use the term 'ethnic group' to denote collectives that have a common proper name, memories of a common past, who possess or assert one or more elements of culture like religion and language, are linked or emotionally attached with a homeland and have a sense of intra-group solidarity.[9]

The primordalist approach that assumes ethnicity as a natural phenomenon cannot adequately explain the empirical situation in the Andamans. The instrumentalist approach that has remained concerned with 'the role of ethnicity in the mediation of social relations and the negotiation of access to resources, primarily economic and political resources' is more suitable for the purpose.[10] Though the latter approach has been criticized for reducing ethnicity to economic and political relationships at the cost of the cultural dimensions, there are numerous situations where economic and political agendas are drawn keeping social and cultural issues like caste, language, and religion at the fore.

The situation was more complex for those Indians who had to migrate from one place to another according to colonial interest (and sometimes out of self-interest and the drive to make use of opportunities created by colonial rule) than those who did not move away from their village, local area or region. The plurality of situations can be understood with reference to differences between multinational and multicultural situations. Multinational situations were or are prevalent in pre-modern empires, colonial plural societies, post-colonial polities, and socialist states, where people with distinct homelands and cultures, particularly language and religion, are found to coexist. Multicultural situations are common in New World settlements, where we find deterritorialized national groups. Though the term 'New World' is biased in favour of colonizers, it has been used here because the Andaman Islands exhibit a close similarity with developments in the Western Hemisphere; in both situations, immigrants came to stay, settled permanently, and showed little regard for the pre-colonial history of the native inhabitants. Oommen has noted how the contemporary multicultural polities differ from the pre-national empires or the pro-ethnic New World settlements and finds multiculturality to be a favoured social value in post-nation-states.[11]

The people of India were subjected to four kinds of migration during the colonial period. First, there were movements from one part of the country to another; plantation workers recruited in Chotanagpur and taken to Assam present one such example. In Assam, the Santals, Mundas, and Kurmis became a faceless mass of tea garden 'coolies'. Under such circumstances, it was not easy for them to maintain social boundaries by observing rules of endogamy or exogamy, but they clung to their cultural identities as far as possible. Here the situation was multi/sub-national and/or multiethnic, and the migrant communities were not deterritorialized. Second, some Indians migrated to neighbouring countries; a number of Tamil, Telugu and Bengali people migrated to Myanmar in search of economic opportunities. As evident in popular Bengali literature, the prospectors looked down upon the people of the land as culturally inferior and maintained social distance. Most of those Indians left Myanmar for their home country when both governments agreed to mutual repatriation after Independence. Here also, the dominant nature of cultural plurality was multinational.

Third, indentured Indian labourers taken to New World destinations like West Indies and Fiji became part of multicultural situations. In Trinidad and Guyana, caste identities have been forgotten by Indians; now they are a deterritorialized people. Experiences of Indian indentured labourers in Fiji and their descendants were not much different from what their counterparts faced in the West Indies. A fourth kind of situation is presented by those who migrated to the Andaman Islands; a New World-like situation in the heart of the Old World that offers a combination of multinational and multicultural situations. Here we find groups of migrants who gradually became or are still becoming deterritorialized but are strongly attached to the immediate space they occupy. In this case, the territories of origin and the territories of present occupation are parts of one nation state, and one can move from one territory to another with ease, so the detachment could never be complete.

GENESIS OF PRE-42 COMMUNITIES

As part of their administrative programme for India and adjacent countries, the British constructed penal settlements initially in Sumatra and then in Singapore and Penang. In 1826, the authorities started sending Indian convicts to newly established penal settlements in Myanmar. In the aftermath of the Indian Rebellion of 1857, the Andaman Islands were declared a penal settlement. The pre-colonial inhabitants of the islands offered resistance to the colonizing activities in the initial years. Soon most of them were infected by new pathogens and disposed by colonial programmes; diseased and alienated from resources, they died in large numbers.

In the initial years of the penal settlement, persons were deported as individuals. The 'free convicts', prisoners who were set free within the settlement and allowed to take part in economic activities of the colony, were allowed to have members of their respective families join them in the Andaman Islands. The response was extremely poor; wives of most of the married male 'free convicts' were not interested in relocating permanently to an open jail. Eventually, a community was formed in the settlement through marriage liaisons between individuals belonging to this group, which came to be known as the 'Local Born'.

A major change took place in 1920s when some Moplahs of the Malabar Coast were imprisoned and deported for participating in a rebellion against the colonial government; they reached the Andaman Islands with their families. The Bhantus of the United Provinces were branded as 'habitually criminal' and many were deported to the islands and rehabilitated there. There was a Burmese or Myanmarese community in the islands whose people were descendants of Myanmarese nationals deported to the penal settlement. They started moving out of India to Myanmar in late 1940s; their repatriation started immediately after both the countries attained independence and continued through to the 1960s and 1970s. By that time, almost all of them had moved away from the Andaman Islands.

Simultaneously, some free citizens were sent to the islands. They were the Karens from Myanmar and the Ranchiwallahs from Chotanagpur Hills, now part of the Indian state of Jharkhand. The Ranchiwallahs are not a homogenous group and represent many social formations. The Moplahs, the Bhantus and the Karens, however, could retain their original social identity in the Andamans. As there are several identifiable sections among those immigrants, the term 'community' has been used to identify each of those groups, and has been used as a cognate expression of 'ethnic group'.

The Japanese Army occupied the Andaman Islands from 1942 to 1945, and upon their arrival, any in- or out-migration of civilian populations came to a complete halt. That is why the communities mentioned above are known as 'Pre-42'. It should be noted that government employees, most of whom were prison guards and officers, were evacuated in 1942 prior to the start of the occupation. After the islands were reoccupied by the British at the end of the war and after India became independent, another phase of immigration and emigration took place. Some members of the Pre-42 communities went back to mainland India to stay, while some eventually returned to the islands.

DYNAMICS OF IDENTITY FORMATION

When considering the factors used by Pre-42 communities to assert their identity, it is important to know how colonial authorities classified immigrants to the Andamans. The period during which migration occurred was important to their categorization; distinctions were made between the free settlers and the penal deportees, and this was a crucial issue in the penal settlement. Further, colonial authorities distinguished between deportees who were brought as individuals and those who came with their kin. At another level, the Moplahs, Bhantus, and Karens were understood as separate from the newly formed communities of Local Born and Ranchiwallahs (see Figure 8.1). However, qualitative differences in the processes of identity formation of the Local Born and the Ranchiwallahs must be noted: though several distinctly different tribal groups residing in Chotanagpur Plateau came to be known by the name 'Ranchiwallahs', the history of formation of the Local Born community was very different. Initially, the authorities identified several distinct endogamous groups, and as a result, the authorities

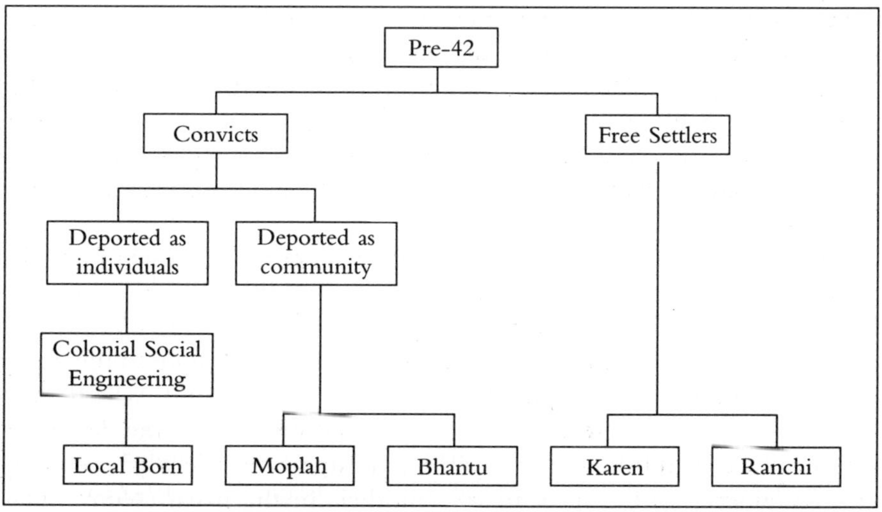

FIGURE 8.1: Categorization of Pre-42 Communities Based on Reasons for Migration.

Source: Prepared by the author.

designated Muslims and Christians, respectively, as intra-marrying groups. The Hindus were treated differently; each varna group was considered to be an endogamous unit. These constructed identities did not last long; most of the Local Born people were unbothered about their caste or varna identity. It was extremely difficult for a single man in the penal colony to find a willing woman of marriageable age as there were very few women in the colony. As such, almost none of the men could afford to bother about caste and varna. However, some members of this community vaguely remember their caste identity in the male line.

The immigrants, however, maintained religious boundaries. Eventually the Hindus, Muslims, and Christians became loosely knit endogamous groups; none of them recognized further internal divisions. In fact, religious identity helped the Muslim Moplahs and the Christian Karens to maintain their ethnic identity, while the Bhantus became almost indistinguishable from the neighbouring Hindu section of the Local Born community.

For the Pre-42 communities, language was never a strong identity marker because they all came to speak Hindustani, the *lingua franca* of the Andamans. Whatever the linguistic identity of an individual before coming to the penal settlement, once there, everyone learned and spoke Hindustani. The Bhantus were from a Hindi-speaking area; they faced no problem in speaking the language. Though the Moplahs and the Karens learnt the *lingua franca*, they also continued to speak their respective mother tongues at home.

As has been mentioned, the authorities of the penal colony decided the occupational status of the immigrants. Though all Pre-42 communities were rehabilitated or settled by the authorities, they were not provided with equal facilities. After serving ten years of their term, an inmate of the penal colony could earn the status of a 'self-supporter'; then they could live in a village as a householder, cultivate land and keep cattle. Each self-supporting family was allotted 5–15 acres of cultivable land and two bullocks as plough animals.

The Moplahs were given the status of self-supporters after six months in the islands. The Bhantus were treated in a similar fashion on their arrival.[12] No settlement package was offered to the coolies who were recruited in and around Ranchi in Chotanagpur Plateau and were brought to the penal colony. Some of them acquired small pieces of forestland, which they began to cultivate. There can be no doubt that variation in the degree of patronage received from the authorities to a large extent decided the status of communities with respect to one another. In the penal colony, such status was closely linked with the identity of a community.

The idea of space and niche among the immigrant communities is important and is closely related to their relative status, which in turn influenced their identity. The first level of contradistinction is made between the Andamans and mainland India. The islands are known as *kala pani*—'dark waters'—a horrific description of the penal colony across the deep seas. The Indian mainland is known as *muluk*—'native place' (see Figure 8.2). Those who could go back to *muluk* at will, the government officials and the free citizens, enjoyed a special status in eyes of the people confined to *kala pani*. In time, for the confined ones, *muluk* was not a specific village and not even a specific province. The entire mainland India became *muluk* for them.

Within *kala pani*, space is divided into several niches. The only urban centre in the Andaman Islands in those days, the town of Port Blair, is known as *bajar*—marketplace. The villages established during the penal colony days, generally located within a radius of 40 km. from the town, are called *basti*. Places beyond *basti* are called *jangal*—wilderness. It follows that the designations *bajarwala*, *bastiwala*, and *jangalwala* denote differential status. The authorities of the penal colony settled those with an urban background and formal education at Port Blair so they could work as clerks or traders. Those from rural backgrounds were settled in rural or forested areas and are still considered to be 'rustic' by the *bajarwala*s.

During the penal colony years, the Local Born community was divided into the *bajarwalas* (townsmen) and *bastiwalas* (villagers). The Moplahs and the Bhantus were primarily *bastiwalas*, as they were settled as cultivators. A few decades ago, Moplah and Bhantu members moved into or closer to the town. A significant number of Local Born families owned cultivable land in *basti* areas and houses in the *bajar*. Some Moplah and Bhantu families also moved into *bajar* leaving other members of their respective families to cultivate their land in *basti*. Thus sections of the same community became *bajarwalas* and *bastiwalas*, the designations were not exclusively specific to a given community.

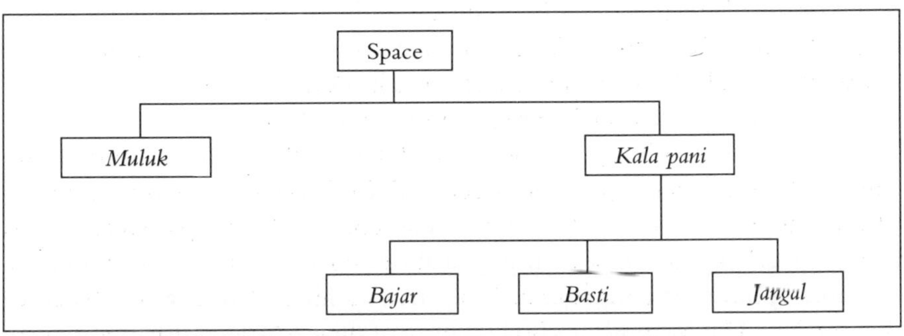

FIGURE 8.2: Categorization of Space Based on Settlement of Pre-42 Communities.

Source: Prepared by the author.

The Karens and the Ranchiwallahs were *jangalwalas* from the perspective of the *bajarwalas* and the *bastiwalas*. Their existence remained marginal to the town-centric society of *kala pani*. However, the term *junglee* or 'forest dweller' was never used for them; it has always been reserved as the description of the indigenous islanders, even though much of their forest habitat was denuded during and after the colonial period.[13]

When examined against the universal attributes of ethnic groups mentioned earlier, the Pre-42 communities are not homogeneous at all. When the matter is examined from an instrumentalist viewpoint without underestimating the cultural dimensions, it is clear that the share of political power and access to educational and job facilities provided by the state are popular rallying points. As none of the Pre-42 communities are provided with exclusive facilities, they need to compete among themselves, and with other groups of immigrants, to secure a greater share of power or more facilities. They have no other choice but to stay close at the cost of community-specific identity. There is no reason to feel that the share of political power or the facilities provided by the state are such a strong draw that the Pre-42 communities have discarded their respective identities; some elements of ethnicity are operative while some non-ethnic divisors observably create conspicuous divisions among the communities.

DIVIDING LINES

Different Pre-42 communities demonstrate conspicuous dissimilarity in their worldview, which can be traced to a variance in their space-consciousness. The first level of such variation is seen *within* the Pre-42 communities; the second, *between* the Pre-42 communities and later migrants. This second category may also include the variation between the Pre-42 communities and mainlander Indians who come to the islands but do not settle there (visitors, sojourners), or non-islanders encountered by Andaman individuals when in mainland India. In the first case, individuals or families are essentially identified by virtue of their connection to a space or specific niche within the islands. In the second, such spatially derived identities lose validity and in many cases, novel identities are fashioned.

The major dividing lines between different Pre-42 communities are still based on the niche they once occupied. In this case, collective identities of the settlers were blurred or at times absent, where people were settled in *bajar*, *basti* or *jangal* based on personal or collective attributes. Thus, the available options for constructing collective identity were closely related to their niches. The *bajarwalas*, who by virtue of their educated urban past were allowed to take up white-collar jobs and settle at the administrative centre of the colony had the opportunity to come into frequent contact with penal colony officials; at times, some of the clerks and traders could, therefore, become close associates of the officials. Such opportunities provided the *bajarwalas* with a window on the world beyond the colony, which was not available to the *bastiwalas*.

At another level, there was a feeling among the Local Borns that the Moplahs, Karens, and Ranchiwallahs preferred to remain segregated from others by retaining ethnic boundaries. The boundary between the Bhantus and the Local Borns, however, were not maintained uniformly everywhere; while the rural Bhantus preferred to stay away from the rest, in *bajar*, such boundaries between them and the Local Borns have become very porous and at times difficult to perceive.

The Local Born people residing in Port Blair or in adjacent villages did not feel close to the Karens even a few years ago, not only because of the ethnic divide that separated them, but also because the latter are *jangalwalas*. As a result of the reservation of seats in educational institutions or government jobs for Pre-42 islanders in recent years, the distinctions between Local Born and Karen communities have begun to soften and the dividing lines have shifted. At the same time, Pre-42 communities generally believe that families living in villages are in a less-favourable position. A gentleman from a village located about 30 km. from Port Blair felt his children could not make full use of the educational facilities offered by the administration to Pre-42 communities as the strong schools and better teachers were in *bajar*. Like many other *basti* parents, he also aspired to send his children to quality institutions on the mainland for higher education. It was difficult for the children from *basti* to compete with those from *bajar*. The children from *bajar* had access to the urban private instructional institutes that trained students allowing them to achieve better results in school leaving examinations or in admission tests for engineering or medical colleges. So, like many other *bastiwala* parents, he had to procure loans to pay for his children's admission to costlier private colleges.

It has been stated that large-scale migration from rural to urban areas has changed the qualitative distinction between residents of *bajar, basti* or *jangal*. In recent years, connotations like *bajarwala* or *bastiwala* are often used without the 'ethnic' connotations of the past. 'Why there are some successful entrepreneurs from among the Local Born but not from the Bhantu, while many Bhantu families have spent more than three generations in the *bajar*', asked one young Local Born entrepreneur. He offered the answer to his own question: 'it was not because they are Bhantus but because they still remain *bastiwala*s in their thought.'

The Pre-42 communities, especially the Local Born, often find it difficult to make mainland Indians, and also people who have migrated to the islands in recent years, understand who they are and where they came from.

It is difficult for most mainlanders to understand why persons with roots and connections to a community that is not indigenous to the islands cannot recollect the village, district or state of their forefathers. Mainland Indians often find it hard to comprehend how there can be Hindu individuals without any caste identity. Almost every person in Pre-42 communities can tell about times they have tackled identity queries from mainlanders. These questions elicit several responses. At times, islanders evade issues and questions related to identity. One elderly gentleman who was born in the islands identified himself as a mainlander because, he argued, only the indigenous islanders could be true islanders. Some islanders respond to identity inquiries by naming any one state of India as their home state, and any caste—usually a high ranking one—as their caste. A Local Born lady who was active in public life used to visit different places in mainland India. Her role required that she met mainlanders within and outside the islands regularly. It was difficult for her to explain Local Born identity to most of the mainlanders, so she used to dodge the subject by telling them that her forefathers were Kshatriyas from Punjab. Such responses are not always composed as a direct result of a question being asked; sometimes, the subject of mainland origin and identity is shared within a family, though not beyond. One Local Born man informed me that he was told by his father and his grandfather that the founder of his family was one Bengali brahman. However, members of that family never claimed brahman status or used the surname they believed belonged to their forefather. The practice of not asserting mainland-style identities has become usual among the Local Born. There are a few Local Born families who do use caste specific surnames, but they almost never claim the concomitant status.

After interviewing several members of Pre-42 communities, it was revealed that proclaiming one's identity in terms of mainland origins and connections is more common among *bajarwalas* than *bastiwalas*. The latter seldom bothered about these identity issues; when interacting with mainlanders, they simply stated that they are people from the Andaman Islands, are not sure about the place(s) their forefathers came from and have no idea what their caste was. When college mates in mainland India asked one village boy about his jati, he said that he was a Hindu. When the question was repeated using the 'caste' word, the boy said he was not sure, he would ask his elders back home. His friends found the response funny but the boy from the islands admitted that he had no better answer.

The variation between rural and urban peoples in their response to queries related to identity suggests a new world-type multicultural situation prevails in the villages more so than in urban areas. It was the *bajarwalas* who accepted the dominance of caste- and territory-based identity to a greater extent, thanks to their greater exposure to *muluk* and mainlander people.

OTHER SPACE

Deterritorialization is a significant factor in the construction of difference between multinational and multicultural polities.[14] In the Andaman Islands, the process helped to establish difference between the Local Born and rest of the Pre-42 communities; while the Local Born could not be identified with any specific part of mainland India and can be considered as completely deterritorialized, some degree of territorial affinity remained part of the identity of other Pre-42 communities. The Bhantu, for example, notionally belong to the state of Uttar Pradesh, whether or not they have any firm footing in that state. Such a group can be described as partially deterritorialized. The difference was sharper between Pre-42 islanders and post-Independence immigrants. At the same time, deterritorialization contributes to evaluative differences between people identified according to different kinds of space or niche.

During the penal colony years, when the Pre-42 communities were largely cut off from the rest of the world, emotional attachment to *muluk* was strong. One Local Born family spoke of a strong attachment to a certain village in Balia District in Uttar Pradesh, their place of origin in mainland India. In pre-Independence years, the term *muluk* was used in that family to denote the specific location of their mainland origin and belonging. After Independence, when people were at last free to move away from the Andamans, many islanders realized that the land they imagined as their *muluk* was very different in reality. When members of a Local Born family visited their natal village in Balia immediately after 1947, relatives made it clear that they were not welcome. The family from the islands was told to forget about any share of property. The disillusionment was sudden and complete. Some years later, a relative from Balia visited the family in the Andamans. It was a courtesy visit, but the islander family did not show interest in keeping in touch with the mainlander relatives. By then, entire mainland India was their *muluk*.

The difference in perception of territoriality between Local Born and other Pre-42 communities is important. For example, many Moplah families maintain close contact with their mainland counterparts in Kerala; this both differentiates and segregates them from other Pre-42 communities. When some members of the Moplah community were asked whether they belonged to both Andaman Islands and Kerala, they did not agree. They cited examples of marriage between Moplah individuals and members of other Muslim communities of the islands. They also admitted that the Moplahs, who reached the Andamans much later than most of the Local Borns, continued to maintain their ethnic identity. However, they asserted that their community belongs primarily to the Andaman Islands and not to Kerala. Their contact with relatives in Kerala is of a casual nature, restricted to occasional mutual visits. Many Andaman Moplahs have foregone any claim over ancestral property in Kerala, as such claims could destroy the cordial nature of their island-mainland family relationships.

'OTHERS'

Since the colonization of the Andamans, the islands have been administered in the main by non-islanders. Islanders have sometimes accused these 'others' of ignorance and insensitivity towards the specific situations and problems of the Andaman Islands. These outsiders primarily understood history of the islands in terms of a linear timeline and categorized islander communities on basis of ethnic identities. Space, as conceived by the islander communities, remained largely a non-issue for them.

The official website of the Andaman and Nicobar Administration portrays the islands primarily as a destination for nature tourism, rarely highlighting them as a space where people have toiled. Under the section 'Know Andaman', the website has a section 'Land and People'.[15] The paragraph on land is full of poetic expressions and romanticizes the spaces of the islands:

> The unparalleled beauty of these islands, create in men a love of nature with a caressing tenderness, a wistful fondness for all its delicate nuances. The enveloping atmosphere with its subtle harmonies of light and shade, fragrance and exhales the paradise, visionary splendours, and the music of the birds that defies definition would develop creative and constructive feelings in the hearts of those people who come here to enjoy the beauty of nature. He would like to rebel against the stereotyped moulds and forms into which life is [*sic*] so called 'modern man' is cast. He would be under the impact of the complex mood of infinite longing and tragic helplessness, 'the yearning that craves for expression, yet defies expression, the inconclusive struggle between emotional apprehension of life and the articulation that must transcend personal emotion'.[16]

A section of the islanders, especially some members of the Pre-42 communities, found such a description far removed from reality. This group perceives the islands as a space shaped by them and their forefathers under rigorous conditions. The colonial authorities tried to tap each possible resource for earning revenue. For them, the islands were a rich repository of timber and other forest produce. The trend continued in the post-Independence years. The paragraph on the people of the islands lacks the élan of the previous paragraph.

> The Andaman and Nicobar Islands have great maritime importance. During the British period political leaders considered dangerous to the interests of the Raj and other dreaded criminals were deported from mainland to the Cellular Jail—the

Indian Bastille, situated on the sea coast of Atlanta Point in the North-Eastern part of Port Blair. Thus these islands were infamously known as the 'Black Water Prison' or 'Kala Pani'.[17]

One gentleman of Pre-42 origin who took an interest in political activities questioned some of the information presented in the above paragraph; he said it is not enough to designate the Cellular Jail, built in the early twentieth century, as a national memorial. The deported freedom fighters of 1850s never stayed there. All places in the islands where they stayed and suffered should be treated as national heritage sites. He felt the bureaucrats have removed the legacy from public memory and, thus, have transformed the Pre-42 people into just another group of immigrants to the islands.

SPACE AND WORLDVIEW

Among some urban elites in India, a preference for multiculturalism as a favoured social value is often expressed in form of defiance towards divisions created by caste, language or religion. The Pre-42 communities and especially the Local Born community were not in a position to exercise preferences or dislike for the divisions, they had to do it under compulsion and they did so very differently. That the major dividing lines between different sections of people in a given space can be urban and rural residence is impossible in mainland India. Another impossibility might be the shaping of space-specific identities which influence both caste and the territorially divided social order.

The heterogeneous present-day Pre-42 communities rarely seem to assert ethnicity as a strategy to distinguish them from other groups. The perception that the Moplahs try to remain distinct has been denied by members of that community. As a Moplah individual explained, two or three generations from now, the Moplah community may become indistinguishable from the Muslim section of the Local Born community. The quest for a common heritage by different sections of the Pre-42 communities is important. This exercise may be interpreted by some as an effort to secure more benefits from the state, but it can go much further. It can redefine the way the Pre-42 communities recognize and understand ethnicity; this is happening through the shifting perceptions of space, the niches within *kala pani* as well as of *muluk*.

Whatever distinctiveness or possibilities are deduced and discussed, all Pre-42 people do not think alike. Some I spoke with were pessimistic; they told of a better past when the people owned prime properties in the islands and were governed by a sympathetic administration. They alleged that money-rich mainlanders, who reached the Andamans as prospectors, have marginalized the Pre-42 people economically, while insensitive bureaucrats have accelerated the process. They were worried because younger Pre-42 persons preferred the more comfortable life of mainland India or of other countries and, given a chance, tended to settle there.

There were optimists as well. A group of young Pre-42 persons moved back to the islands after completing higher education in the mainland and leaving behind better career options. One of them, a young entrepreneur, wanted to do something for the Pre-42 people but was not sure how to go about it. He was planning to join an organization called the 'Local Born Association'. He was designing t-shirts with the message 'I am a proud Andamanese', and he was considering creating a blog for like-minded people.

It is interesting to note that the people who expressed opinions on the subject, both optimists and pessimists, were *bajarwalas*. Though I also asked several *bastiwalas* for their thoughts, their general attitude was one of indifference; they did not feel that the identity of the Pre-42 communities was under threat, and as such did not feel the need to act or do anything about it.

COROLLARY

It has been noted that, unlike the native islanders, the Pre-42 communities considered the Andaman Islands primarily as a place of residence and not as a resource base. This understanding was based in their status as mere tenants in the Andamans, while the government owned the resources. As such, they did what the authorities asked them to do to implement the colonialization scheme.[18] On the other hand, when compared with the post-Independence immigrants, the Pre-42 communities were found to possess better knowledge and distinctive cognition about the space in which they reside.

Coexistence of multinational and multicultural polities in a limited space not only suggests heterogeneity among the inhabitants, it is indicative of the colonized character of the space. Such a dichotomy could hardly occur in a space where immigrants do not dominate native inhabitants. Another dichotomy is also observable in the Andaman Islands. While some immigrants preferred to identify themselves primarily according to the space they or their forebears occupied in the past, there were others who were more attached to their spaces of residence in the present. This again is typical of a situation compelled by involuntary migration and prolonged habitation. Temporality is an important factor in this case; while attachment to the past has been found to be stronger among relatively recent immigrants, those who have stayed longer at the new location showed less attachment to the past than the present.

Finally, it can be said that consciousness about space, like ethnicity, is an instrumentalist construction based on the experience of material conditions. For those who were relatively more conversant about the ways of the mainlanders, it was largely a matter of convenience to claim a fictitious identity that mainlanders might find 'noble'. Still, there were others who preferred not to pursue lucrative careers in mainland India, but chose to return to the islands and be identified as islanders. Whichever way identity issues are manipulated by different sections of a group's members, space consciousness can not only outlive the conditions that were responsible for its creation, it can act as a cementing factor for a long-lasting collective identity.

NOTES

1. First-hand information cited in this chapter was collected between 1998 and 2013; the author stayed with people in the Andamans intermittently over a number of years. This permitted the discussion of several issues with many interlocutors at different locations. While preparing this chapter certain specific issues were discussed with a cross-section of these people in 2012–13.
2. Akhil Gupta and James Ferguson, 'Beyond "Culture": Space, Identity, and the Politics of Difference', *Cultural Anthropology*, vol. 7, no. 1, 1992, pp. 6–23.
3. Alfred Reginald Radcliffe-Brown, *The Andaman Islanders*, Glencoe, Illinois: The Free Press, 1922; repr., 1948, p. 26.
4. Vishvajit Pandya, 'Above the Forest: A Study of Andamanese Ethno Anemology, Cosmology and the Power of Ritual', New Delhi: Oxford University Press, 1993, pp. 21–3.
5. Pierre Bourdieu quoted in Sankha Priya Guha, *Anthropology of Space*, Memari, Burdwan: Avenel Press, 2014, p. 12.
6. Guha, *Anthropology of Space*, pp. 12–13.
7. Setha Low and Denise Lawrence-Zuñiga, 'Locating Culture', in *The Anthropology of Space and Place: Locating Culture*, ed. Setha Low and Denise Lawrence-Zuñiga, Malden and Oxford: Blackwell Publishing, 2003, pp. 1–47.
8. Daniel C. Dennett, *Consciousness Explained*, Boston: Little, Brown and Co., 1991.
9. John Hutchinson and Anthony D. Smith, 'Introduction', in *Ethnicity*, ed. John Hutchinson and Anthony D. Smith, Oxford and New York: Oxford University Press, 1996, pp. 1–14.
10. Sian Jones, *The Archaeology of Ethnicity: Constructing Identities in the Past and Present*, London and New York: Routledge Press, 1997.
11. T.K. Oommen, 'Cultural Pluralism and the State: Situating South Asia', in *Identity, Cultural Pluralism and State: South Asia in Perspective*, ed. N.K. Das and V.R. Rao, Delhi: Anthropological Survey of India and Macmillan, 2009, pp. 1–21.
12. P.K. Sen, *Land and People of the Andamans*, Calcutta: Postgraduate Book Mart, 1962.

13. Kanchan Mukhopadhyay, 'Society in Andaman Islands: In Search of its Centre and Margin', *Journal of the Anthropological Survey of India*, vol. 51, 2002, pp. 139–63.
14. Oommen, 'Cultural Pluralism and the State'.
15. The Andaman and Nicobar Administration official website, 'Know Andaman' [http://www.and.nic.in/andaman/knowabt.php], accessed 12 November 2014.
16. Ibid.
17. Ibid.
18. Kanchan Mukhopadhyay, 'Time, Space, and Belongingness: Some Experiences from the Andaman Islands', *Practising Geographer*, vol. 18, no. 2, 2014, pp. 11–25.

9

The Ethnohistory of 'Uninhabited' Nicobar Islands

The Relevance of Perceiving History and Collective Identity from Legend and Folklore

MANISH CHANDI

Folktales and legends are often emic narratives of history, mirrors, and expressions of people's experiences and also rationales for socio-cultural practices. The fundamental concern of this chapter is in using such perceptions of history to understand their resonance within local meanings attached to land and waterscapes in the Nicobar Islands.

In many traditional societies, taboos are associated with legend, folklore and myth, and they are viewed as the basis of regulatory resource access and environmental conservation.[1] Resource regulation and sociological systems are facets of resource management, but another, if not equally or more important, aspect is that of understanding rationales of ownership

* I would first like to thank the organizers of the conference 'Manifestations of History in the Andaman Islands', Professor Dr Frank Heidemann and Dr Philipp Zehmisch for the opportunity to present this facet of understanding communities, their notions of history and sense of place. I am indebted to many Nicobarese interlocutors who have shared their time, spaces, points of view, and information on issues which I continue to work on. Any faults in the telling or analysis of these narratives are my own. In particular, I would like to thank the late Revd Isaac of Changpin Village on Nancowry Island for his narration of the legend of Tillanchong and for sharing his hand-drawn map with local place names; Mr S. Prakash of Kakana Village, Kamorta Island; Mr Potifer of Ukchuaka Village, Trinket Island for inviting me to accompany the team to Tillanchong Island on each occasion over three years; Mr. Moses of Pulomilo Island (Makachua Village) for the narrative of the legend of Meroë; from Little Nicobar Island Mr Joseph and Obedia of Pulo

and stewardship of the user. In this chapter, I attempt to point out frames of reference to ownership embedded in local perceptions of history. Local perspective is a crucial aspect in comprehending use of and conservation mechanisms for landscapes and seascapes. As Bob Johannes succinctly put it, 'Understanding a conservation system means understanding not only the nature of what is being conserved, but also the viewpoint of the conserver.'[2]

An increasingly common feature across traditional communities is the influence of cultural change on traditional resource management systems. Invariably, over-exploitation of resources or breakdowns in resource sharing mechanisms are frequent outcomes. Common property resource theory recognizes the use of interdisciplinary research to empirically understand resource management strategies used by local communities.[3] This approach recognizes equal opportunities among stakeholders for developing robust strategies in managing commonly used resources. There have been significant contributions in understanding various traditional communities, through their systems of traditional knowledge and utilization practices and the anthropology of cultural landscapes.[4]

Little has been written on indigenous conservation practices and cultural geography of the Nicobar Islanders over the past century.[5] The Nicobar Islands comprise twenty-one islands, of which eleven are inhabited.[6] The islanders spread across the archipelago can be divided into five dialect groups, excluding the Shompen tribe who reside in the interior forests of Great Nicobar Island. The Nicobarese are coastal dwellers dependent on coconut cultivation, subsistence from the sea, and the husbandry of pigs and chicken in villages. Some native species from these ecosystems are featured in oral traditions in the islands. In many stories from the Nicobar Islands, interconnections with animal and plant life on the islands are reflected in various forms with islanders as the principal characters. Two published accounts on folktales from the Nicobar Islands are of Car Nicobarese

Ulon; the late Mr Jackson and Mr Hajoon of Muhincohn; the late Mr P. Joora of Pulo Bahaun; and from Kondul Island (Afra Bay), Mr James, Mr Ramesh, and Mr Mohoh, for their individual narratives regarding the tale of 'Hindra-tö-Pu'. They all shared their stories with pride and humour as narratives of their own people. I have only provided a brief sketch of these legends for the purpose of this volume; there remains much to be written on this oral tradition and its stories that is beyond the scope of my chapter. Last but not the least, I thank the late Dr Ravi Sankaran, a friend, ornithologist, and intrepid explorer of the Nicobar Islands, for encouraging me to visit these spaces and work to understand the issues with regard to the use of Tillanchong Island many years ago.

origin.[7] They provide a glimpse into the genesis of belief systems of the 'natural' word around their island, as well as stories of ancestral concerns and imaginations. These stories are not very well known to the younger generation in the present day, especially given the changed circumstances after the tsunami of 2004 and increasingly market-dependent livelihoods. Islanders often use these narratives in describing rationales for behavioural mores or customary rules and regulations of their systems of natural resource management and regulation. Frequently, they integrate perceptions of natural history with methods of resource use, conservation, and resource partitioning. These resource management systems are influenced by the historical experience of living on their island with limited resources, and beliefs regarding the natural world through these oral traditions. In other instances, they influenced the formation of taboos relating to species or a resource region, and thereby regulate harvests and induce behavioural norms. Such practices vary geographically across different land- and seascapes of the Nicobar archipelago. During my fieldwork on natural resource management systems, I was often told of prescriptions instantiated by stories and oral traditions that provide the basis of accepted norms and practices.[8]

These practices often controlled over-exploitation through seasonal regulation and taboos with regard to use of many resources as well as specific regions, such as geographical regions on an island which had season-specific uses. The cause-and-effect outcomes are both epiphenomenal as well as conscious decisions based on the limitations to resource availability. Though I will not dwell on the nuances of epiphenomena in this account, I use three narratives from these oral traditions to describe how an emic perspective of history regarding uninhabited islands and spaces construe their ownership by various Nicobar islanders. I will briefly present these stories as I understand them; they describe how affinities and ownership of assets such as land and other resources on such 'uninhabited' islands are understood and appropriated by the islanders. These three legends are among many others regarding the origin of islands, differences between islander communities, and metaphysical phenomena, and span just a small portion of the central and southern Nicobar Islands. They are also explained through ancestral experiences in relation to the practices of taboos and behavioural norms.

THE LEGEND OF MEROË ISLAND

The term for native islanders in the south and central Nicobar Islands is 'Payuh'.[9] Southern Nicobarese call the island of Meroë—'Piruii'.[10] Their legend says that Payuh lived on the now uninhabited island of Meroë in earlier times. The Payuh of Meroë were related to those on Pulomilo, Little Nicobar and Kondul, but spoke a different dialect. Their dialect was only spoken on Meroë. The inhabitants were associated with magic powers of healing and epitomized strength. Despite these powers, they were known as peaceful islanders. They lived off the coconut trees that they cultivated. As seasoned medicine men (*minluanö*), they were able to sustain a large population on the small island and shared their resources with those friends among the neighbouring islanders from Pulomilo, Little Nicobar and Kondul Islands.

This story describes the decimation of the people of Meroë Island as it took place many years ago, when sailors and traders visited the island periodically. One such sailing ship arrived from the southern ocean and anchored off the island of Pulomilo, known for its safe harbour and water. The sailors spent a few weeks in the harbour and interacted with the residents of Pulomilo, sharing gifts. One of the sailors who came to the island was a man from the island of Minicoy;[11] he made good friends with a family on the island and wished to stay on Pulomilo Island. He was a friendly man, and was welcomed by the family, and the ship's captain let him leave the ship without much ado. In a few months, his life changed. Despite making friends, he was not able to live off the land by hunting and was dependent on the family for everything. He did not know how to climb coconut trees nor did he know where to fish; the family soon grew tired of his many demands and told him to work for them to earn his living and he became their servant. It is said that, in due course, he got on everyone's nerves. There was no way he could return to his home country, as no ship passed by or stopped at Pulomilo for many years. The man was desperate for relief and was fed up with the drudgery of his chores on Pulomilo. He yearned to leave. He sulked a lot and was diffident, but did not upset anyone, despite his angst. One day, as he went down to the beach to wash cooking utensils, he saw that somebody had left a large mud pot[12] near the beach. He took this large mud pot, stored food in it, and set sail. No one knows how long his voyage took, but he finally reached his native island of Minicoy. He retold his tale of suffering to his friends and they planned to take revenge on the islanders of Pulomilo. They set sail in large numbers, armed with weapons and food for the journey. They finally reached the southern Nicobar region but mistook the island of Meroë for Pulomilo and went ashore. Much to the consternation of the peaceful islanders of Meroë, they were attacked. A massacre took place despite the magical powers of the Meroë islanders. Only a few people survived, and these fled to Pulomilo where they told the tale. Much innocent Meroë islander blood was shed that day. Their blood flowed from the island of Meroë into the sea, colouring the clay beach red.[13] This is the only beach of clayey soil on the island that remains red to this day; a reminder to other Payuh of the gory massacre. Since that time, Meroë has remained uninhabited but to this day, it is visited by islanders who have plantations there, to harvest produce during the dry season. Those islanders who escaped the massacre entrusted the ownership of Meroë to a former chief of Kondul Island and his lineage. Ever since, the stewardship of the island is maintained by the descendants of that family. The present trustee is an elderly man, Mohoh (also known as Layuh). Mohoh and his father divided the plantations on Meroë amongst kin groups of the Payuh of Little Nicobar, Kondul, and Pulomilo for their use. Restrictions are invoked on hunting birds and robber crabs, on the use of modern fishing gear, and the cutting of timber or the bamboo clump when Payuh visit Meroë.

THE STORY OF TILLANCHONG ISLAND

Tillanchong Island is located along the eastern extremity of the Central Nicobar Islands. It is a long, thin island approximately 16 sq. km. in area. Its coast is interspersed with thin beaches of sand and pebble along the west, though its eastern shores are mostly rocky and form a ledge dropping into the sea; the island is covered with dense jungle all along a steep central ridge. Coconut palms fringe four sandy beaches, while the rest of the coast is mostly rocky. Col. Gerini, in his treatise on Ptolemaic geography published in 1909, attributes the etymological meaning to the Chinese phrase *Tswe lan chang*, meaning island of blue waters.[14] Tillanchong Island is called Lö-uk in the Central Nicobarese dialect. Its use, visitation, and the ownership of plantations by Nicobarese of Kamorta was mentioned by Kloss in 1903.[15] Kloss refers to an instance recorded by Hamilton, in which islanders of the Nancowry group rescued shipwrecked sailors in 1708.

The first person from Central Nicobar who established the use and ownership of the plantations was Lawaöh, an ancestor of the clan Nyi Takaru of Trinket Island. Legend has it that Lawaöh was one among the people taken by a European vessel which had sailed into Nancowry harbour and planned to visit Tillanchong Island for some days; the ship took with them four islanders, one each from Ukchuaka Village (Trinket Island), Enaka and Kakana (villages on Kamorta Island), and from Tapong Village (on Nancowry Island). The vessel ran aground along the west coast of Tillanchong and the crew, including the Nicobarese, swam over to the island.[16] They returned to Kamorta Island after repairing the vessel. During this visit, the Nicobarese on board noticed coconut trees at four beaches.

After his return, Lawaöh took his friend Kotėklòng from the clan Nyi Sumyeuh at Kakana Village to revisit the island in order to examine the coconut plantations there. They sailed over, found the plantations to be productive, and staked their claim of ownership on them. Then the tradition of sharing coconuts and few other natural resources on the island began between these clans. Ever since, the island has been under the ownership and use of two extended families from the central Nicobar Islands of Kamorta (clan Nyi Sumyeuh) and Trinket (clan Nyi Takaru). More recently, another clan from Trinket Island, called Nyi Mumallö, has been included.

At that point (over a century ago), trade in coconuts was meagre as only few sailing ships passed by. Given the importance of coconuts in Nicobarese tradition—both in terms of livelihood and economic value—these plantations were shared by the members of the clans of Lawaöh and his friend Kotėklòng. Lawaöh was known to be an exceptional man among the islanders of yore and was remembered through his Kareav.[17] His descendants are at Vikas Nagar (Nyi Takaru, formerly on Trinket Island), and that of his partner, Kotėklòng, are at Kakana Village (Nyi Sumyeuh, House Milehren, Kamorta Island).

In those years, traditional customs associated with the island were established according to the belief systems and metaphysical experiences of visitors. These include living off the land and its resources, though no trees may be cut and the only animals that may be hunted for food are wild pigs, fish and sea turtles close to the shore. Many elaborate behavioural norms also exist including the use of the dialect of Tillanchong, known only by the initiated few that use the island on a frequent basis, along with the customary owners. The dialect of Tillanchong is locally believed to be a relic of its past inhabitants. Between the two clans, they devised a sharing mechanism of alternating their visits to the island in the dry season so as to allow each group to maximize their returns from the harvests on the island.[18]

The story continues and describes an instance in the ancient past when Chowra islanders tried to colonize Tillanchong and rid the island of its original inhabitants. The Chowra islanders were driven away with spears, rocks, and knives. That incident set in place a rule in vogue among the customary owners that islanders from Chowra and Terassa are not favoured by the spirits on Tillanchong Island and they will fall ill or die if they attempt to colonize or use the island. The island is the exclusive property of the clan members and can be used by friends from their own islands, but not from Terassa or Chowra Islands.[19] The arrival of Myanmarese poachers and other outsiders defies customary law of the island, and risks attracting malevolent spirits who could bring death and illness in various forms. Therefore, all men and women from the clans who visit the island are prepared, through a process of initiation and rituals conducted on the island, to propitiate the spirits and ancestors of the original inhabitants of Tillanchong Island. This practice continues today, and it is the only location in the Nicobars where such a ritual continues.

THE STORY OF HINDRA TÖ PU AND THE ISLAND OF KOMVING

Komvingö is the name in Little Nicobarese for the islet of Kabra, situated north-east of the southern Great Nicobar Island. This islet is known for excellent whetstones found along its coast. The stones of Komvingö are used by the Little Nicobarese to maintain their knives, machetes, spears and axes. The tools when sharpened on stones from this island retain a sharp edge formed by the perfect grain found on stones from this islet. Pre-tsunami (2004), almost every village on Little Nicobar had a pair of stones from this islet to sharpen a range of tools used to hunt prey, to construct houses and to do carpentry.

Legend has it that long ago, all the islands of the Nicobar group were closer to each other, clustered together.[20] The island of Car Nicobar was then situated along the eastern coast of Great Nicobar Island. The islanders of Komvingö traded the renowned whetstones with other islanders for resources not found on their little islet. The islanders of Car Nicobar were closest to the islet and often complained of having to put up with the horrible smell of the faeces of people from Komvingö every morning. Eventually, fed up with the morning ordeal, the islanders pleaded with the best medicine men (*minluanö*) from their island and others, and convinced them to move the island of Car Nicobar away from the eastern coast of Great Nicobar. When the island was moved away by magic, a small portion was left behind, a large rock called 'Hindra tö-Pu'. The literal translation of this name is 'a portion/rock of Car Nicobar' (Pu). From then on, any islanders north of the southern Nicobar Islands were not allowed to take rocks as whetstones from Komvingö. The belief remains that the *minluanö* cast a spell on the island of Komvingö after Car Nicobar Island was moved away; ever since then, all other islanders beyond the vicinity of the southern Nicobar would be stricken with disease if they took any stone from Komvingö.

This story is used by many southerners as an explanation of the cultural differences between the northerners and southerners. They believe it explains why the northerners are uncomfortable in their rugged terrain of forests and hills. The whetstones are now the exclusive property of the Little Nicobarese and Great Nicobarese, the southerners.

UNINHABITED ISLANDS AND COLONIZED SPACES

Nicobarese history is fairly well documented from the eighteenth century onward.[21] This history relies on written documents by sailors, colonizers, and missionaries, but there is also a range of oral histories narrated by the elderly and held in collective memory, stories, and myths. Except-ing the documentation by Revd Whitehead on Car Nicobar Island in 1921, the stories and oral histories of other islands have so far remained undocumented. In many ways, the three narratives portray the islanders' historical relationships with their natural environment.[22] Events of colonization and trade are not the focus of this oral tradition; rather, it is focused on more pressing concerns such as the use of spaces (islands) and resources. Unlike eurocentric approaches to history that emphasize the importance of singular events and linear chronologies, Nicobar oral history, like that of other traditional communities, dwells more on references to locations, ancestors, and events rendering their history. These influence conceptualizations of origin, identity, and the history of sharing or maintaining exclusive rights to resources.

Rarely does an individual own important livelihood resources; the clan or group are institutions through which ownership of such limited assets and articles is organized and thus made accessible to all their members. This is recognized throughout the archipelago of Nicobar Islands with local variations around kinship or corporate relationships in social organization.[23] As a crucial aspect of natural resource management, resource sharing occurs within and between kin groups. The social structure of the Nicobar islanders is based on variations of the concept of a clan being composed of affinal and consanguineous members who form a kin group;[24] a collective of clans make up villages and the island population. All basic economic assets such as land and plantations are, thus, partitioned among various clans. Consequently, all land and its produce on each island was partitioned by ancestral leaders of large clans leading to ownership by successive generations of kin groups. Gifting of land, or partitioning of land as payments for fines or punishment are other means by which ownership of land may be transferred without cash transactions.[25]

On nearly all islands,[26] resources are divided by the axiom 'the island is small and has limited resources; to live and prosper, islanders have to share limited resources'. This important aspect of sharing and ownership in the islands is deeply entrenched in some legends. They are also illustrative and used by local islanders in various oral histories that are used to establish land ownership, as well as the need to share resources.

Sharing also brings about a sense of collective ownership of land and other resources therein, and of a sense of stewardship and association with kin groups of natal islands.[27] It is this phenomenon of collective ownership, as well as sharing land and other resources that are often overlooked in the larger developmental schemes initiated by the Andaman and Nicobar Islands Administration. More recently, after the tsunami of 2004, the government-induced rehabilitation process influenced changes in the structure of Nicobarese society. This impacted social collectives and clan groups to nuclear/unitary households through the resettlement and rehabilitation process thanks to a badly planned housing scheme and disaster aid.[28] Another instance of misunderstanding mechanisms of ownership of islands as resource spaces was evident a few years ago: virtually all uninhabited islands[29] are within the purview of neighbouring islanders, with established resource catchments on some, while others feature in oral histories and legends. These uninhabited islands are, in this sense, already controlled by the indigenous islanders. Two islands, in particular, stand out for the resource sharing practices established by the Nicobarese who customarily use and own the islands: Tillanchong Island is a declared Sanctuary in the Protected Area network of the Andaman and Nicobar Islands Administration; Meroë Island is left unclassified like other small uninhabited islets. These two islands were recently proposed for use in national defence-related developments such as missile testing.[30] This was eventually turned down by the Ministry of Environment, Government of India, after activists, conservation organizations and indigenous islanders expressed their concern and displeasure over the proposal. Another issue regarding land ownership and colonization of limited habitable lands is a festering problem in Central Nicobar. The defence apparatus, especially the Indian Navy, was keen to develop a stretch of land that was apparently granted to them by a former influential matriarch of Nancowry Island;[31] this is disputed by local residents and descendants of the matriarch and for more than a decade has failed to achieve resolution.[32] The issue has now assumed greater magnitude since the development of facilities for the defence forces increased the importance of this site; simultaneously, local islanders experienced land scarcity after the 2004 tsunami.

Increasingly, the more market-linked economies of the archipelago have provoked changes, including the erosion of sharing mechanisms, alterations of perspectives on modernity, and changing dynamics among younger generations of Nicobar islanders.[33] Given this situation, it is useful to consider integrating customary practices with mechanisms that are acceptable and adaptable to both the islanders and the Andaman and Nicobar Islands Administration. If by this amalgamation, cultural and socio-economic stability can be strengthened, the continuity of resource sharing systems will be a critical component in socio-ecological adaptability and resilience for future generations.

These perceptions partially emerge through oral histories and legends, which are of importance to the islanders in establishing a chronology and anchoring their sense of place and collective identity. Narratives such as these legends and stories provide but a window through which reading and perceiving the 'viewpoint of the conserver' becomes possible. Offshore and coastal reefs, a few uninhabited islands, the large acreage of undisturbed forests and beaches are ecological habitats spread across the Nicobar archipelago. All these are biologically diverse and conserved according to the use and protection afforded through taboos and the epiphenomenal effect of customary use. These can continually evolve with changing worldviews of the islanders and need not be understood as frozen in time. The uninhabited spaces and islands are already colonized by indigenous islanders through their periodic use and conserved through customary law. Though community rights to access natural resources have been given due recognition,[34] acknowledging the values attached to customary law and resource partitioning will provide pathways for better understanding and future governance with respect to land and marine tenure as well as their use. There is immense scope for recognizing community-conserved regions (landscapes and seascapes) of the Nicobar archipelago with tenure rights and stewardship of natural resources that can develop along with economic growth and cultural evolution. Should such understandings be implemented, indigenous livelihood processes will find ample space for cultural continuity and change as well as improving and integrating relations with the state.

NOTES

1. Gbadebo J. Osemeobo, 'The Role of Folklore in Environmental Conservation: Evidence from Edo State, Nigeria', *The International Journal of Sustainable Development & World Ecology*, vol. 1, no. 1, 1994, pp. 48–55; Johan Colding and Carl Folke, 'Social Taboos: "Invisible" Systems of Local Resource Management and Biological Conservation', *Ecological Applications*, vol. 11, no. 2, 2001, pp. 584–600.
2. Robert E. Johannes, 'Traditional Marine Conservation Methods and their Demise in Oceania', *Annual Review of Ecological Systems*, vol. 9, 1978, pp. 349–64.
3. E. Ostrom, *Self-governance of Common-pool Resources in W97-2 Workshop in Political Theory and Policy Analysis*, Bloomington: Indiana University Press, 1997; idem, 'Design Principles and Threats to Sustainable Organizations that Manage Commons', in *VI Conferencia Electronica y Exposicion Virtual en Internet 'De Cara*

a la Globalizacion: Organizaciones Economicas Campesinas en America Latina y el Caribe', 1999 [http://www.fidamerica.cl/actividades/conferencias/oec/ostroing.html], accessed 10 November 2007.

4. Some references from a huge body of work with a focus on traditional knowledge used in managing often scarce natural resources are the following: F. Berkes, J. Colding, and C. Folke, 'Rediscovery of Traditional Ecological Knowledge as Adaptive Management', *Ecological Applications*, vol. 10, no. 5, 2000; James R.A. Butler, Alifereti Tawake, Tim Skewes, Lavenia Tawake, and Vic McGrath, 'Integrating Traditional Ecological Knowledge and Fisheries Management in the Torres Strait, Australia: the Catalytic Role of Turtles and Dugong as Cultural Keystone Species', *Ecology and Society*, vol. 17, no. 4, 2012, p. 34; J.E. Cinner, M.J. Marnane, and T.R. McClanahan, 'Periodic Closures as Adaptive Coral Reef Management in the Indo-Pacific', *Ecology and Society*, vol. 11, 2005, p. 31; I. Davidson-Hunt and F. Berkes, 'Learning as You Journey: Anishnaabe Perception of Socio-ecological Environmental and Adaptive Learning', *Conservation Ecology*, vol. 8, no. 1, 2003; Debal Deb and K.C. Malhotra, 'Conservation Ethos in Local Traditions: The West Bengal Heritage', *Society & Natural Resources*, vol. 14, no. 8, 2001, pp. 711–24; Joshua A. Drew, 'Application of Traditional Ecological Knowledge in Marine Conservation', *Conservation Biology*, vol. 19, no. 4, 2005, pp. 1286–93.
5. See Vijoy S. Sahay, 'The Nicobarese: A Study in Nature-Man-Spirit Complex', in *Nature-Man-Spirit Complex in Tribal India*, ed. R. Mann and Vijoy S. Sahay, New Delhi: Concept Publishers, 1981, pp. 209–68; Simron Jit Singh, 'Winds over the Nicobars', *The Human Landscape*, India International Centre Quarter, vol. 28, no. 1, 2001, p. 15; Lucas Robert, 'Kanacho or Nicobari Seasonal Festival', *Daily Telegrams*, Port Blair: Government Press, South Point, 29 May 2004; Manish Chandi, 'The Use and Knowledge of Herpetofauna on Little Nicobar Island, India', *Conservation and Society*, vol. 4, no. 1, 2006, pp. 155–65.
6. Prior to the Asian tsunami of 2004, the Nicobar Islands comprised twenty-two islands (including islets) of which twelve were inhabited; after the tsunami, Megapode Islet (of Great Nicobar) was submerged, and Kondul Island became uninhabited as a result of geomorphological changes.
7. G. Whitehead, 'Folktales of the Nicobarese', *The Indian Antiquary*, August–October 1921, Calcutta: Government Press, pp. 234–87; Rabin Roychowdhury, *Folktales of Nicobar*, New Delhi: Sahitya Akademi, 2002. Roychoudhury's account uses all the stories originally collected by Revd Whitehead, who was with the colonial administration stationed at Car Nicobar Island.
8. These stories were documented during the course of fieldwork conducted in various parts of the Nicobar Islands over many years, beginning from 2001 until the present, during various research projects and yearly visits. I did not specifically focus my attention on documenting stories and oral traditions, rather they were mechanisms used by various respondents trying to explain the rationales and basis for beliefs and customary practices. I subsequently

included them as part of my work due to their importance and relevance in resource sharing mechanisms and in emic representations of identity. These were often narrated during a discussion regarding the genesis of resource use systems, or when explaining why it was not wise to visit certain regions at certain times of the year.

9. 'Payuh' is a generic Nicobarese term for native islanders in the central and southern Nicobar Islands. In this context, it refers to the islanders of Little Nicobar, Pulomilo and Kondul Islands.
10. The island was named Meroë probably by early Danish or Portuguese sailors due to the difficulty of landing on the island (the historical island of Meroë in Africa is surrounded by the swirling waters of the Nile and two other rivers), with sharp rocks washed by large swells all along its coast. The partitioning of plantation resources among clans brought on collective ownership of the island. In customary law, various taboos are in place regarding the use of its resources.
11. Minicoy Island is a part of the Lakshadweep Islands, a chain of atolls north of the Maldivian Islands.
12. These mud pots were originally gifted to the central and southern Nicobarese by Malay sailors and pirates. The Little Nicobarese call these mud pots *kuichi*, differentiating them from the mud pots made on Chowra Island in the Nicobar archipelago which are called *kariang*. The Chowra pots were historically traded between islanders and were valued for their cultural origin and attributed properties of healing (the earliest account of Nicobar pots are found in an article by Edward Horace Man in 1894 published in *The Journal of the Anthropological Institute of Great Britain and Ireland*, vol. 23, pp. 21–7).
13. On the south-western coast, there is a red clay beach, interspersed with limestone rocks that form a cliff toward, the south.
14. G.E. Gerini, *Researches on Ptolemy's Geography of Eastern Asia*, London: Royal Geographic Society, London, 1909; repr., New Delhi: Oriental Books, 1974.
15. C. Boden Kloss, *In the Andaman and Nicobars: The Narrative of a Cruise in the Schooner 'Terrapin,' with Notices of the Islands, their Fauna, Ethnology, Etc.*, London: John Murray, 1903.
16. It is unclear whether the shipwreck of 1708 mentioned by Kloss is being referred to in the legend, or if another ship had wrecked on the island.
17. A Kareav/Kareyu (wooden carved effigy) of Lawaöh used to exist under the care of a shaman Halakka, at Trinket Island in Ukchuaka Village prior to the tsunami of 2004. Halakka died in the tsunami and the entire village was washed out by the tidal waves. Kareav are usually carved in human form representative of ancestors or of benevolent spirits (from the past); the form can be animal or anthropomorphic. These symbols and artefacts, expressive of ancestral reverence and of a metaphysical worldview of the islanders were common in many houses before the spread and greater acceptance of Christianity. After the tsunami of 2004, almost all old heirlooms including

material culture were washed away. A Kareav was often carved in remembrance of a respected ancestor, whose status was celebrated during a great ossuary feast (*Kinróak*) and celebration held in his or her honour, when crop and food production was bounteous, to be shared with the community at large. They were also used in rituals of healing by shamans across the Nicobar Islands.

18. This practice is still in vogue, despite one of the descendants not having visited the island after the 2004 tsunami, due to various logistic and personal reasons.
19. In 2012, a person originally from Terassa Island was on deputation at the Police outpost on Tillanchong. After some weeks of living with his team on the island, he went missing. He was last seen by a few of his colleagues early in the morning near the beach. He is presumed dead; since that day there has been no trace of his whereabouts. Islanders of Kamorta and Trinket, who are aware of this incident, claim that his death goes back to the legend, and he could have been swallowed by a large shark.
20. This phenomenon of islands existing at locations different from the present is not restricted to this story; the Chowra islanders have their own version, and so does the story of 'The Little One' on the origin of Battimalv (Kuonö–little one) with its genesis on the southern edge of Car Nicobar.
21. Simron Jit Singh, 'In the Sea of Influence: A World System Perspective of the Nicobar Islands', *Lund Studies in Human Ecology*, vol. 6, 2003.
22. For example, see the following folktales: 'The Creation of Car Nicobar', 'The Man who Became a Python', 'The Boy and a Whale', 'The Kind Shark', 'The Story of Coconut Palms', and 'Why Trees Stopped Moving', in Roychowdhury, *Folktales of Nicobar* and Whitehead, 'Folktales of the Nicobarese'.
23. See Manish Chandi, Charudutt Mishra and Rohan Arthur, 'Sharing Mechanisms in Corporate Groups may be More Resilient to Natural Disasters than Kin Groups in the Nicobar Islands', *Human Ecology*, 2015, pp. 1–12.
24. For more details on social organization in the Nicobar Islands, see T.N. Pandit and A. Justin, 'The Authority Structure in the Nicobarese Society', in *Polity, Political Process and Social Control in South Asia: The Tribal and Rural Perspective*, ed. Manis Kumar Raha and Iar Ali Khan, New Delhi: Gyan Publishing House, 1993, pp. 322–47; Anstice Justin, *The Nicobarese*, Calcutta: Seagull Books, on behalf of the Anthropological Survey of India, 1990; N.K. Symachaudhuri, *The Social Structure of Car Nicobar Islanders: An Ethnic Study of Cognation*, Kolkata: Anthropological Survey of India, Government of India, 1977.
25. For historical information in this regard, see R.F. Lowis, Census of India 1911: The Andaman & Nicobar Islands, Part 1–Report, Part 2–Tables, Calcutta: Superintendent of Government Printing, India, 1912, p. 169.
26. The islands of the southern group, consisting of Little Nicobar and Great Nicobar, are relatively larger, thickly forested and inhabited by a dispersed

and relatively sparse human population; cultivable and habitable land is in short supply.

27. Some relevant discussion in this regard is found in Michael Gurven, 'The Evolution of Contingent Cooperation', *Current Anthropology*, vol. 47, no. 1, February 2006, pp. 185–92; Duran Bell, 'On the Nature of Sharing: Beyond Methodological Individualism', *Current Anthropology*, vol. 36, no. 5, 1995, pp. 826–30; N.S. Jodha, 'Rural Common Property Resources: Contributions and Crisis', *Economic and Political Weekly*, vol. 25, no. 26, 1990, pp. A65–A78.
28. M. Rajshekhar, 'How the Tsunami and "One-size fits-all" Relief and Rehabilitation has led to the Reconfiguration of the Nicobar Islands', *The Economic Times*, 31 January 2015; Venkat Ramanujam Ramani, 'Gifts Without Dignity? Gift-giving, Reciprocity and the Tsunami Response in the Andaman and Nicobar Islands, India', M.A. thesis, University of Cambridge, 2010, p. 51; R. Venkat Ramanujam, Simron Jit Singh and Arild Vatn, 'From the Ashes into the Fire? Institutional Change in the Post-Tsunami Nicobar Islands, India', *Society & Natural Resources*, vol. 25, no. 11, 2012, pp. 1152–66.
29. The uninhabited islands in the Nicobar archipelago include the following islands and islets: Battimalv, Tillanchong, Isle of Man, Meroë, Treis, Trak, Menchal, Kabra, Kondul, and Pigeon Island.
30. Janaki Lenin, 'Indian Navy Jeopardising Pristine Nicobar Island?' *Firstpost*, 16 September 2012, p. 1; Manish Chandi, 'Targetting Tillanchong', *The Hindu*, Sunday Magazine edn., 22 January 2012, p. 1.
31. The 'Rani' or Islon, as she was named, was a prominent matriarch of a large extended family from Nancowry Island during the British regime. She was given the title 'Rani' or queen by the colonial British for her bravery in single handedly deflecting the advances of invading Japanese warships with soldiers during World War II. The title was given to her in recognition of her acumen and services to the empire. There is no monarchy nor kingdom in Nancowry as is often implied in news reports or articles misleadingly referring to her female descendants as the 'Queen of Nancowry' and as royalty; her title remained after Indian Independence and the occupation of the islands because she earned enduring respect by acting as a major arbiter for the Nancowry islanders with the British as well as her descendants with the Indian Government.
32. Pankaj Sekhsaria, 'Disaster as a Catalyst for Military Expansionism: The Case of the Nicobar Islands', *Economic and Political Weekly*, vol. 50, no. 1, 3 January 2015, pp. 37–43; Ajay Saini, 'The Nicobarese "Letters of Sufferings: In Protest, Respectfully Yours"', *Economic and Political Weekly*, vol. 50, no. 8, 21 February 2015.
33. Ajay Saini, 'Consumerism Among the Nicobarese: The Post Tsunami Phase in Nicobar Islands', *Economic and Political Weekly*, vol. 49, no. 46, 15 November 2014.

34. The Nicobarese and Andamanese (by default) are the only tribal communities in India exempt from the rules of hunting and gathering for their bona fide subsistence use, as instituted through the Indian Wildlife Protection Act (1972). A recent instance of conflict between a government-run agency and local islanders is described in Zubair Ahmed 'Forest Department and Tribals at Odds?' in *The Light of Andamans*, vol. 36, no. 5, 15 November 2012, pp. 2–3.

10

Afterword

From the Andamans to the Antipodes and other Origin Stories

SITA VENKATESWAR

> Time present and time past
> Are both perhaps present in time future
> And time future contained in time past.
>
> —T.S. ELIOT, *Four Quartets*

> We walk backwards into the future, our eyes fixed on the past.
>
> —*Maori proverb*

> Whakapapa is a taxonomic framework that links all animate and inanimate, known and unknown phenomena in the terrestrial and spiritual worlds. Whakapapa therefore binds all things. It maps relationships so that mythology, legend, history, knowledge, tikanga (custom), philosophies and spiritualities are organised, preserved and transmitted from one generation to the next.
>
> —*Te Ara Encyclopedia of New Zealand*

When the editors of this collection approached me to contribute an 'Afterword', I perceived the invitation as an acknowledgement of the continuing value of my scholarship to Andaman research.[1] Cognizant of the privileges of inclusion amidst so many distinguished scholars drawn from across the world, I spent many days thereafter puzzling over the implications of what I seemed to have so unthinkingly consented to without properly defining the parameters of the task. Several decades have elapsed since I conducted fieldwork in the islands. Although I have remained an interlocutor engaged with developments there, it is at a distance from the cut and thrust of direct involvement with the various contentious issues confronting the Andamans and its inhabitants, often represented through animated discussions on various forums. Without the facility of an ongoing research connection, what can I contribute from such a distanced positionality? What precedents are available to serve as models to provide me with the bearings I need to orient myself to writing the requested 'Afterword'?

Two examples do come to mind, one, eminent anthropologist Talal Asad's 1991 essay in George Stocking's well-thumbed collection that set the tone for historical anthropology at the time.[2] Asad's piece became the basis for situating anthropology's relationship to colonialism in the years that followed the publication. What is also interesting to note are the shifts in emphases that Asad brought to bear in representing anthropology's relationship to colonialism, attending to the conditions of production of anthropological knowledge yet moderating the significance attributed to the discipline's origins within colonialism, even in its subsidiary 'handmaiden' role. Often attributed to Claude Levi-Strauss, that much-quoted phrase 'a handmaiden to colonialism', is more directly linked to Talal Asad's volume *Anthropology and the Colonial Encounter.*[3] This 1970s intervention in which Asad interrogated the colonial apparatus and the roles played by individual anthropologists through their complicities (or not) with the structures of colonial power in place, renders evident why he was invited to contribute to George Stocking's book that followed almost two decades later. The passage of time offers subtle changes to one's cognitive processes, often an important component of scholarship!

The second example that I turned to was Piya Chatterjee's critical meditations in *Critical Transnational Feminist Praxis.*[4] As a component in a larger group dialogue and commentary beyond the confines of the chapters that everyone else in that working group contributed to in the edited collection, it is similar to the final dialogic concluding chapter in my own co-edited book.[5] Titled *Continuing Conversations*, Chatterjee's position reminds me of my own insertion into this collection. Starting as an intended participant at the 'Manifestations of History' workshop in Munich, which I was ultimately unable to attend, followed by a last-minute, unexpected invitation to contribute to the publication, my efforts through these musings are to comprehend what I can glean of the specificities of the task required of me.

Unlike Chatterjee's mode of engagement that follows a trajectory typical of feminist praxis, there is no basis in this particular Afterword for a collective set of reflections. Nor is it intended as a commentary on the other contributors' chapters. Having established what it is not, what then *is* the work that an Afterword accomplishes in an edited collection such as this one?

Talal Asad's illustrious example suggests the possibility of a series of reflections, reminiscent of Chatterjee's chapter in tone, that moderate my earlier research in the islands with the enhancement of hindsight brought about by the passage of time. Emulating Asad's attention to the wider context in which he wrote means not losing sight of the continuing grip of colonial configurations modulating the lives of indigenous peoples in the Andaman Islands.[6] Piya Chatterjee's precedent offers a timely reminder for a gendered lens, a strongly threaded *leitmotif* in my own prior research in the islands, marking a point of rupture with existing anthropological scholarship in the Andamans.

Inflecting my responses is my location in the Antipodes where the colonial and the post-colonial can be construed as locked in embrace (or mortal combat)![7] Such a perception confers a bifocal vision to the specificities of Māori in Aotearoa and those of Australian Aboriginal people, situated within the contingencies of settler colonialism as deployed from each site. The view from 'down under' firmly locates the indigenous peoples of the Andaman Islands within the Indian variant of the same, with many elements that are similar to the Australian context for the deployment of biopower, yet where the assemblage for 'the governance of the prior'[8] in its Indian materialization deliberately elides its own traces.

To advance with this task, I intend to follow the injunction in the Māori proverb from the series of epigraphs at the beginning of this chapter, and move forward with my sights set on the past! As a callow Ph.D. student, my entry into the islands was informed by Eric Wolf's *Europe and the Peoples without History*, Frederik Barth's *Ritual and Knowledge among the Baktaman of New Guinea* and Edwin Wilmsen's *Land Filled with Flies: A Political Economy of the Kalahari.*[9] This corpus served as precepts for my own quest when I arrived in the Andamans, to decipher, comprehend and unravel the workings of memory as entwined with the transmission of knowledge in an oral society like the Onge. Comprehending how concepts of the past and the historical were both constitutive of their lives and constituted them was at the centre of my endeavours at the time. Not for long though as evidenced in my ethnography,[10] when the series of events that I confronted during my residence in Dugong Creek and Strait Island forced me to reorient my engagement with the historical. Instead, I traced how the present came into being to become what it was and impact as it did on the lives of indigenous groups. Alternatively, to restate that intent with the recognition triggered by my attention to the thematic focus for this collection, *manifestations of history* were also embodied in and through the lives 'as lived' by the Onge and the Andamanese. My task as an ethnographer was to discern how the historical played out in the present, in configuring the lives available for the Onge and the Andamanese to lead. Whether through the deployment and performance of gender,[11] or the dialectics of mundane modes of resistance to colonial interventions of the past and present, I registered the rhythms of the everyday that constituted those lives.

Bhrigupati Singh alerts us to the ways in which we are preconditioned to register particular facets of the ethnographic encounter derived from the conceptual 'baggage' we carry with us to the field.[12] What might I have observed and responded to in the Andaman Islands had I arrived there without the scholarly corpus that I mentioned above or a different repertoire that I 'eavesdropped' on?[13] Such contingencies, illustrated in the contrasts provided by the series of ethnographers who have worked in the islands or the preoccupations that informed their intellectual endeavours, emphasize the fluidity of the processes that constitute 'scholarly knowledge production'. More importantly, how each is positioned through their complicities with the colonial-post-colonial assemblage in the Andamans speaks to the ways in which the deployment of biopower through the structures of governance in 'time present and time past' (and possibly in time future as well!) are entwined with and legible in processes of knowledge production. Much has changed, yet nothing has changed at all since Talal Asad first wrote about anthropology and the (post-)colonial encounter. Anthropologists and cultural historians of the islands are locked in step, shaping how we come to 'know' to render legible the politics of biopower[14] as inscribed on the bodies and lives of the indigenous peoples of the islands.

Attention to the nuances of the everyday, drawn from zones of social abandonment, characterizes the work of João Biehl.[15] His portrayal of his ethnographic subject Catarina resonates with Lichu and Nāo, Andamanese women whose lives I glimpsed during my time in the islands, and their efforts like Catarina's, to 'refuse' their own 'erasure'. 'Attempting to grasp the intricate infrastructural and intersubjective tensions'[16] that constituted Andamanese and Onge lifeworlds 'revealed the present as embattled and unfinished'.[17] The sad figure of Lichu that I encountered during a brief visit in 2004 or the diminished one of Nāo that Madhusree Mukherjee observed recently in 2014, stripped of the vitality that characterized their personalities, embodies what became of their lives. If the modes of biopower derived from colonial interventions are inscribed on the bodies of the indigenes, then the lifeworlds of the indigenous are a palimpsest on which the history of the islands can also be read.

The Māori concept of *whakapapa* as defined in the last epigraph to this essay operates as a concept and process of tracing genealogies, encompassing, simultaneously, 'a method and the materials used in this form of text-building'.[18] As a layering across time-space continuums, *whakapapa* exists as a palimpsest of identifications through relationships that bridge human/non-human, animate/inanimate, landscape and movements across multiple realms of life. In practice, *whakapapa* is invoked through an oral recitation that maps the multiple domains of relationships, which position an individual within a temporal and spatial landscape.

Whakapapa, therefore, simultaneously combines the chronological *and* spatial modes of conceptualizing the past within the present (a mode of historicization highlighted as alternatives in this collection), to securely position and harness a sense of 'place' for an individual and community across the landscape. *Whakapapa* is also inscribed on the body as a metonym for these wider relationships through complex tattooing practices that serve as markers for rites of passage.[19]

My antipodean immersion offers more insight as I recall other inscriptions, both transient and enduring, encountered on the bodies of the Andamanese and the Onge, to remind me of my own inattention to such complex practices of writing and reading the body when I conducted research in the Andamans. What might I have read if I was able to harness the augmented perspective that I now bear to embody and inscribe my own place in the world? What expanded grounds for dialogue might have emerged if I had met Lichu and Nāo with the tattoos that I currently wear on my person? 'Ethnographic subjects allow us to return to the places where thought is born.'[20] Alternatively, drawing on the clarity voiced by T.S. Eliot, 'and the end of all exploring will be to arrive where we started and know the place for the first time.'[21] Foucault too reminds us that 'the return to ... constitutes an effective and necessary task of transforming the discursive practice itself.'[22]

Will I return to Dugong Creek and Strait Island 'where thought was born' as Madhusree Mukherjee urges me, to retrace the steps I walked earlier a lifetime later? The 'return to' then is not just a discursive practice but entails an embodied re-engagement with the site. I remain uncertain; the impediments to access combined with the exigencies of fieldwork in those locations make me pause. Complicity with the administrative apparatus will be demanded at several levels to enable knowledge production anew. Nevertheless, it is a possibility that I will leave open for the future. In the interim though, I will not abandon Lichu or Nāo, Totanange or Bada Raju or Boke, Kakeyi or Sheila and many others, who remain vivid in my memory, to intellectual oblivion. Like Biehl's Catarina, my Andaman interlocutors' luminous presence haunts all my anthropological endeavours, whether in implicit or explicit forms.[23]

In the concluding section of the Ph.D. thesis I completed on my return from the Andaman Islands, I paraphrased in part irony and jest, a famous query from Lenin, 'What is to be done?', as I groped for a solution to the immiseration of the Andamanese and the Onge, trapped within the colonial structures of the welfare apparatus in the islands. Several decades later, we are no closer to arriving at an answer. The colonial-post-colonial assemblage of the twenty-first century now encompasses Jarawa, who present the next frontier for scholarly knowledge production in the islands. Scholars of the future who are alert to the nuances of 'governance of the prior' will glimpse other manifestations of conjunctures-to-come of histories-in-the-making as inscribed on Jarawa bodies, just as it was embodied by the Andamanese and the Onge in the past. Some may be brave enough to bear witness by interrogating the conditions of production of their scholarship in their capacities as anthropologists or cultural historians of the Andamans. Such a stance could potentially counter the strategic absence of an archive that documents the colonial-post-colonial assemblage for indigenous 'welfare' in the islands available for critical scrutiny.

To write about the indigenous groups of the Andaman Islands at this conjuncture demands an elegiac register, the more distanced abstraction of scholarly work falls short of the emotional clarity demanded to construe the conditions of their life within the colonial-post-colonial settler assemblage in place in the Andaman Islands. Hence, I turn to T.S. Eliot yet again who elucidated so thoughtfully that: 'Time present and time past/Are both perhaps present in time future/And time future contained in time past.'

The essays brought together in this collection from anthropologists and cultural historians draw on a range of narratives to engage with processes of historicization that constitute the past. Each contributor applies distinct perspectives and methodologies to addressing the thematic focus for the collection. I have applied the lens of hindsight to review my earlier research in the islands. I argue that manifestations of history in the 'colonial-post-colonial' settler space of the Andamans are embodied within the lifeworlds of the indigenous groups and can be glimpsed through the modes of living they are able to achieve or the traces that colonial biopower leaves on their bodies.

NOTES

1. A more pragmatic inference can be based on the gaps left by the absence of any other scholar addressing the indigenous Andamanese, hence the editors' attempt to ensure more comprehensive coverage by soliciting a contribution from me, structured as an 'Afterword' at the end of the collection.
2. Talal Asad, *Colonial Situations: Essays on the Contextualizations of Ethnographic Knowledge*, Madison, Wisconsin: University of Wisconsin Press, 1991.
3. Kamari M. Clarke, 'Toward a Critically Engaged Ethnographic Practice', *Current Anthropology*, vol. 51, no. S2, 2010, pp. S302–S312. Clarke was referring to Talal Asad, *Anthropology and the Colonial Encounter*, London: Ithaca Press, 1973.
4. Piya Chatterjee, 'Continuing Conversations', in *Critical Transnational Feminist Praxis*, ed. R. Nagar and A.L. Swarr, Albany: State University of New York, 2010, pp. 206–18.
5. Sita Venkateswar and Emma Hughes, *The Politics of Indigeneity: Dialogues and Reflections on Indigenous Activism*, London: Zed Books, 2011.

6. Despite India's contention that all its citizens are indigenous and hence, is not a signatory to the 2007 United Declaration on the Rights of Indigenous Peoples (UNDRIP), such a claim is clearly untenable in the Andaman and Nicobar Islands. Also, see Sita Venkateswar, 'Indigeneity and International Indigenous Rights Organisations and Forums', in *The Politics of Indigeneity: Dialogues and Reflections on Indigenous Activism*, pp. 191–245.
7. I take a conjunctural approach in my responses to this task in that *how* I respond is contingent to the moment and the other influences that interface with me while engaged in writing this piece. See note 12 for additional details about the conjuncture within which I am currently located.
8. Elizabeth Povinelli, 'The Governance of the Prior', *Interventions: International Journal of Postcolonial Studies*, vol. 13, no. 1, 2011, pp. 113–30.
9. Eric Wolf, *Europe and the Peoples Without History*, Berkeley: University of California Press, 1982; Frederik Barth, *Ritual and Knowledge Among the Baktaman of New Guinea*, New Haven: Yale University Press, 1975; Edwin Wilmsen, *Land Filled With Flies: A Political Economy of the Kalahari*, Chicago: University of Chicago Press, 1989.
10. See Sita Venkateswar, 'Policing Power, Governing Gender and Re-imagining Resistance: Perspectives on the Andaman Islanders', Ph.D. diss., Rutgers University, 1997; Sita Venkateswar, *Development and Ethnocide: Colonial Practices in the Andaman Islands*, Copenhagen: International Work Group for Indigenous Affairs, 2004.
11. Judith Butler, *Gender Trouble: Feminism and Subversion of Identity*, London: Routledge, 2006.
12. Bhrigupati Singh, 'How Concepts Make the World Look Different: Affirmative and Negative Genealogies of Thought', in *The Ground Between: Anthropologists Engage Philosophy*, ed. Veena Das, Michael D. Jackson, Arthur Kleinman and Bhrigupati Singh, Durham and London: Duke University Press, 2014, pp. 159–87. Bhrigupati Singh and other anthropologists who I cite from the 2014 collection of essays are drawn from this edited volume, *The Ground Between*, the main textbook in the postgraduate seminar that I teach during the first semester of any year. My immersion in the intellectual space set out by the collection in contiguity with the invitation to contribute this Afterword, 'primed' my receptivity to what I read, highlighting the contingencies of scholarly production and the kinds of engagements that emerge from such serendipitous conceptual encounters to frame our perspectives of the world.
13. Ghassan Hage, 'Eavesdropping on Bourdieu's Philosophers', in *The Ground Between*, pp. 138–58.
14. Didier Fassin, 'The Parallel Lives of Philosophy and Anthropology', in *The Ground Between*, pp. 50–70.
15. João Biehl, 'Ethnography in the Way of Theory', in *The Ground Between*, pp. 94–118.
16. Ibid., p. 99.
17. Ibid.

18. David Farrier, *Unsettled Narratives: The Pacific Writings of Stevenson*, Ellis, Melville and London: Taylor & Francis, 2007, p. 105.
19. In contemporary times, such rites of passage are transposed to include other life events but are applied using an enduring palette of idioms to construe relationships across space and time within which the individual is embedded.
20. Biehl, 'Ethnography in the Way of Theory', p. 99.
21. T.S. Eliot, *Four Quartets*, London: Faber and Faber, 1968.
22. Michel Foucault, 'What is an Author', in *Aesthetics, Method and Epistemology: Essential Works of Michel Foucault (1954–1984)*, ed. J.D. Faubion and P. Rabinow, New York: New Press, 1999, pp. 205–22, see especially p. 219.
23. See Venkateswar, 'Indigeneity and International Indigenous Rights Organisations and Forums'; idem, 'Manifesto for a Public Anthropologist: Insights from Fieldwork', *India Review*, vol. 5, nos. 3–4, 2006, pp. 263–93.

Editors and Contributors

FRANK HEIDEMANN is Professor of Social and Cultural Anthropology, Ludwig-Maximilians-University (LMU) of Munich. He conducted fieldwork among the repatriates from Sri Lanka in Tamil Nadu in the 1980s. Since the 1990s, most of his fieldwork has been with the Badaga community, based in the Nilgiri Hills. His publications include *The Modern Anthropology of India: Ethnography, Themes and Theory* (2013, co-edited with Peter Berger) and *Kanganies in Sri Lanka and Malaysia: Tamil Recruiter-cum-Foreman as a Sociological Category in the Nineteenth and Twentieth Century* (1992).

PHILIPP ZEHMISCH is a Postdoctoral Research Fellow at the Center for Advanced Studies and the Department of Social and Cultural Anthropology, LMU Munich. His research interest lies at the intersection of post-colonial studies, political anthropology, and migration studies with a regional focus on South Asia. He conducted twenty months of fieldwork in the Andamans between 2006 and 2012. His Ph.D. dissertation, 'Mini-India: The Politics of Migration and Subalternity in the Andaman Islands', won the Dissertation Prize of the Faculty for the Study of Culture, LMU Munich, as well as the Frobenius Society's Research Award 2015 and will be published in 2017.

CLARE ANDERSON is Professor of History, University of Leicester. She has recently worked on the collaborative, international, and interdisciplinary Economic and Social Research Council-funded project, 'Integrated Histories of the Andaman Islands' (with Madhumita Mazumdar and Vishvajit Pandya, 2009–13). Her published works include *Subaltern Lives: Biographies of Colonialism in the Indian Ocean World, 1790–1920* (2012); *The Indian Uprising of 1857–8: Prisons, Prisoners and Rebellion* (2007, 2012); and *Legible Bodies: Race, Criminality and Colonialism in South Asia* (2004).

MANISH CHANDI is Assistant Director of the Andaman and Nicobar Islands Environmental Team (ANET). For the past nineteen years, he has conducted work with team members on surveys for sea turtles and salt-water crocodiles, and profiled some of the human communities of the islands. His Ph.D. through the Nature Conservation Foundation, Mysore focussed on studying common property resource regimes and natural resource management in the Nicobar Islands. He has published extensively in both natural science and social science journals.

JAMAL MALIK is Chair of Religious Studies/Islamic Studies, University of Erfurt. He is presently affiliated to the Käte Hamburger Center 'Law as Culture', Bonn. His publications include *Islam in South Asia: A Short History* (2008, 2012); *Madrasas in South Asia: Teaching Terror?* (2008); and *Sufism in the West* (2006, co-edited with John Hinnells).

KANCHAN MUKHOPADHYAY is a cultural anthropologist who has spent most of his professional career working for the Anthropological Survey of India. He has published numerous papers on the social and cultural identity of refugees and migrants, and relations between the Indian nation-state and scheduled tribes. He is a member of an expert committee reviewing policies of the Indian state towards the indigenous people of the Andaman Islands.

SATADRU SEN is Professor of South Asian History, Queens College and The Graduate Center, City University of New York. He has authored several works on modern South Asia, including *Traces of Empire: India, America and Postcolonial Cultures—Essays and Criticism* (2014); *Disciplined Natives: Race, Freedom and Confinement in Colonial India* (2012); *Savagery and Colonialism in the Indian Ocean: Power, Pleasure and the Andaman Islanders* (2010); and *Disciplining Punishment: Colonialism and Convict Society in the Andaman Islands* (2000).

SITA VENKATESWAR is International Director of the College of Humanities and Social Sciences and Senior Lecturer in the Social Anthropology programme at Massey University, Palmerston North. She is also Associate Director of the Massey chapter of the recently established New Zealand India Research Institute, Victoria University of Wellington. Her ethnography *Development and Ethnocide: Colonial Practices in the Andaman Islands* (2004) is based on her Ph.D. fieldwork in the Andaman Islands from 1989 to 1992 funded by the National Science Foundation Dissertation Improvement Grant. Her other publications include *Globalisation and the Challenges of Development in Contemporary India* (2016, co-edited with Sekhar Bandyopadhyay) and *The Politics of Indigeneity: Dialogues and Reflections on Indigenous Activism* (2011, co-edited with Emma Hughes).

CLAIRE WINTLE is Senior Lecturer in the History of Art and Design, University of Brighton. She curated the exhibition 'Temple, Man and Tuson: Collecting the Andaman and Nicobar Islands' for the Brighton Museum & Art Gallery and has published several articles about representations of material culture in museums. She is the author of *Colonial Collecting and Display: Encounters with Material Culture in the Andaman and Nicobar Islands* (2013).

Index